# LORENZO

## Books by EMILY HAHN

Once Upon a Pedestal
On the Side of the Apes
Times and Places
Animal Gardens
Romantic Rebels
With Naked Foot
Africa to Me: Person to Person
China to Me
China Only Yesterday
The Tiger House Party
Diamond
Chiang Kai-shek
Love Conquers Nothing
Purple Passage
England to Me
Miss Jill
Raffles of Singapore
Hongkong Holiday

# LORENZO

## D. H. Lawrence
## and the
## Women Who Loved Him ·

### by EMILY HAHN

J. B. LIPPINCOTT COMPANY
Philadelphia and New York

U.S. Library of Congress Cataloging in Publication Data

Hahn, Emily, birth date
    Lorenzo: D. H. Lawrence and the women who loved
him.

    Bibliography: p.
    Includes index.
    1. Lawrence, David Herbert, 1885–1930—Relation-
ship with women. I. Title.
PR6023.A93Z63117    823'.9'12 [B]    75–11865
ISBN–0–397–00772–8

The author wishes to thank the following publishers for permission to make use of the materials from the books indicated. Special acknowledgment is made to Edward Nehls's three-volume compilation, *D. H. Lawrence: A Composite Biography* (Madison: The University of Wisconsin Press, 1957, 1958, and 1959), which made accessible a good deal of the material on which this book is based, and without which no book on Lawrence can well be written.

John Carswell for quotations from *The Savage Pilgrimage: A Narrative of D. H. Lawrence* by Catherine Carswell.

Frank Cass & Co. Ltd. for quotations from *D. H. Lawrence: A Personal Record* by Jessie Chambers, edited by J. D. Chambers.

The John Day Company for portions of letters and excerpts from *Journey with Genius: Recollections and Reflections Concerning the D. H. Lawrences* by Witter Bynner. Copyright © 1951 by Witter Bynner.

Farrar, Straus & Giroux, Inc., for quotations from *The Priest of Love* (revised edition of *The Intelligent Heart*) by Harry T. Moore, Copyright © 1954, 1962, 1974 by Harry T. Moore.

Holt, Rinehart and Winston, Inc., for portions of a letter from *Carrington Letters and Extracts from Her Diaries* chosen and with an introduction by David Garnett. Copyright © 1970 by David Garnett and The Sophie Partridge Trust. Reprinted by permission of Holt, Rinehart and Winston, Publishers.

Alfred A. Knopf, Inc., for permission to quote from *Frieda Lawrence: The Memoirs and Correspondence*, edited by E. W. Tedlock, Jr., and from Katherine Mansfield's *Letters to John Middleton Murry, 1913–1922*, edited by John Middleton Murry.

Norman Holmes Pearson, owner of the copyright, for quotations from *Bid Me to Live* by Hilda Doolittle.

The Society of Authors as the literary representative of the Estate of Katherine Mansfield for portions of *Letters to John Middleton Murry, 1913–1922*, edited by John Middleton Murry.

Southern Illinois University Press for quotations from *"Not I, But the Wind . . ."* by Frieda Lawrence. Copyright 1934 by Frieda Lawrence. Reprinted by permission from Southern Illinois University Press, Laurence Pollinger Ltd., and the Estate of the late Mrs. Frieda Lawrence.

The Sunstone Press for selections from *Lawrence and Brett: A Friendship* by Dorothy Brett.

Selections from letters of D. H. Lawrence are reprinted by permission of Laurence Pollinger Ltd. and the Estate of the late Mrs. Frieda Lawrence, and by permission of The Viking Press, Inc., publishers of *The Collected Letters of D. H. Lawrence* edited by Harry T. Moore and *The Letters of D. H. Lawrence* edited by Aldous Huxley. Copyright 1932 by the Estate of D. H. Lawrence, and 1934 by Frieda Lawrence; copyright © 1933, 1948, 1953, 1954, and each year 1956–1962 by Angelo Ravagli and C. M. Weekley, Executors of the Estate of Frieda Lawrence Ravagli. All rights reserved.

Excerpts from "Lilies in the Fire," "The Bride," "The Hands of the Betrothed," "Last Words to Miriam," and "Whether or Not" are reprinted by permission of Laurence Pollinger Ltd., the Estate of the late Mrs. Frieda Lawrence, and The Viking Press, Inc., from *The Complete Poems of D. H. Lawrence* edited by Vivian de Sola Pinto and F. Warren Roberts. Copyright © 1964, 1971 by Angelo Ravagli and C. M. Weekley, Executors of the Estate of Frieda Lawrence Ravagli. All rights reserved.

*To John, Jimmy, and Fred*

# Contents

# *Author's Note*

D. H. Lawrence's life was dominated by women. While there were many years in which he had no close male friends, during almost every moment of his life there was at least one woman—and often more than one—with whom he had a close, special, and hectic relationship. I wish I could say that I have solved what was a mystery to me before I began research on the subject: namely, what did women see in Lawrence? Why did so many of them fall in love with him?

His own portrayal of the irresistible male bore little resemblance to himself. His heroes were tall and strong and handsome and ruthless, reeking with masculinity. They spoke in deep, throbbing tones. Lawrence was slight, delicate in health, equally delicate in appearance, and his voice was high and piping. He was not masterful save with words. There, of course, he excelled, in speech as well as on paper. He could be nastier, in his oddly high voice, than anyone else his friends had ever met, but it is not a quality generally thought to be sexually attractive. In other moods he was vastly more appealing, but even at his most engaging he usually frustrated women by refusing to take what they offered. To me, therefore, the mystery remains a mystery. Why *did* they love him? Nonetheless, they most certainly did: they fought over him, wept for him, and pined when he rejected their advances.

Immediately after Lawrence's death in 1930, women in numbers (and some men too) hastened to set down their memories of him. I do not think the criticism voiced at that time—that the memoirists were merely trying to capitalize on their acquaintance with a great man—is justified. Lawrence was an extraordinary person who attracted love and also had great power to hurt, and it was natural, or so it seems to me, that when he died his friends and lovers felt an urge to talk about what had happened to them through him.

I have leaned quite heavily on these memoirs in writing this book, and it is, therefore, a view of Lawrence refracted from the eyes of those who knew him. It is not a discussion of his written works, except where his writing reflects his own experience. Admittedly this is a large exception, for Lawrence, like other novelists, drew on his life and surroundings for material. However, if anyone has opened this book expecting yet another critical appraisal of the works of D. H. Lawrence, I apologize; it isn't here. What I have tried to appraise instead is his life with his women. Here, at any rate, is the story as the women told it.

EMILY HAHN

*New York City*
*December, 1974*

# LORENZO

# 1

## *Lydia: "Poured her very soul into him"*

D. H. LAWRENCE'S MOTHER, Lydia, was the most important woman in his life until the day she died. She had a strong influence over him even after her death, and her example lingered even after his marriage. She had made an imprint too deep to be forgotten. Not only did he try to make his wife, Frieda—and various other women—conform to Lydia's notions of dress and comportment; he cooked as he had learned to cook from his mother, kept his living quarters scrupulously clean as that busy little miner's wife had done, and scrubbed his floor just as Lydia had scrubbed hers in his childhood. He adopted her code of propriety as well. It astonished a friend of his later years to be told by the man considered the arch-master of pornography that sexual intercourse is indecent in the afternoon, or for that matter at any time except during the dark of night.

Those who have read *Sons and Lovers*—which includes most of us, as it is required reading in literature courses—may feel we know all that it is possible to know about the author's mother. But it is not wise to take everything for gospel that one finds in novels, however autobiographical they are known to be. "Mrs. Morel" was Lawrence's mother as he saw her, but he saw her in his individual way, with his own prejudices. Not everyone who knew his model agreed with the picture he gives.

For example, there was her behavior toward her husband, Lawrence's father, which was ungenerous in the extreme. The writer made his mother in fiction more of a saint than she appeared to observers in real life, and he continued to exaggerate in this respect in an outright factual sketch, a scrap of autobiography written for *Phoenix,* a collection of Lawrence's shorter pieces. After giving the usual facts—that he was born in Eastwood, Nottinghamshire, in 1885, in coal-mining country—he continued:

"My father was a collier, and only a collier, nothing praiseworthy about him. He wasn't even respectable, in so far as he got drunk rather frequently, never went near a chapel, and was usually rather rude to his little immediate bosses at the pit."

On this point Lawrence was never accurate, any more than his mother was. In fact his father, Arthur John Lawrence, did sometimes attend chapel, and, what is more important, according to his daughter Emily he didn't drink all that much. Only on Friday and Saturday evenings, said Emily, certainly never on Sunday. However, it must be admitted that he did spend most of his evenings in public houses, to get away from his Little Woman, as her children called her. The atmosphere at home was not pleasant for him, which is putting it mildly. Even the younger girl, Ada, though she professed to be a staunch admirer of her mother, put in a few words in favor of her father when she wrote a book about her famous brother. She said that Arthur Lawrence, when he came home drunk, was at first cheerful and pleasant, and would have gone on in this agreeable mood if only his wife had let him alone. But she never did. She would rail at him, until in reaction he became "brutal and coarse" and sometimes frightened the children by roaring at Lydia and hitting furniture. Nevertheless, Ada insisted, when he was sober nobody could have been more charming. He was very handy about the house and loved to repair the family's footgear or stop up leaks in the pots and kettles.

It was the mother who turned the children against him and

filled them with her bitterness, until when they grew older they ignored him, coldly shutting him out of their lives. He reacted to this treatment as he did to his wife's scoldings: he deliberately behaved as badly as possible, and things got worse and worse. In maturity, Ada regretted having joined in the family conspiracy to put her father down. Even Lawrence, a long time after his mother's death, showed signs of softening, but by then it was too late.

"My mother was, I suppose, superior," Lawrence wrote in his autobiographical sketch. "She came from town, and belonged really to the lower bourgeoisie. She spoke King's English, without an accent, and never in her life could even imitate a sentence of the dialect which my father spoke, and which we children spoke out of doors. . . . But she was a working man's wife, and nothing else, in her shabby little black bonnet and her shrewd, clear, 'different' face."

Lawrence, who was notoriously sensitive to social distinctions, fudged the facts a little. There was not as much difference as he implied between his father's background and his mother's; they were noticeably similar, and the families were connected by marriage (of their cousins) even before his mother, Lydia Beardsall, and his father, Arthur Lawrence, met one another. Arthur's grandfather was a silk and lace manufacturer who lost his money in a trade depression; Arthur's father, John Lawrence, was a tailor in Brinsley, Notts. Arthur himself went down into the pits at the age of seven. Lydia's grandparents, too, were lacemakers, though one ancestor was also a well-known writer of hymns. Her family too had lost their money. Her father, a dockyards foreman, came from Kent to Nottingham so that his six daughters might go into lacemaking. He liked to preach in the Methodist chapel, and Lydia herself was very pious. She had taught school in Sheerness before the move; she wrote verses and for a time expected to marry a certain "superior" young man, who let her down by marrying a rich widow instead. Still brooding over being jilted,

Lydia went to a relative's party in Nottingham and there met good-looking young Arthur Lawrence, who had imposing black whiskers and beard and was a splendid dancer. He was attracted to her ladylike daintiness, and she to his beauty and strange manner of speech. Prim Lydia did not dance, but she found it pleasant to watch him. He promised to take the pledge and never drink again. And so the young couple married and went to live in Eastwood, a mining community of about four thousand souls near Brinsley, where Arthur worked in the colliery.

Until then the bride knew nothing about coal mining. It was a famous story in the family that her husband came home from work on the first night so black with coal dust that she didn't recognize him. To her ladylike disgust, he insisted on having his meal before taking a bath, because it was *"clean dirt."* His young wife could scarcely swallow a bite. Afterward he ordered her to prepare water, and bathed right there in front of her, before the kitchen fire. He even insisted that she scrub his back. In later life Lawrence was sometimes shocked at the sight of exposed flesh or underwear, but the operative word there is "sometimes." In such matters you never knew where you were with him. Many of his attitudes were his mother's, for he was always to carry her encapsulated in his heart. Lydia Lawrence recoiled from the exposure of flesh or underclothing; ergo, at times so did Lawrence. At other times, as readers of his works will remember, he most certainly did not.

Of course colliers were not prosperous, but it seems that biographers have made too much of the extreme poverty suffered by the Lawrences: no doubt the middle-class conscience was at work here. Dr. J. D. Chambers, who knew the Lawrences well in childhood, as did his whole family, was explicit about this in his introduction to his sister Jessie's book. He said that Arthur Lawrence was a "butty" or underground contractor in charge of a stall and a gang of stall men. "He was a highly skilled man, bringing home good money, occupying a house with a bay window and separate 'entry' of which the Lawrences were immensely proud, and handing over to his wife

enough money to give three of their five children a good education." However, the house Chambers described was the best
one occupied by the Lawrence family, which moved three
times before Lydia's death. There were undoubtedly difficult
days for them too. Another friend of the family told Chambers
that Lawrence was recognized and respected by his work mates
as a skilled miner, but lacked technical knowledge and often
argued with his immediate superiors, which habit impaired his
chances of getting more profitable places in the pit. "Of this
Mrs. Lawrence made much. . . . Lawrence senior had no welcome except in the pub," wrote Chambers. She was determined
to bring up her children to a better sort of life than hers. The
boys must not go into the pits and must not drink; the girls
must marry refined men. She was a fighter and had her way in
these matters. At first, to make extra money, she even tried
keeping a little shop in the house, but the project was unsuc-
cessful. There was no Methodist chapel in Eastwood, so she
went regularly to the Congregational one and made sure the
children did too—first-born George, Emily Una, William
Ernest, David Herbert (or Bert), and, last, Lettice Ada.

From babyhood Bert was delicate and sensitive, a mother's
boy who preferred playing with girls to joining in the robust
pastimes of the other miners' sons. His brother George, who
became a textile engineer, said in reminiscence that Bert was
always getting female playmates together and leading them on
blackberrying excursions and the like. He was wonderful, too,
at thinking up party games, said George.

They all petted and spoiled Bert at home; George said his
mother "poured her very soul into him." But outside Bert found
unfriendly critics. The boys at school called him "mardy" or
"mardarse"—babyish, cowardly, sissy. William Henry Hopkin,
town councilor, recalled in later years how he once met the
boy walking home from school between two girls, while behind
the trio a group of boys trailed, shouting, "Dicky Dicky
Denches plays with the Wenches."

"Sock 'em, Lad!" called Hopkin encouragingly, but Bert

did not, though his eyes were full of anger and mortification. Rather, he held up his chin defiantly and marched on with his girl friends. Certainly this took moral courage. Bert was tough in his way, and he had to be. Eastwood was no place for weaklings.

Still, he *was* a mother's boy. He was not ashamed to help her with the household chores: he learned from her how to cook and clean and remembered these lessons all his life. He even picked up her mannerism of tossing the head scornfully, though he did not go so far as to give her characteristic scornful sniff.

Both George and D. H. Lawrence himself have implied that Lydia Lawrence's maternal passion was concentrated on Bert, but this was not the case. In the early days her particular pet was Ernest—"our Ern"—though she loved all three boys more than the girls, who had to be content with the leavings. We have all seen women like her, jealously possessive of their sons. If she could have done so, Lydia Lawrence would have kept them forever devoted only to herself. This is plain from the evidence of May Chambers, later Mrs. William Holbrook, who became acquainted with the family when she was a child playing with other children in the neighborhood. The Chambers family lived in Eastwood like the Lawrences; their friendship began when Mrs. Lawrence and Mrs. Chambers met at chapel. Like so many people in small country towns, Mr. Chambers was a combination of townsman and farmer. At first he had a shop, but when this palled he decided to move into the country outright and become a farmer. His chance came when the tenancy of a farm called The Haggs fell vacant. He moved his family into the farmhouse and set to work to make a go of this new life by becoming a delivery milkman as well as a mixed farmer, for which work he utilized the labor of his older sons. In Eastwood, the Chambers family and the Lawrences had been fairly intimate, and the friendship continued after the move to

The Haggs—though the distance that now had to be traversed caused them to meet with less frequency.

There were seven Chambers children, but it was the two oldest girls who would become Lawrence's special friends: May, who was two years older, and Jessie, who was a year younger. However, Bert never so much as noticed Jessie until he went to The Haggs, judging by his fictional account in *Sons and Lovers*. There would come a time when he made up for this lapse, but at first we have only May's account of her impressions of the Lawrences, gathered while the Chambers were still neighbors of theirs in Eastwood.

May remembered Bert's mother as "a short, robust woman with a heavy, plodding step, [who] drooped slightly, and carried her head bent to one side a little, as if weary and discouraged." She usually wore black, with a dirty apron. She complained a lot about the work she had to do, and the subject of most of her complaints was her husband, a fact that puzzled the child, for Arthur Lawrence, on the few occasions when she saw him, seemed charming and friendly. Still, though Mrs. Lawrence impressed May as being "bitter, disillusioned, and austere," the little girl must have liked her, for she often went to the Lawrence house, and so did other children from round about. May knew all about the Lawrence boys because their mother talked about them constantly, and of course she knew Emily, who was older than herself, and Ada, who was younger; but her real friend—one might almost say companion —was the mother. May regarded the big boys with proper respect: George, who was the best-looking though rather short, and Ern, who had red hair. She knew that Ern was bright; he went into office work and rose rapidly until he got a well-paid job as shipping clerk in London. Mrs. Lawrence was happy then, and very proud of him, until he committed the unforgivable sin of falling in love. When he brought his girl, a pretty London stenographer named Gypsy Dennis, home with him for the holidays, May heard all about it; and she saw Gypsy with the young people at a band concert in the park. They were obviously enjoying themselves, but Mrs. Lawrence was not with them, and May thought of her with pity, picturing her brooding alone at home.

A few days later when she dropped in at the Lawrence house she found Mrs. Lawrence in a raging temper and Bert vainly trying to calm her down. Lydia never suffered from repression, and now she cried out on sight of her young friend, "They're gone! Aye, they're gone, and I for one am not sorry. Why, child, she lets him buy her boots!"

Bert, while protesting that there was nothing wrong in a man's buying presents for his fiancée, was nevertheless somewhat shocked, if pleasurably, by the sum his brother had paid for the boots. He told May how much it was, and she too was shocked. All three seem to have been awed. The fact that Ernest no longer sent money to his mother, but squandered it instead on Gypsy, infuriated Mrs. Lawrence, but his true offense lay in his infidelity.

Ern was probably his mother's favorite, but George, too, betrayed her. Not long afterward she was giving May a tragic message for Mrs. Chambers: "Eh, child, tell your mother not to spoil her sons. Mine's married! Aye, he's married."

George, cleverer than Ern for once, had committed his crime secretly, and the *fait accompli* cut down his mother's ability to make scenes, but the affair badly frightened poor little May. Overwhelmed by George's wickedness in getting married, she resolved that *she* would never, never do such a dreadful thing to *her* mother.

Everything considered, it seems clear that Mrs. Lawrence's behavior was not that of the woman we have read of in her son's novel, preoccupied with a crippling fondness for her sensitive little boy. She was not a monomaniac, as she has been described. Admittedly she was neurotic, but so are many other mothers. If her adored Ernest had not died young, if George had not wriggled out from under, Bert, her last son, would not have been nearly smothered by her love.

As it was, she tried her best to discourage him from developing independence. With Emily's help, she kept him indoors on the frequent occasions that he had a cough and did her best to obstruct him in his projects. We have the record of one such attempt because May has written it down. By this time Bert was about thirteen; it was 1898. May found mother and son in the middle of a tense discussion. Mrs. Lawrence was standing in a typically tragic attitude, head on hand. "In her black dress and soiled apron she impressed me as one in deep misery," May recalled. She thought Mrs. Lawrence must be suffering from a bad headache, but it was not that; the trouble was that Bert had won a scholarship to Nottingham High School. Though he was exultant, his mother found it an occasion for gloom. It took money to go to high school, she reminded him, and when Bert replied that money was included in the scholarship, she said that it wouldn't be nearly enough.

"Skimp, skimp, I'm tired of skimping," she declared, and moved off with her usual weary step, her shoulders bowed. No doubt Bert was so used to this sort of thing that it didn't worry him as much as it did May, but the message was not lost on either child: Mrs. Lawrence was suffering for her boy's sake. Of course, he accepted the scholarship and went to high school. There was never any likelihood that he would not.

It comes as a relief in May's account to read of one occasion when Mrs. Lawrence was *not* soaked in gloom. One afternoon when Bert answered the door to the constant visitor he announced excitedly that his mother was writing poetry. The lady herself did not deny the impeachment, though she made a halfhearted effort to hide the exercise book she had been writing in. Yes, she admitted; she was trying to write something, though Bert shouldn't talk so much. It was seldom enough that they had the house to themselves, she added tartly. She would send her efforts to a magazine, but she doubted if it would come to anything. Evidently it didn't, since that was the last May heard of Mrs. Lawrence's verse.

Ada Lawrence described her mother in a very different

light. She seems to have harbored no resentment about being
,treated as a second-rate citizen: "I marvel now at the housework she could do, and the wonderful way in which she managed on the little money my father gave her," she said. "No
wonder we all idolised her." Mrs. Lawrence, she said, was short
and slender, with graying brown hair, blue eyes, and a nose
that was slightly crooked because of a girlhood accident. She
had small hands and feet and a proud carriage—not the down-
trodden gait described by May Chambers—and read a lot of
books. The minister liked to hold philosophical and religious
discussions with her. She had a dry sense of humor. She always
wore black and white, or gray. The children thought she looked
very ladylike when she was dressed for chapel all in black, with
a black silk blouse, and a little black bonnet trimmed with black
and white feathers. No mention was made of a dirty apron.

Jessie Chambers gave a third impression. "She struck me
as a bright, vivacious little woman, full of vitality, and amusingly emphatic in her way of speaking," she wrote. "Her face
changed rapidly as she talked and she had a habit of driving
home her views with vigorous shakes of the head. She took a
keen interest in things around her." At the Lawrence house
Jessie noticed a tenseness always present in the air, a curious,
powerful vibration. In another passage she again described this
woman who was to become her bitter rival in Bert's affections:
an arresting figure in spite of her smallness, she said, with shrewd
gray eyes in a pale face, and light-colored hair. "Her smallness
was more than compensated for by her vigour and determination. All her energy was expended upon her children, who
adored her; she was such a contrast to the poor, disinherited
father." An excellent housewife, a kind neighbor. "Her confidence in herself and her pronouncements upon people and
things excited my wonder. It was new to me to meet anyone
so certain of herself and of her own rightness," confessed Jessie.
"But she could be vivid in speech, gay and amusing; and in
spite of a keen edge to her tongue, she was warm-hearted. She

said quite frankly that she was interested mainly in her sons." Jessie found it curious, though not at first a nuisance, that various girls from the neighborhood would drift casually into the house, talk a little, then drift out again. Sometimes Bert strolled out to meet members of the Chambers family; he was usually accompanied by several girls. His mother would smile about this and say there was safety in numbers.

By this time the Chambers family had made that important change in their way of life and moved out to The Haggs, about four miles from Eastwood. A possible visit by the Lawrences to The Haggs was mooted, but it did not take place for some time. In fact, the Chamberses had been at The Haggs three years before Lydia Lawrence and Bert, then fifteen, set out to pay the promised visit, walking by short cut through a wooded valley and past the Moorgreen reservoir under a great hill which was, wrote May, "clothed with a remnant of Sherwood Forest." May knew the way well; she was now a pupil teacher, and her school was on the far side of Eastwood. Pupil teachers learned their profession rather as substitutes do in the United States except that they remained in one place after they had been assigned to it, teaching the smaller children and being taught in turn by more experienced students. That day she stopped by at the Lawrences' house and picked them up, and they all walked over together.

Everything went so well on this visit that Mrs. Lawrence was in a fine humor and suggested that Bert come out every week on his school half day for the sake of the healthy country air. The family thought this a splendid idea, so did Bert, and the program was duly followed. The Chamberses would not permit him to bring out his own tea, so Mrs. Lawrence, in an effort to return hospitality, insisted that May come to her house for tea at least once. "Tea" in Eastwood, of course, was high tea, a substantial supper rather than the little in-between meal of the middle classes. It was the first time May had been there to tea, and she found the situation somewhat bizarre. Mrs. Lawrence and Bert were the life of the party until Mr. Lawrence came in, when everything changed. Bert's manner was transformed: instead of sparkling and laughing, he drew himself together, as it were, "humping himself up and bending his head over his plate." His father seemed not to notice this phenomenon but behaved in a normal, genial way as befitted the man of the house, addressing remarks to everyone in turn. Bert scarcely answered him, and Mrs. Lawrence, too, hardly raised her eyes and spoke only when necessary. Little Ada said something or other that made them laugh—at least, Mr. Lawrence laughed, and so did May until Bert angrily nudged her. It was a horrid sensation.

"There was such a hateful feeling coming from Bert that I was almost frightened," she wrote. "It was as if Prince Charming had changed into a toad."

As soon as the meal was over Mr. Lawrence left, probably aiming as fast as he could go for the nearest pub, and Bert became merry and sparkling once more.

"He hates his father," said Mrs. Lawrence complacently.

In the summer of 1901, when Bert's scholarship ended, he went to work, though not for long, as junior clerk in the Nottingham firm of J. H. Haywood, maker of surgical appliances and elastic stockings. That summer Ern brought his Gypsy home again, this time for two weeks, and her presence put the mother into an unusually sour mood. Bert told May, "Mother's wild because they lay on the sofa all one afternoon. It was raining, and they couldn't go out, and they lay on the sofa and talked. Mother's furious about it, but I can't see how it matters, can you? . . . Mother's carried on ever since they went about it. I wish she'd let the matter drop." But soon all Mrs. Lawrence's fury was forgotten, for a dreadful thing happened. In the autumn Ern fell ill of pneumonia and erysipelas, and died.

It was a terrible blow to the Lawrences, especially the Little Woman, though she managed even then to turn some of her rage against her husband. He was no help at all, she said bitterly to Jessie Chambers; all he did was fetch Ern's body home, leaving her to arrange the funeral and attendant matters. She grieved deeply. Nothing seemed to rouse her. For weeks she sat staring at nothing, listening to nothing, going through the day like a zombie, until in December she was jerked out of her apathy by another threatened tragedy. Now it was sixteen-year-old Bert who came down with pneumonia. One immediately jumps to the conclusion that he did it on purpose, as a kind of "me too" gesture to focus his mother's attention and love on himself, but an old friend, George Neville, thought otherwise. He happened to know, he told Lawrence's biographer Harry T. Moore, that the factory girls where Bert worked, a rough lot, had badly shocked and frightened him by cornering him in a storeroom and trying to expose his genital organs. He escaped this ultimate shame, but the experience made him vomit, and soon afterward he came down with pneumonia.

Whatever brought it on, the illness rudely shook Mrs. Lawrence out of her stupor. If Bert should die too! . . . She busied herself and nursed him with fierce devotion, and he recovered. But it was a long ordeal, and he seems to have thought the pneumonia laid the foundation for the tuberculosis that dogged his later years and finally killed him—not that he ever admitted it was TB. He might have been right about the aftereffect of pneumonia, but a doctor who was asked by Moore for a post-mortem opinion thought it unlikely that Lawrence contracted the disease until later in life. Possibly, however, this early complaint had an effect on the youth's voice. For the rest of his life it remained oddly high-pitched, growing even more shrill in moments of excitement.

"A curious hollow voice, like the soft hoot of an owl," Rebecca West said of it.

# 2

## *Jessie: "An ineradicable loyalty"*

As soon as Bert was convalescent, Mr. Chambers called for him with the milk cart and took him, carefully wrapped up, for a happy afternoon at The Haggs, and after a month's stay at an aunt's boardinghouse in Skegness he returned to his old program of visiting the farm, nowadays usually on Saturday. Even May's brothers were at last willing to like Bert, though at first acquaintance they had held him off. Alan, the eldest, was his favorite and was to be a model for the character of George Saxon in Lawrence's first novel, *The White Peacock*. Lawrence's character drawings were not quite like those of his contemporaries. Except in *Sons and Lovers* he did not make the portrait consistent with its model. Often he simply selected someone who caught his attention and transferred the person's appearance, manner of dress, and way of speaking to paper, almost as if he were drawing a paper doll. Then, to continue the analogy, he cut out this character and pasted it on the page, or rather shuffled it about the book, where it behaved and spoke as he dictated, rather than as the original would have behaved or spoken.

In the autumn of 1902, his health restored, Bert started on a new job better suited to his talents than clerking for a surgical-stocking manufacturer; through the good offices of Mrs.

Lawrence's friend the minister, he was given the post of pupil
teacher at the British School in Eastwood. About this time, too,
Lawrence's friendship with Jessie Chambers became important.

Ada Lawrence described Jessie under the name Lawrence
used for her in *Sons and Lovers:*

> Miriam inherited her mother's large brown eyes. Her figure
> was a little ungainly as she walked with her head and shoulders
> bent forward, but her black silky hair had a natural wave and
> from her shoulders upward she was beautiful.
>
> I think she first attracted Bert because she was so different
> from the gay, thoughtless girls we knew in the district. She was
> always very much in earnest about something or other, either
> her school work or a book, or her failing to understand her
> younger brothers or be understood by them. They delighted
> to offend her with little vulgarities.
>
> Unlike us, she was not interested in new clothes or sweet-
> hearts, and until her meeting with my brother she had made no
> friend.

Jessie was a year younger than Bert, fourteen years old
when he first came to The Haggs, and she was undergoing an
emotional crisis. For some reason her parents had decided that
she should stay at home and help her mother run the house,
though she longed passionately to go on with her education.
Every weekday morning she had to watch bright, self-assertive
May set out for school, then turn back to the kitchen. Jessie,
who was close to her mother, had adopted Mrs. Chambers's
fervent attachment to religion and took seriously the admonition to turn the other cheek; Lawrence was to write of Miriam's
humility in *Sons and Lovers* as an outstanding—and irritating—
characteristic. But all the humility in the world could not keep
Jessie from feeling miserable at home.

"I was the family drudge and hated it. My lack of education was a constant humiliation. The desire for knowledge and a
longing for beauty tortured me." The dreadful despondency of
adolescence weighed heavily on her. "I quarrelled continually

with my brothers, who tried to order me about. I felt an Ish-
mael, with my hand against everybody, and everybody's hand
against me."

When Bert Lawrence arrived in all his glory as a scholarship boy, she resented him as fiercely as she did May, and he
felt it and reacted characteristically. Throughout his life Lawrence took special notice of shy, retiring women. They presented him with a challenge, and he always set to work to draw
them out. So he encouraged Jessie to talk, plucked chords in
her spirit, and, finally, gave her courage. One afternoon when he
was outdoors with her he wrote in chalk on the stable door
*Nil desperandum*—Never despair—and ran away. (Like many
schoolboys, Bert loved to use tags in foreign languages, and he
never outgrew the habit.) Jessie took this as an incitement to
fight for what she wanted. She grew so insistent and "disagree-
able," as she put it, that her mother changed her mind about
keeping her at home. Jessie happily returned to school and became a pupil teacher at Underwood School a mile from the
farm, willingly making the time to do household chores when
she wasn't working at her job. Bert insisted on helping her with
her homework. The two friends would study at the side table
in the kitchen while the evening routine went on around them
—milking, bathing the small children, baking. There in the
kitchen they carried on animated discussions about books and
life and religion. On fine afternoons, with a group of other
young people, they went on tours to beauty spots, by train or
tram or on foot for long distances, Lawrence the leading spirit
as always, telling the other about the birds and flowers they saw.
And on Thursday afternoons, when the Mechanics' Library was
open for two hours in Eastwood, Jessie and Lawrence would
meet to turn over the stock of books and make selections.

Jessie was valuable to Lawrence partly because of her love
of books and docility in being taught, but also, no doubt, because she was rosy and handsome. She was deeply serious:
fervent, gentle, and not very sure of herself. She did not laugh

readily and was probably slow to see the point of a joke, but this was no drawback in a pretty girl who so patently admired everything he said or did. One day a member of May's class at school reported enthusiastically that she had seen on the railway platform a lovely girl who resembled an Italian painting. Who could it be? Tracked down by the description of her clothes, it turned out that this romantic vision was seventeen-year-old Jessie Chambers. Yes, she was valuable to Lawrence, but he seems not to have forgotten his mother's dictum about safety in numbers. He still laughed and larked with May, and the group that went on tours together, the Pagans as they named themselves, were for the most part girls.

For several years now he had been going out to The Haggs at least once a week, and his mother began to resent it. Though it was through her suggestion that he had at first begun to visit the Chambers family, and everybody still believed in the efficacy of the pine-laden air for his weak lungs, Mrs. Lawrence thought it was becoming too much of a good thing. Sarcastically she mentioned to Mr. Chambers that "Bert might as well pack his box" and move in on them for good, but it was never any use being sarcastic with Mr. Chambers; he just laughed and said that the family would like it if Bert did. Even so, young Lawrence did most of his studying at home where, as May observed, his book-laden table was usually surrounded by the inevitable neighborhood girls, who chatted with Mrs. Lawrence as he tried to concentrate. His mother entertained the girls with her clever remarks but her sharp eyes followed every move if one of the maidens should ask Bert for help on a school problem. Nothing slipped past Mrs. Lawrence. She often said that it kept her young, having so many youthful creatures about—and, as she inevitably added, there was safety in numbers. At these times the bright little woman appeared to May quite unlike the moaning housewife one saw in the morning, but the girls around her were never allowed to forget even then how heavy a cross she bore, married as she was to a

man who spent his evenings and his money in taverns. When
Eastwood inhabitants discussed the Lawrences, and Arthur's
friends among the men were brave enough to speak up for him
and say he wasn't so bad, the neighborhood girls were quick to
take Mrs. Lawrence's side. Like Bert, they were thoroughly
indoctrinated. She told them, more than once, of the dreadful
night when Arthur, in a drunken rage because she remonstrated
with him, had put her out of the house—and she pregnant.
(This scene occurs, of course, in *Sons and Lovers.*)

"He put me out and locked the door," said the Little
Woman. "Aye, there's a reason for hate and nasty temper. It
was in them before they were born."

But the loyal little band of believers could not change the
minds of those townspeople who had fixed ideas about Bert.
One of these was the salesman in a store where Bert chatted
with May about his purchases and other household matters.
"He's not right in his head!" said the salesman as the door
closed behind young Lawrence. "Anybody'll tell you he's not
right in his head! Do you know another lad as 'ud stand and
talk like a woman about groceries? Do you ever see him with
a gang o' lads? Do you ever see him without two, three girls?
You can't tell me he's right in his head. Anybody'll tell you
the same!"

"Eh, that Bertie Lawrence is none long for this world, I'm
thinking," said May's grandmother. But it was well known that
the Chamberses had a prejudice in Bert's favor, and most Eastwood boys went on laughing at him.

"Kindly folk dubbed him 'Jack among the Maidens,'"
wrote May. "Youths passed him up as a 'tea leaf,' but the majority were harsh in their judgment, the general remark being
'He should see a doctor.' He was well aware of all this but
disdained it." Dicky Dicky Denches kept his chin up and went
his way.

In 1903, as part of her schedule, Jessie had to go to Ilkeston
several days a week to study at the Training Centre. At Law-

rence's suggestion, on her way home on Friday evening she would stop at his house for a French lesson, after which he walked back with her at least part of the way. Mrs. Lawrence and her elder daughter, Emily, who was now Mrs. Samuel King, seem to have discussed this new development (as they discussed everything to do with Bert) and agreed that it was not a good thing. Both Chambers girls, May and Jessie, were obviously after their treasure, but which girl did he really like? In any case it was an outrage that he should spend so much time at the farm, and one day when May went to see Mrs. Lawrence the women asked so many probing questions, in such a catty way, that May got angry. She complained to Bert about it, but he refused to take it seriously, and his visits to The Haggs continued.

May tried to follow his example. One evening she even dropped in at his house after chapel with a number of other young people, to sing at the piano and eat cake as she had often done before, but she could see that Mrs. Lawrence was coldly furious with her, and she resolved that this would be the last time. Anything would be better, she thought, than courting his mother's deep aversion: "She tried to hide it under witty sallies; but whether she took refuge in irony or sarcasm, it flashed from her eyes, and the bitter curl of her lip, and the turn of her head."

May could not understand why others in her family remained blind to such signs of enmity, but they did; her brothers and Jessie continued to accept Bert's invitations to go home with him.

Soon ill-natured scraps of gossip came to May's ears, things that the Lawrence women were saying about the farm's family —that they were stealing Bert from his mother; that Jessie took up too much of his time and kept him indoors when he should have been in the open air; that she was taking too much for granted; that he only went to The Haggs for his health's sake, not because of fondness for any particular member of the family. When May repeated these rumors to her parents and begged them to forbid Bert to come over any more, her father laughed at her. "If his mother doesn't want him to come, she must stop him. I shan't," he said, and she had to give up.

In any case it was not so much her battle as Jessie's. She herself was engaged to be married, and her fiancé, a young stonemason named Will Holbrook, was at the house even more of the time than Bert Lawrence. J. D. Chambers said that Will was lively and full of tall stories that kept the young children in shrieks of laughter. Chambers thought, probably correctly, that Lawrence was jealous of Holbrook. He generally took care to keep out of his rival's way. Then Will made a stone carving, a portrait of his beloved, which Lawrence said was an atrocious piece of work. One day—doubtless during Will's absence—Bert actually took a coal pick and smashed the thing. Such an arbitrary, malicious act would have called down the elder Chamberses' wrath on any less favored youth, but Bert could do no harm in their eyes and they forgave even that crime, though what May thought of it is not recorded.

Jessie listed the books she and Lawrence read through the years, from their first youthful enthusiasms—James Fenimore Cooper and *Rupert of Hentzau* and *The Prisoner of Zenda* (solemn Jessie found the latter two somewhat trivial)—through Robert Louis Stevenson to George Eliot. They read *Jane Eyre* and moved on to Thackeray. When she was eighteen Lawrence brought *The Golden Treasury* to the farm in his pocket, and through the following weeks he read it to her from cover to cover. Bacon, Emerson, Thoreau, Carlyle. They were happy, untroubled days for Jessie, at home and at school. She loved the Training Centre and everything to do with it: the long early morning walk to the station, the novelty of the short train journey to Ilkeston, and, most of all, the Friday-evening French lesson with Lawrence. With any luck his mother went out marketing then, like most of Eastwood, and Ada too was often out, so Jessie and Lawrence could talk without interruption. Lawrence spoke of himself and what he meant to do in the future about his career. For example, he wanted to have a big house where his mother, himself, and all the people he liked could live together; wouldn't that be fine?

One day, suddenly, he asked her if she had ever thought of writing. Yes, said Jessie, of course she had, all her life, and what of him? It was the same with him, Lawrence said. "Well, let's make a start," he continued. "I'm sure we could do something if we tried. Lots of the things we say, the things you say, would go ever so well into a book."

So the weeks went on for Jessie from Friday to Friday. Not all of the French-lesson evenings were perfect, it is true. As long as she and Lawrence were alone there was magic in the air, but Mrs. Lawrence and Ada would sometimes interrupt them and drive them from that world in which they shared each intense feeling and thought. Writing of their relations even years later, poor Jessie insisted again and again that they had been perfectly pure, as if she were still answering the brooding, censorious ghost of Lawrence's mother.

"We talked about books and writers, and about life, gropingly, trying to find the hidden reality behind the appearance of things. Towards one another we were utterly unself-conscious except for a strong feeling of mutual sympathy," she protested. "We were too content with the present to look into the future." She had the feeling, moreover, that their walks and talks on the way home after study were important and would be memorable: there was something creative about them. "An ineradicable loyalty to Lawrence grew up in me; his significance seemed beyond that of an ordinary man. I felt that I was in the presence of greatness." It is small wonder that he should have said to her earnestly, "Every great man—every man who achieves anything, I mean—is founded in some woman. Why shouldn't *you* be the woman I am founded in?"

Mrs. Lawrence knew why Jessie shouldn't. Unfortunately, even the Friday lessons were not always private. Frequently Mrs. Lawrence and her baleful chorus of maidens were there too. The girls would sit watching the students quizzically, making significant remarks which Jessie was not able to brush off. One girl was especially good at this; "her gibes flew like arrows." Meantime the Little Woman would go about housewifely affairs with a subtle smile, well pleased with the proceedings. Lawrence ignored it all and went ahead with his work, but Jessie could not, though she understood the cause of it as far as the girls were concerned: the collier people were clannish and resented her as a farmer's daughter. Once she reproached Lawrence for not defending her, but he only replied in a high-and-mighty way, "I never take sides."

Because of all this, at the end of term the Friday lessons were given up, and such studying as the friends had together was carried on in the farm kitchen. Even then the friendship flourished.

"We did not speak of love although we knew it lay ahead, something that would have to be faced," Jessie remembered. "But the time was not ripe." Poor girl: hers was no unusual story. It often happened to women in love with Lawrence that the time was not ripe.

If she had been older or wiser—but she wasn't, so she didn't recognize the first hint of trouble on the horizon. Lawrence invited her to a Christmas party at his house, and added, "I *would* come and meet you, but already they're beginning to say I care more for you than for them. It isn't that . . . they don't understand."

His visits continued, regular as ever, until Easter, when Jessie attended chapel in Eastwood and after the service went to the Lawrence house with him. Emily was there, supporting her mother with a heavy air of disapproval. Her reinforcement made Jessie a little uncomfortable, more than usually aware of hostility, but she had got used to undercurrents in that house and so took no warning. When Lawrence escorted her back as far as the field path he leaned over to say softly, "I shall come up to-morrow—early."

Jessie went home, she says, with a singing in her heart. She could imagine nothing better to look forward to. Her brothers would be out on their bicycles and May was going to Liverpool with Will Holbrook, leaving her at home, but what matter? Bert was coming early.

He didn't come. Jessie helped her mother in the house all morning, expecting him to arrive. He didn't come at noon, and when he cycled in at last, late in the afternoon, and she reproached him, he was silent. Not until after tea, when they went outdoors to read French, did he make a clean breast of what was troubling him. His mother and Emily had been lecturing him and asking his intentions toward Jessie: were they or weren't they courting?

"I thought, I don't know, you might be getting to care too much for me," he went on haltingly. Now this was an exceedingly difficult remark to react to, implying as it did that Jessie had been unmaidenly enough to have feelings. Remember the year, 1906. It was, in fact, the first cannon shot in all-out war. Jessie's words in reply may sound unreasonable now, but they made sense then:

"Ah—I always thought your mother didn't like me."

No, no, said Lawrence, it was not like that, not like that at all. His mother hadn't anything against Jessie. In fact, it was for Jessie's sake that she had spoken. Going on as they were was not fair to the girl because it kept her out of circulation, prevented her from finding someone else to care for.

Someone else? Jessie, who had never cared about clothes or parties or beaux, or anyone but Lawrence, was staggered. She sat like a stone figure while Lawrence went on, reciting the lesson he had been filled with. His mother, he said, had shown him the error of his selfish ways and insisted that he work out for himself how he felt about Jessie, in all fairness to the girl. And he had done so, he continued; he had looked into his heart "and I cannot find that I love you as a husband should love his wife. Perhaps I shall, in time. If ever I find I

do, I'll tell you. What about you? If you think you love me,
tell me, and we'll be engaged. What do you think?"

Mrs. Lawrence's ploy does not seem so very extraordinary.
Many another mother has used a similar strategy—"It's not fair
to the girl." It is Lawrence himself who sounds peculiar. No
girls within Jessie's knowledge, practical or literary, had ever
received such a grudging proposal, and it is no wonder that at
first she found it difficult to speak at all. At last she mustered
up enough pride to refuse his offer—if that is what it was—and
to go on, in ladylike fashion, to say that they should stop seeing each other.

Certainly they must go on seeing each other, said Lawrence
decidedly. "Mother said we needn't give everything up, only
we must know what footing we're on, that's all." And when
Jessie said that there was no footing, he insisted. "We shall not
give everything up. It means too much to us." There was far
too much to talk about; they had to talk about writing, and
the French lessons should go on, only they would have to read
in the house, or where "they" could see them. There must be
no more walks and talks by themselves, that was all. For example, said Lawrence, he would tell Alan not to cycle to chapel
on Sunday, so he could walk home with them, and when they
went out into the fields, one or two of the younger children
could go with them.

Jessie was torn to pieces. In implying that a nice girl might
have sexual impulses toward Lawrence, Mrs. Lawrence was
breaking all the rules and accusing her of immodest behavior.

On the other hand, Lawrence could not be blamed, Jessie
felt; he was innocent, sometimes, indeed, exasperatingly so, as
when, after laying down the rules that afternoon, he actually
asked, "Will you tell your mother?"

No, said Jessie, she would not.

"Shall I tell them, then?" he asked, and he seemed surprised
and distressed when she said no to that too, and burst into tears.

"They'd be awfully angry and tell you never to come
again," she sobbed.

Afterward he went indoors with her as if nothing had happened and stayed a little while, brushing off Mrs. Chambers's anxious fussing over him because he looked pale. Jessie was left to deal alone with her humiliation and "sense of irreparable loss."

For the rest of her life she felt that Lawrence's mother had deliberately destroyed something diaphanous and beautiful. They were still immature and unprepared, she said, when "the issue of love in its crudest sense" was forced upon them.

Yet after this crisis things went on much as before, except that the new rules made by Lawrence were carefully observed. When Alan, in spite of directions, cycled to chapel after all, and Jessie started out to walk home on her own, Lawrence ran after her and insisted on accompanying her—bringing with him a young man he knew she disliked—and scolded her for not waiting. At least once he even made her come home to tea and see his mother.

"We exchanged a seared glance," wrote Jessie, "but never made any reference to what was uppermost in our thoughts."

Mrs. Lawrence now grudgingly accepted Jessie's presence, even, oddly enough, on the rare holiday trips that Lawrence and his parents made to the seaside. The girl had been warned, she probably felt, and the young people would not now easily forget themselves. Nor did they. When a youth of their acquaintance made a girl pregnant, Mrs. Lawrence lectured Bert —now nearly twenty-one—on the pitfalls of what she called five minutes of forgetfulness, and the lecture did not fall on deaf ears. White with emotion, he said to Jessie, "Thank God . . . I've been saved from that . . . so far."

Not surprisingly, things were no longer free and easy between Lawrence and Jessie. He was irritable and hypercritical. He scolded her when she caressed flowers or hugged her little brother: why must she keep *touching* things? She ought to learn detachment, he said, and at least once, unwittingly, he put his finger on the trouble. "If only you'd been a man," he told her, "things might have been perfect."

Jessie found him mystifying in this mood, though when he said, "You'd be easier to understand, you know, if you would be a bit naughty sometimes," she knew perfectly well what he meant and saw the justice of his complaint. The trouble was that she had become too self-conscious of the barrier raised between them to relax; she could not ignore it. She could only remain silent and listen to his criticisms, to which there seemed no reply. She scarcely protested when he picked her to pieces and told her that she had no humor, or pointed out that she wasn't popular—why was that?—or said scornfully that she had no intellect and was governed by her feelings rather than her mind. Suddenly he changed direction and announced that the real trouble lay in himself: he was two men, not one. One part of his nature needed Jessie deeply, he explained, but the other part, his animal side, needed someone else. Every man should be allowed two wives, he once declared, and on her twenty-first birthday he wrote her a letter making the idea clearer:

> When I look at you, what I see is not the kissable and embraceable part of you, although it is so fine to look at, with the silken toss of hair curling over your ears. What I see is the deep spirit within. That I love and can go on loving all my life. . . . Look, you are a nun, I give you what I would give a holy nun. So you must let me marry a woman I can kiss and embrace and make the mother of my children.

In spite of this he still seems to have considered himself engaged to Jessie, and there is no doubt that he, at least half of him, needed her. He had begun to write his first novel, "Nethermere," eventually published under the title *The White Peacock*, and he had to have her advice. He would give her several pages at a time, as he finished them, and wait impatiently for her to read them and give her opinion. The friends had most of their discussions at Ilkeston, meeting in the street after a lecture where no Eastwood neighbors could spy; there Jessie gave her careful opinions and afterward Lawrence ran to catch an early train back home. Having finished her classwork, Jessie took a later train and usually met him again at The Haggs, over the tea table. By the end of the year he had finished the first draft and was writing poems at the same time, and all his writing, poems and book, invariably went to Jessie for judgment.

He must have shown "Nethermere" to his mother too, because she said to Jessie, "To think that *my* son should have written such a story."

We will never know what she found to disapprove of, because he later wrote the book all over again, but it is hard to imagine anything in it that might have offended the most modest reader. Subsequent books, yes, but the poor "Peacock"? It is useless to conjecture. Jessie's dislike of the first version was on other grounds than propriety; she found it bookish and unreal. The final one she thought much improved.

It was autumn, 1907, when Lawrence, embarking on the second and last year of his college course, saw a notice in the local paper offering a prize of three guineas for the best Christmas story submitted to the editor. Each contestant was permitted only one try, but Lawrence thought of a way around that. He wrote three stories and asked Jessie and another friend, Louise Burrows, to submit one, each under her name, while he sent in the third. The story submitted by Jessie got the prize and was printed. Mr. Chambers was in on the secret and amiably congratulated Bert as he cashed the check for Jessie and handed the money over to the real author, but May, careful May, who always listened to what people were saying, heard the rumor that Bert was writing stories and letting Jessie take the credit. This upset her and she demanded the truth of Bert. He denied that there was anything in the gossip—the tale was Jessie's, he said—but May found out eventually and was angry.

"If she had stolen that story from him, her integrity could not have been more bitterly assailed," she declared. The teacup storm soon died down; it is retailed here merely to illustrate how precarious a girl's position was in that society, at that time.

# 3

## *Jessie and Helen: "A unique bond"*

WHEN the college course ended for Lawrence in 1908 he drew a deep sigh of relief. It had been a waste of time, he declared. He urged Mr. Chambers not to consider sending Jessie for similar training, because he regretted every minute he had spent there. But now came the question familiar to graduates: what to do next. The teaching jobs he first investigated were ludicrously underpaid and he refused to consider them. For three months he did nothing. Then came a reasonable offer of an assistant mastership at the Davidson Road School in Croydon, a suburb of London, which paid £95 a year, and he accepted. "What shall *I* do when he's gone?" moaned Mrs. Lawrence to Jessie. "And where would he have been without me to call him up in a morning, and have his porridge and everything ready for him? He'd never have got off to College every day if I hadn't seen to things."

Jessie thought it ridiculous to make so much of these motherly duties. But then, the girl decided, Mrs. Lawrence very probably didn't see Lawrence, or even want to see him, as a genius; it would set him apart from her. Her own sense of loss was tempered by the pride she must always keep close at hand. On his farewell visit to The Haggs, she walked with him to the last gate and he said, indicating the surrounding farmland and

woods, *"La dernière fois."* Jessie promptly burst into tears, at
which Lawrence put his arms around her, kissed her and soothed
her, murmuring, "I'm so sorry, so sorry, so sorry."

"His words scalded me," said Jessie, and she drew away and
dried her tears.

"I'm so sorry for this. But it can't be helped, it can't be
helped," he repeated.

"Never mind, it doesn't matter," said Jessie.

He wrote a letter to her the day after he got to Croydon
—"like a howl of terror," she said. He was in an agony of
homesickness and dreaded going to work, but he begged her to
say nothing of this to his mother. At any rate, soon he was
feeling better and enjoying London, even able to start a second
revision of *The White Peacock.* During his Christmas fortnight
at home he described his rooms in Croydon and the people he
lived with, the family of School Attendance Officer John William Jones from Lancashire, who had a small child and a baby
named Hilda. Lawrence immediately struck up a special relationship with Hilda.

"I was glad when I knew there was a baby. It will keep
him pure," said Mrs. Lawrence rather obscurely to Jessie.

Lawrence still wrote to Jessie almost every week. When
he came home they continued seeing each other as much as ever,
but there was a change in him; he began to discuss sex. Perhaps, said Jessie scrupulously, "began to" was not the right
phrase, because he had mentioned the thing directly twice before. Once, for example, after asking if she minded the word,
he quoted Chesterton to the effect that the man who talked
about sex to a woman is a brute. Jessie said to that, "Why,
surely, it's the other way about. The man who can't speak
properly to a woman about sex is a brute."

Lawrence agreed. He had been shocked, he implied, by a
conversation he overheard on the train between some commercial travelers discussing the taboo subject. "If you had heard
them, you'd have had to rush away," he said darkly. On the

other occasion he had expressed the idea that while it was proper for him, as a man, to know all about the worldly attitude to sex, Jessie should remain in comparative ignorance.

"I *must* know about those things," he said, "but why should you want to?"

Jessie, a well-brought-up girl, assured him that she didn't want to because such matters didn't interest her, but when he went on to state firmly that she should never try to experience love and marriage, she felt that she had to protest. Why, she demanded, should one half of life be forbidden to her, especially as Lawrence was explicit about the marriage *he* intended to make—to satisfy the purely "animal" side of his nature? He even mentioned the girl he thought would fill the role: Louise Burrows. Jessie refused to take him seriously.

"He was too vehement; I felt that he was trying to force himself in that direction," she said. Yet she could not forget that one summer afternoon a year or so earlier he had gone to Louie Burrows's home for tea on purpose, he gave Jessie to understand, to find out whether his feelings for Louie were truly animal. Some days later, "with a significant glance," he handed Jessie the poem "Snapdragon," one of the most sexually explicit that he ever wrote.

Louie was slightly younger than Jessie. She had grown up in the nearby village of Cossall, the eldest of the eight children of a draftsman in a lace factory, and had known Lawrence as long as Jessie had and had much in common with the other girl. She too was a pupil teacher, she too attended the Centre, and she too was one of the Pagans. Though her parents were not as fond of Lawrence as the Chamberses were, he knew them well; in his novel *The Rainbow*, the Brangwens share many of the Burrows family's interests and live in the Burrows cottage. Louie had aspirations to be a writer, and from 1906 on she and Lawrence wrote to each other on such matters. She attended Nottingham University College at the same time as he and took her degree when he did. She was quicker at finding a situation than he was, no doubt because she didn't hold out for as much salary; during his idle summer she began teaching in Leicestershire, and her people moved to Quorn near Leicester.

Little by little, after Lawrence decided that Louie would satisfy his animal yearnings, his letters to her became more personal. On April 21, 1908, he finished one of his notes with the apprehensive passage:

*Au revoir—jusqu'à jeudi.* I trust you and [Jessie] are having a good time—have you yet fallen on each other's necks and poured out your hearts in girlish sympathy?
*"Est et fideli tuta silentio.*
*Merces."*
Which is "There is a safe reward awaits faithful silence."

Why was he nervous about the girls' talking him over? Surely it was not in order to spare Jessie; he never tried very hard to do that. More likely he worried for fear Louie would find out too much. After he went to Croydon, the friendship lagged for a while.

When, years later, an interviewer asked Mr. Jones about his famous lodger, the landlord had plenty to say. Most men considered Lawrence effeminate, he recollected, but they must have been wrong because he had great appeal for women. There was one especially, a red-haired girl named Agnes Holt who was a teacher at Davidson Road along with Lawrence; Lawrence, said Mr. Jones, "was very bitter against her because she would not fall in with his wishes"—but he was no more explicit, and we are left wondering. While they were still friendly she did some copying for him. A friend of hers saw and recognized her writing on portions of the manuscript of *The White Peacock.* There were also traces in Lawrence's letters of otherwise unknown girls of the Croydon period. "I am having one or two delightful little flirtations—quite little, but piquant," he wrote to a friend, Blanche Jennings, but after seeing Louie that Christmas he wrote to the same friend of an old fire that had burned up afresh, adding:

She knows me through and through, and I know her. . . .
We have fine, mad little scenes now and again, she and I—so
strange, after ten years, and I had hardly kissed her all that
time. She has black hair, and wonderful eyes, big and very
dark, and very vulnerable; she lifts up her face to me and clings
to me, and the time goes like a falling star, swallowed up immediately; it is wonderful, that time, long avenues of minutes
—hours—should be swept up with one sweep of the hand, and
the moment for parting has arrived when the first kiss seems
hardly overkissed. . . . What would my people and hers say?—
but what do I care— not a damn!

As the editor of Lawrence's letters to Louie rightly remarks, however, obviously he did care, for when he wrote her
to arrange this very meeting—the letter was dated December
11, 1909—he said, "I *must* squeeze in a day this time, at Quorn.
I will see what mother says."

When he lost his virginity Lawrence was careful to keep
quiet about it, though it must have been difficult not to tell
Jessie at least, out of sheer habit. The identity of the woman
is known because somebody else blabbed—Councilor William
Hopkin, the man who had urged the child Bert to stick up for
himself.

Willie Hopkin was a man with an interesting career and a
pleasant personality. A Socialist, he was in his time, to quote
biographer Edward Nehls's list, "Colliery clerk, cobbler, pro-
prietor of boot-shop in Eastwood, magistrate and member of
County Council, antiquarian, local historian." His first wife,
Sallie, had a great friend named Alice Dax, wife of the local
pharmacist, Henry Dax; she was the lady who seduced Lawrence. Alice, according to Sallie Hopkin's daughter, Enid Hilton, was years ahead of her time—uninhibited—an original who
refused to have any clutter in her house and who was herself
"clear, direct, uncluttered in thought and action, to the point
of harshness." She and Mrs. Hopkin used to take little Enid to

women's rights meetings in Nottingham and bring the speakers home afterward to stay with the Hopkins. Socialists such as Keir Hardy, Ramsay MacDonald, the Webbs, and Margaret Bondfield were among them. The Hopkins held open house for the villagers at these times, and Lawrence was often a guest then, though he never accepted Socialism. Enid Hilton said that Alice Dax was "one of the kindest persons I have ever met, but most men of her generation feared her. She represented a kind of ramrod, forcing the future into their present in an uncomfortable and uncomprehended manner."

It comes as a surprise to learn that she was a small, petite blonde, but the word "uninhibited" does seem justified to describe her. Councilor Hopkin overheard her telling his wife, "Sallie, I gave Bert sex. I had to. He was over at our house struggling with a poem he couldn't finish, so I took him upstairs and gave him sex. He came downstairs and finished the poem." One wonders which poem.

Alice Dax was considerably older than Lawrence, which is not remarkable; probably the majority of men are introduced to the facts of life by more mature females. But Lawrence after his initiation (at about twenty-three) continued through life to find attraction in older women rather than younger ones. Jessie was younger, and he railed at her with monotonous regularity for—it seems obvious—failing to seduce him, for not taking the initiative. He seems to have wanted to reenact the fall from grace in the garden of Eden; the woman should have tempted him. When she didn't, he blamed her.

The affair between Mrs. Dax and Lawrence went smoothly for a while at least. It was a closely guarded secret from all but Alice's best friends, and they, unlike many other friends, really held their tongues. It would have been dangerous to gossip about it in Eastwood; not many inhabitants would have cared to get into trouble with Mrs. Lawrence, and, for another thing, there was Henry Dax. The secrecy was hard on Alice Dax because she really fell in love with Lawrence, so much so that when she bore a child she hoped fervently it would be his. However, the boy was obviously Henry's, and she had to relinquish her dream and Lawrence too when he outgrew the affair. After they parted, she never let another man, not even her husband, touch her.

In springtime, 1908, when Lawrence had not yet found his Croydon job, he and Jessie talked seriously about trying to get some of his work published, but his first attempt (if we forget the Christmas stories) was lamentably amateurish. He simply picked out the name of a newspaper columnist whose work he thought good and sent the man something he had written, along with a letter asking for the professional's opinion. The writer took a long time to reply and then only said that he had no time to give advice. Lawrence felt rebuffed and wounded. He said to Jessie, "I've tried, and been turned down, and I shall try no more. And I don't care if I never have a line published."

Jessie knew this for a lie but was wise enough not to argue the point, and nothing more was said about it until summer, 1909, when he was at home on holiday. A new magazine, the *English Review*, had been introduced to his Eastwood friends by Lawrence, and Jessie always read it eagerly. One day she came on a notice in its pages that the editor was prepared to welcome new talent. She showed it to Lawrence and proposed that he try his luck, but the prideful young man was still determined to make no more humiliating efforts to get himself into print. At last, when Jessie persisted, he said that if she wished she might send in some of his poems, anything she liked; he didn't care as long as she provided a nom de plume, because, he said, he didn't want people in Croydon to know that he wrote poetry.

Jessie sent off half a dozen poems with a covering letter to the editor about the young man who had written them, who, she said, would be grateful for a little recognition. Soon afterward Lawrence, temporarily abandoning his pose of indifference, asked if she had sent anything. When he learned that she had, he said, immediately that they'd never print them—which was patently the equivalent of crossing his fingers.

Novelist Ford Madox Hueffer, who was to change his name during the First World War to the less Teutonic-sounding Ford Madox Ford, was editor of the *Review*. In his memoirs in later life he declared that it was not so much Lawrence's poetry as a short story by him, included with Jessie's letter, that caught his attention. Jessie's story is different, but never mind; the editor sniffed talent. He wrote to Miss Chambers suggesting that the young man come to see him next time he was in London.

It was then August, and the letter arrived at the farm while Lawrence was away at Shanklin, Isle of Wight, disporting with a few of the Pagans under the chaperonage of Mrs. Lawrence and Ada, so Jessie saved her momentous news until he got back. One can imagine with what pleasure she then handed him the magic piece of paper. He was tremendously excited. "*You* are my luck," he exclaimed. "Let me take it to show mother."

"And I never saw it again," wrote Jessie.

A more sophisticated man might have dashed straight to London, but Lawrence did not. Fame and fortune could wait; he still had several weeks of holiday. Not having shared the Pagans' seaside outing, Jessie too wanted a jaunt, and now she reminded Lawrence that they had talked of a one-day trip to Nottingham to look at historical remains. His mother and Ada were to come along, according to the plan, and Jessie would spend the following night with the Holbrooks, who lived close by. From something in his manner she gathered that he was doubtful if the idea would attract his mother; still, they arranged to go. She was to pick up the Lawrences at their house, but when she got there she found Mrs. Lawrence very stiff and distant. No mention was made of Ford's letter, and Jessie suspected that she was in disgrace for having written to him. No, Mrs. Lawrence was not coming, she said, nor was Ada.

The two young people set out for Nottingham in a state of

gloom. As usual in such circumstances Lawrence seemed determined to take revenge on Jessie for his mother's bad temper.
He behaved in an arrogant, unpleasant manner all day and took
every opportunity to snub her. When he bought some photographs of Greek statues he said that one of them, "Amor et
Psyche," was for her, because Jessie was Psyche, the soul, and
had no other significance for him. He harped on this theme,
embellished it, and railed at her until she was quite beaten down.
In the evening, at the door of May's cottage, he refused to come
in but made one more dramatic speech of abuse and glared at
her for a time before stamping off into the darkness. For a day
or so Jessie coped with misery; then she came to a decision. It
was the end of Lawrence for her. She couldn't bear it any
longer. No more waiting for him to make up his mind whether
he did or didn't love her, she said to herself. She went back to
Nottingham and left her name at an agency for teachers, as one
in search of a position.

It was a calmer Lawrence who came to say good-bye to
her before leaving again for his job in Croydon, but she could
never be sure how long his calm would last. Walking back with
him as far as the farm's outer gate, she tried to avoid controversial subjects, but soon the conversation led back to the old
theme, with which he seemed to have become obsessed, of how,
when, and whom he should marry.

"It isn't that I don't want to marry," said Lawrence, "I'd
marry to-morrow, if I could only find someone I *could* marry.
I'd marry *you* if only I could. As I am at present I shall go
from woman to woman until I am satisfied."

Jessie was shocked. "I looked at him in horror and com-
passion . . ." she wrote. "I could say nothing, and left him. I
crossed the field path in the soft starlight. . . . It was midnight
when I went to the house."

What are we to make of all this? Possibly Lawrence was
already acting out the argument he was later to develop in
*Sons and Lovers*, the story of the boy whose mother held him

so tightly he was unable to love anyone else as long as she lived. But there seems something more in his treatment of Jessie, which was so adroitly cruel that one cannot give him the benefit of the doubt by saying he didn't realize what he was doing. Why should he go on proving his power to hurt, over and over again? There is nothing mysterious about Jessie's reactions, she was a born victim not only of Lawrence but of the social and religious code in which she had been reared. It is his actions that are not easy to interpret.

Of course this was not the end of their friendship; as he would have explained, there was still far too much to tell her. First, he had to go and visit the *English Review* office, an encounter Ford described in his memoirs, *Portraits from Life*. Ford was really excited, he said; on the evening after he got Jessie's letter with its enclosures he had babbled about his new discovery at a London party of literati, though his enthusiasms were an old story to them.

"Hurray, Fordie's discovered another genius!" cried H. G. Wells, but before the party had ended two publishers were asking to see the new genius's first novel. Ford explained their interest: everyone at that time was eager to find working-class writers, but nobody had yet succeeded in doing so. Gissing and Wells were not really working-class, only lower-middle. The "artisan," said Ford, was a different animal, "as sharply divided from the ruling or even the mere white-collar classes as was the Negro from the gentry of Virginia." A rare specimen indeed—and he had caught it!

He expected gratitude and eagerness from the man he had chosen as a protégé, and it was disconcerting not to get a reply to his kindly letter. However, all was forgiven when the editor learned that the genius had been away from home when it arrived; "as one can well believe," said Ford, grandly indulgent, "holidays on the seashore from a Croydon board-school were moments too precious to be interrupted even for a visit to a first editor."

Then too, a teacher's time during the week is not his own. At last, on a Saturday in September, without bothering to make an appointment, Lawrence dropped in at Ford's office. The genius was not quite what the editor had expected. He did not stand there twisting his cap; he didn't even wear a cap. He was self-confident and reasonably well-spoken. This, one feels, was disappointing to Ford, and it was even more annoying that the working-class man should have refused to be overawed by the editor or the editor's luxurious appointments, which he failed to recognize as genuine antiques. He had expected something grander, he admitted. Ford forgave him, and even overlooked, in the kindest manner, Lawrence's brash announcement that he intended to earn a lot of money with his writing, something like two thousand a year. And when the self-appointed guide and counselor advised his discovery to stop teaching in order to devote his whole time to writing, Lawrence balked. His was a regular job, he said, and the pay was good; he would have to think things over very carefully before taking such a perilous step.

In his memoirs Ford confessed that he didn't like Lawrence much; he was too upsetting to like. He saw to it that everyone with whom he came in contact was forever aware of his problems. "He claimed moral support imperiously—and physical care too," wrote Ford. "I don't mean that he whined. He just ordered you to consider that there he was in Croydon subject to the drag of the minds of the school-children for hours every day in a fetid atmosphere," and after a while he made everybody else miserable about it too. Important figures like Galsworthy —"and of course several ladies" wrote Ford bitterly—began looking worried "because Lawrence was writing masterpieces and teaching in a fetid atmosphere." But to do Ford justice, he himself seems to have exhibited a considerable amount of solicitude. (It was to be through him, for instance, that Heinemann would publish Lawrence's second novel, *The White Peacock*, a book Ford didn't like, but this is anticipating.)

Lawrence wrote exultantly to Jessie about his interview with Ford, urging her to come up for a visit to Croydon and witness his triumph for herself. She could stay at the Jones house. She really must come; he had a lot to show her. He had written a play and some poems that he didn't have the time to copy out, and, as if this were not enough inducement for any girl, he wanted her to meet the girl he had almost decided to marry—Agnes Holt. How could any woman resist such blandishments? Yet Jessie hesitated, the memory of their last encounter still vivid in her mind. However, Lawrence persuaded her, and at the end of November she went to London by the morning train.

He met her at the station and outlined his plans. They would spend the day sightseeing, he said, going around the shops. And so they did, lunching at Selfridge's. It was all marvelous, thought Jessie, though she felt how trivial was all the wealth displayed in those shops compared with the joy of being with him—this in spite of the fact that he took the time to send a postcard to Miss Holt announcing that he would bring Jessie to meet her next morning.

"Will she really like to see me?" asked Jessie, incurably meek.

"Oh yes, she's keen on seeing you," said Lawrence, adding artlessly, "She thought herself great shakes until she met me and heard about you."

They saw a play in the evening. It was late when they got home and everyone had gone to bed, but Mrs. Jones had left them supper. Tired out after all the excitement, Jessie looked forward to bed, but Lawrence brought out the play and the poems and expected her to read them then and there, so she tried. It was no use; she would have to take them home, she told him, and read them again before she could give any sensible criticism. He accepted this dictum like a reasonable man, but he still didn't want her to retire. Couldn't she sit up one more hour? Yes, Jessie supposed she could.

What followed was for the most part familiar, but something new was mixed in. Lawrence asked her seriously what she hoped for in the future. What did she expect from life? Such questions usually made Jessie cry, and they did this time, but she replied steadily that she didn't know, couldn't tell, didn't hope for much, but would get along somehow, and wasn't afraid.

So much for politeness. After a seemly pause, Lawrence began talking about himself. He said he found all this, his new life, a terrible strain—the excitement, meeting such different people. It was hard to bear the stress alone, he said; he needed to be married.

"You know, I could so easily peg out," he said. Jessie, wiping her eyes, had a vision of a candle puffed out in a gust of wind, and it nearly set her off again. But, she pointed out to him, he had only to make a choice of brides. "Have I?" He sat thinking. "But I've no money," he said at last, "I shan't be able to marry for ever so long. I think I shall ask some girl if she will give me . . . that . . . without marriage. Do you think any girl would?"

"I don't know," she answered like the 1909 lady she was. "The kind of girl who would, I think you wouldn't like."

But would she think it wrong? he asked.

Not wrong, said Jessie, but it would be very difficult. And to herself she thought, in the words of the New Testament, "Whoso giveth a cup of cold water in My name . . ."

At this psychological moment Lawrence chose to say, "Well, I think I shall ask *her*. Do you think she would?"

It was a good try, but for the moment at least it didn't work. Jessie said, "It depends on how much she is in love with you. . . . Look, Bert, it's two o'clock. I really am tired now." He protested still, but she was firm and left him. After she was in bed she thought she heard a soft knock on the door, but she did not answer it and nothing more happened. This detail, which she omitted from her book, came out in the correspondence that she carried on much later with Emile Delavenay. It is thanks to him that we know much more about Jessie's relations with D. H. Lawrence than she wished to divulge herself, even under a nom de plume. Indeed, it was because of M. Delavenay's interest, and the questions of eager scholars as well as publishers, that she ever wrote her memoirs at all. Her husband, Jack—John R. Wood—pointed out to her that since everyone else was trying to use the material it would be better for her to publish it herself, and she saw the justice of the suggestion. But there were items she could not bring herself to include even then, in middle age. These she told—in part at least—to M. Delavenay.

That morning, after Jessie had refused to open her door, Lawrence took her to meet Agnes Holt as he had arranged. Miss Holt, Jessie thought, was pleasant enough, especially as she talked to Lawrence like an elder sister rather than a lover. She pinned a spray of red berries on Jessie's coat, evidently thinking that they were becoming to a dark-haired, dark-eyed girl. Somewhat ostentatiously Lawrence arranged to meet Agnes later, after his guest had left, and he and Jessie moved on. They were on their way to a luncheon at the house of Violet Hunt, reader on the *English Review* and Ford's mistress, but first they went to the combination flat and office where the editor lived to pick him up. Ford was kind to Jessie, though he had certain cut-and-dried ideas about working-class girls.

"You're a sort of Socialist, I suppose?" he said genially.

Jessie, who had never given a thought to politics, was startled, but she began thinking about it: was she or wasn't she? In the end she did, in fact, become an ardent Socialist and pacifist, but that did not happen for some years.

The three moved on to Miss Hunt's house, actually her old mother's in Kensington, where the other luncheon guests included a young American poet named Ezra Pound. He showed off a bit, but that was all right with Jessie; anything that drew attention from herself was welcome. Shy enough to begin with, she was doubly confused to realize that she was there under false colors, because both Ford and Miss Hunt treated her as if she were Lawrence's fiancée. She felt guilty and wondered if she could not tell them about Agnes Holt, but there seemed no way to bring the topic into the open.

In Violet Hunt's account of the party she did refer to Jessie as the girl engaged to Lawrence: "D. H. Lawrence brought his fiancée to lunch. She was like a brown bird, bright-eyed, her little head covered with curling russet locks like feathers. Obviously, when at home, a dashing young party. Here she was obviously nervous, but pulled it off all right."

During a walk after lunch Ford asked Jessie why she didn't come and teach in London and then suggested that she write something about herself. Lawrence cut in at this point—after all, *he* was the genius, not Jessie. He said, "It wouldn't be any good. She's incommunicable." When they had parted from Ford he was still ruffled, saying impatiently, "Isn't he fat, and doesn't he walk *slow!*" Jessie replied sedately that the editor was wonderfully kind. "Oh, he's kind, he's *kind*," said Lawrence. Then he suddenly asked Jessie how she liked having champagne with her lunch. "I said I didn't know it was champagne, but that anyhow I liked it," she reported. "Then he said: 'Did you hear where [Ford] said he was going next? He was going to see Lady——' " As he pronounced the title he gave Jessie one of his significant glances, to show that he was impressed and thought she should be too. It always made her a little impatient that so talented a man should be impressed by titles, but that was the way Lawrence was and she accepted the trait because it was his.

Seeing her off at the station, he asked her to go and call on his mother when she got back to Eastwood, saying, "She'll like to hear how we went on."

Though this seemed questionable to Jessie, she did as she had promised, went to see Mrs. Lawrence, and duly described the lunch party.

"Well, it would be very interesting," said Mrs. Lawrence almost genially. But a few minutes afterward, discussing one of Ford's stories, she said with heavy meaning, "When two women are in love with the same man, one of them usually has to be disappointed."

Yes, Jessie agreed evenly, that was usually the way. Inwardly she comforted herself with the thought that all this would soon be over. She had a job and was going to take it up after the beginning of the new year. Her family too were leaving the neighborhood, moving to another farm near Nottingham.

"I was glad to be leaving the valley, that I had completely outgrown, and almost come to hate," she wrote. "I expected that Lawrence would marry the auburn-haired teacher, and tried to accustom myself to the idea. He had said to me many times, vehemently: 'It doesn't matter *who* one marries!' "

Then Lawrence came home for Christmas with startling news. Everything had changed, he told Jessie. He had been absolutely wrong to think of marrying Agnes Holt and had told her so, and she had left Croydon. (In fact she had refused to go to bed with him before marriage, hence the break.) It was Jessie he loved, said Lawrence; he had loved her the whole time without realizing it. They would be married in due course, but in the meantime their engagement had better remain a secret—everyone would make such a fuss otherwise and ask so many questions. Jessie knew, of course, who he meant by "everyone," and agreed. She even agreed at last to go to bed with him in advance of the wedding, since they could not possibly marry as yet; the only thing she demurred at was to "take advantage" of his landlady in Croydon by carrying on a liaison under her roof. This misgiving was eventually conquered, though she said nothing of the fact in her book, referring to it only obliquely: "I felt how sincere was his desire to be convinced. And on my side was the bond of love, and the long loyalty."

Their first encounter was probably in March, during a visit she made to Croydon. Was it rapturous, and did they live happily ever after? Alas, no; it wasn't good, at least not good enough to satisfy Lawrence. His first letter after the week end was loving and thankful. She had done him a lot of good, he said; he needed her and wished that they could be close together in a little house. But within a month or two he was finding fault with her, as some of his poems from this period indicate. In "Lilies in the Fire," for example, he wrote:

> I am ashamed, you wanted me not to-night.
> And it is always so, you sigh against me.
> Your brightness dims when I draw too near, and my free
> Fire enters you like a frost, like a cruel blight.

It seems not to have occurred to him that Jessie's lack of fire was natural in an inexperienced girl who was full of in- hibitions. With Lawrence it was always the woman's fault, and he blamed her bitterly not only because of her frosty reactions but because he found himself not immune to the attractions of other women. When he came home at Easter he told her that he had met Alice Dax in London and taken her to a concert, where the music so affected him that he was nearly unfaithful to Jessie. As if this were not enough, Mrs. Dax followed up Lawrence's account with her own, which she retailed in a letter to the girl. The implication was plain: Jessie had better warm up or she would lose her man.

Jessie tried. During Lawrence's next holiday, at Whitsun, the lovers got together a few times out of doors in the fields. As Delavenay has pointed out, these were not the best of con- ditions for a sensitive girl, plagued by various fears, chief of which was that she might get pregnant, and the indissoluble pangs of religious conscience. Nor did Lawrence give her much chance to get used to his love-making. She later told Delavenay that their encounters in all—including the first one at Croydon —were no more than four or five. And all the time, between bouts, Lawrence scolded her, threatened her, and broke down her self-esteem. For her part Jessie thought that there was a forced note in *his* attitude, a lack of spontaneity, and she was probably correct.

Then there was the added complication of Helen Corke. At Easter, when Lawrence saw Jessie only fleetingly and spent most of the time with his mother, he had spoken of an association recently formed with Helen Corke, a teacher at another Croydon school. Lawrence had known Miss Corke ever since he first arrived in Croydon early in 1909, but they had had little to do with each other until she came back from a holiday in a state of shock brought on by a tragic experience. As was his usual way with subdued ladies in distress, Lawrence immediately set to work to help her get better.

"She was attractive, the only one among Lawrence's girl friends who was small physically," wrote Harry T. Moore of Helen Corke, evidently forgetting the description he had furnished of the petite Alice Dax. "And she had a fiery nature."

They took long walks on Saturdays while Helen talked of the tragedy that obsessed her. Lawrence was fascinated by the story. She had fallen in love with her music master, a married man, and gone away with him for five days, after which escapade they returned to their respective homes and the man killed himself. Helen gave Lawrence her diary to read and various other fragments she had written—for she too was literary and meant to write up her experience when she could face putting it down on paper. It happened that Lawrence was in the kind of vacuum writers enter when they have just finished a piece of work and have not yet embarked on another. *The White Peacock* was with Heinemann, and he was only squaring up to the task of beginning *Sons and Lovers*. It is not remarkable that his imagination seized on Helen Corke's story and filled him with longing to make it his own, but it does seem strange that she should have been willing to let him have it. However, Lawrence was often successful in persuading people to give him their material, though in other cases he was known to go ahead and use such material without first getting permission. Besides, it would be a stony-hearted young woman—Miss Corke was twenty-eight—who could withstand the request of a man who was paying her such ardent attention, taking her out for expeditions and writing her poem after poem. It must have been an immense relief for her to pour out to a sympathetic listener all her guilt and grief, aware the whole time that a real genius did not condemn her.

He suggested that he expand the diary and notes into what he planned as a long poem (though in the end it became a novel), and she agreed, only stipulating that he wait five years after the suicide before publishing the work. (In the end, as we shall see, she released him even from this promise.) Women were kind to Lawrence. He got to work on it immediately, still in 1909, and by July of 1910 had finished the first draft of *The Trespasser,* at first called "The Saga of Siegmund." In the meantime he had begun to argue with Jessie that everything depended on his freedom to love Helen. This affair would not be permanent, he assured the unfortunate girl; he simply had to have it for the sake of the book.

"Lawrence implored me not to attempt to hold him," wrote Jessie. "He told me most impressively the story of the Shirt of Nessus. Something of that kind, he said, something fatal, perhaps, might happen if I insisted on holding him: 'For this I need Helen, but I must *always* return to you,' he said earnestly, 'only you must leave me free.' "

Helplessly, Jessie agreed to lend him to Helen for the sake of his genius. Perhaps it was not really so great a sacrifice considering the fact that their love affair was, as he never failed to explain, a great disappointment to him, but she couldn't pretend to be happy about it, and when she learned that the first draft of the book was finished she waited in vain to hear from Lawrence that he and Helen had separated. Time went on, July was nearly over, and an agreement is an agreement, Jessie thought, so she wrote to Miss Corke herself. Either Lawrence gave up Helen, she said, or all was over between him and Jessie. It was not an angry letter; it was even reasonable in a crazy way, but of course it made Lawrence angry. Very well, he told Jessie; he and she would part. All was over. They were not even to write to each other.

Jessie had heard this before; however, she took it seriously enough to write again to Helen Corke, this time assuring her that the field was now clear and Miss Corke would have Lawrence unimpeded. Yet not long afterward we find him writing to Jessie, persuading her to come again to Croydon. Jessie did go, and Lawrence was able once more to indulge in one of his favorite exercises: he introduced his two girls to each other. But this time things were different, for Helen and Jessie took a great liking to each other and formed a friendship that lasted longer than he did.

Helen Corke described the meeting years later in *D. H. Lawrence's "Princess,"* a name chosen because Lawrence had said in his autobiographical sketch, about Jessie's sending his poems to the *English Review*, "The girl had launched me, so easily, on my literary career, like a princess cutting a thread, launching a ship."

At that first meeting Helen thought "Muriel," as Lawrence often referred to Jessie when speaking of her, as vivid as Lawrence described her. But she had more warmth than he had suggested, said Helen, with her short curly hair and gypsy tan. Between the two women there developed what Helen called "a unique bond based upon our mutual recognition of Lawrence's genius," which Helen felt Jessie had fostered to a degree even Lawrence did not realize.

That day they all took a walk and then went back to Lawrence's rooms for tea. Lawrence at first was cheerful, as well he might be with two attractive girls adoring him, but then, as he often did, he became difficult and lost his temper, this time over some verse he read as he sprawled before the fire.

Jessie, obviously accustomed to such behavior, was gentle, treating him, Helen said, "rather as Mary of Bethany might have treated Christ. He reacted irritably; the harmony of the day was gone, and I left as soon as tea was over." After having put Jessie on the train, Lawrence went to see Helen that evening and told her that he and Jessie were engaged, but his mother didn't like her and he knew she would never consent to the marriage. If it came to that, he continued, he wasn't quite sure himself that he wanted it.

Deservedly confident that his friends were always interested in his *affaires de coeur,* the genius wrote Miss Corke further on the subject in August, from Eastwood, to say that Jessie had met him, that she was very pretty and wistful, and he was going to stay at the Chambers farm. "I must tell her that we ought finally and definitely to part—if I have the heart to tell her," he wrote.

In the event he canceled his visit but met Jessie outside and told her—well, something. Jessie's account of the interview is terse; she said only that he had returned to his old attitude of uncertainty and that she had put her foot down and declared that it must be all or nothing, to which he replied, "Then I am afraid it must be nothing." They agreed that they would not even correspond, but within a week he wrote again, an importunate note begging her to read Barrie's *Sentimental Tommy* and *Tommy and Grizel,* which would help her, he said, to understand, since he was in exactly the same predicament.

Evidently Lawrence's and Helen Corke's affair was no more successful than the one carried on between him and Jessie. His poems show slowly developing impatience and anger with her, though in all fairness he would have been equally impatient and angry if she had refused his attentions; with the Lawrence of those days a woman might be damned if she didn't, but she was decidedly damned if she did. Helen seems not to have accepted the blame for this failure, but then she was not like Jessie at all. She was not meek and her youth had not been devoted to Lawrence; she could be angry with him and often was. We see a spark of that anger in a conversation she held with Malcolm Muggeridge about Lawrence as recently as 1969, which was broadcast by the BBC and rebroadcast in 1974. In this interview she told Muggeridge how Lawrence had written to her early in 1912 from Edward Garnett's house where he was resting after a serious illness. The letter did not please her, she said, because he suggested that she come and see him there, since Garnett, he assured her, was beautifully unconventional.

As Miss Corke said, with emphasis, everybody knows what *that* means. It is clear that public demonstrations of free love, even with a genius, were not to her taste.

That Lawrence's mind should have been preoccupied with his amorous entanglements is no wonder. Not only did he have Jessie and Helen—and Helen's diary—on his mind; there was Mrs. Dax in the background, and probably he had several other girl friends of less importance stashed away here and there. His preoccupation spilled over at times in unexpected directions, as for instance during the social evenings he occasionally spent at the house of his headmaster, Philip F. T. Smith. They were quiet evenings, according to Mr. Smith, with only himself and his wife to entertain the young man. Mrs. Smith shared with Lawrence a liking for French literature and French songs, which they sang together, but between songs Lawrence boasted of his amorous conquests until Mrs. Smith, out of female solidarity, took him to task for speaking so harshly. Her rebukes did not turn him off. Smith wrote dryly of Lawrence's impenitent accounts, "When he cancelled out a period of endearment at which the lady invariably wept, the outburst only provoked him to the extent of, 'My dear, how you are enjoying yourself.'"

Rachel Annand Taylor, a Scottish poet whom Lawrence met through the *English Review*, had a similar experience and felt the same reaction as had the Smiths. Because Lawrence was preparing a lecture on her work, she invited him to tea on October 15, 1910, to discuss it. There in her drawing room, however, instead of talking about her and her work, he immediately started talking of himself and his affairs, "stating to begin with that his mother was the person who meant most to him." The Oedipus complex was not yet a commonplace, observed Mrs. Taylor, so she gave Lawrence the benefit of considering him sincere in this. He went on to tell her about Jessie, saying that he owed her a lot—but "evidently felt," said Mrs. Taylor acidly, that she "seemed a little provincial in the lofty realms of Violet Hunt." She summed up: "He was a terrific snob, he was definitely a cad, yet in this early period he was touching, he was so artlessly trying to find his way."

When not playing the role of the Demon Heartbreaker of Davidson Road, Lawrence worked on "The Saga of Siegmund." Whether it be considered a poem or a novel, it is so much better than *The White Peacock*—at least in my estimation—that one can understand why he resented Ford's criticism. To read Helen Corke's version of the story, *Neutral Ground,* which she published in 1933 after Lawrence's death, is an interesting exercise, but—again in my estimation—Lawrence did far better with the story than she.

Whatever the deficiencies of their sexual relations, Helen was surely the most amiable colleague in literary history, as witness a tale told by herself. She showed him a poem she had written, saying that it did not satisfy her, and he exclaimed after reading it, "I always feel, when you give me an idea, how much better I could work it out myself!" And he promptly proved it.

# 4

## *Jessie and Louie: "A glorious girl"*

THAT AUGUST in 1910 Mrs. Lawrence fell gravely ill, and the trouble proved to be cancer, well advanced. Of course Lawrence, home for the holidays, was distracted; yet as she lay in bed rapidly getting worse, he complicated his affairs of the heart, which one would have thought quite tangled enough, by falling in love all over—again—with his old flame Louie Burrows.

He had been in touch with Louie all along, sometimes seeing her and often exchanging letters, but they were not love letters until late in 1910. For instance, in 1909, when he was planning his holiday in Shanklin with his mother and the Pagans, he invited Louie to join them on the Isle of Wight. She didn't go. He also invited her to Croydon, and sometimes they worked on short stories by correspondence. Of course he wrote at length to her about his new prospects through the *English Review* and the acceptance of *The White Peacock* novel and so on; he wrote to everyone he knew about these triumphs. But the correspondence throughout the first three quarters of 1910 languished, for he was working very hard on "Siegmund."

When Mrs. Lawrence was struck down she happened to be visiting her sister, Mrs. Fritz Krenkow, who lived in Leicester. Lawrence often went up to see her there, and Louie, who still lived with her family at Quorn not far away, was able to see

Lydia often and help in a dozen other little ways. Back at work at Croydon, Lawrence was under tremendous strain, for he had to get away as much as possible to check up on his mother, now sinking fast. On December 5 he wrote from Eastwood to A. W. McLeod, his best friend on the faculty at Davidson Road. It was a long letter about his mother, some school matters, and, at the end, a startling account of his new love affair with Louie. The passage starts out in an oddly kittenish way:

"Oh, there's one thing I'll tell you—if you promise not to give me away." He went on to say that it happened in the train from Leicester, on his way back to Eastwood, when Louie was riding with him as far as Quorn. There in a carriage full of buxom farm women they talked about his mother, and Louie asked him what he planned to do after Christmas when— though neither of them said it—Mrs. Lawrence would almost certainly be dead. Out of nowhere, according to Lawrence, came his inspiration.

"Why, I should like to get married," he said, watching her as she hung her head in maidenly embarrassment. "Should *you?*"

Louie murmured that she didn't know.

"I should like to marry you," said Lawrence. Hearing his own words, he told his friend in the letter, he opened his eyes in surprise. "Should you?" he went on.

"What?" asked the blushing girl in husky tones.

"Like to marry me?"

He wrote in the letter:

She turned to me quickly, and her face shone like a luminous thing. "Later," she said. I was very glad. . . .

So I have written to my other girls, and I have written to Louie's father. She is a glorious girl: about as tall as I, straight and strong as a caryatid . . . and swarthy and ruddy as a pomegranate, and bright and vital as a pitcher of wine. I'm jolly glad I asked her. What made me do it, I cannot tell. Twas an inspiration. But I can't tell mother.

Well, what did make him do it, and was he really so surprised at himself? Not if we are to believe another letter, written to his fiancée the next day, December 6. In the McLeod missive he placed the proposal during the Saturday just past, but to Louie, in his first love letter, he wrote:

> It is funny. I said—but you know, my mother has been passionately fond of me, and fiercely jealous. She hated [Jessie]—& would have risen from the grave to prevent my marrying her. So I said carefully, about a month or six weeks ago, "Mother, do you think it would be all right for me to marry Louie—later?"
>
> Immediately she said "No—I don't"—and then, after half a minute, "Well—if you think you'd be happy with her—yes." So you see, I know she approves, & she always liked you.

Which account are we to believe? If he actually talked it over with his mother "a month or six weeks ago," then he didn't take himself by surprise that day on the train. Furthermore, in that case there is no sense in the phrase "But I can't tell mother." Or was the talk of the exchange with his mother just a tarradiddle to please Louie, to reassure her of his mother's feelings or perhaps convince her that he had long intended to propose to her? Never mind. We are dealing with a novelist—or, rather, Louie was, and so was Jessie, and so was Alice Dax. So, of course, was Helen Corke, who got yet another story from Lawrence: that the only thing he could do in the presence of his mother's suffering was to "deny" Jessie Chambers. Deliberately, according to Helen, he proposed to marry a girl in his mother's world: Louie. This is confusing too, for why should Louie be considered any more of his mother's world than Jessie was? After all, Arthur Lawrence's niece Alvina Lawrence married Alan Chambers, who was Jessie's brother, and nobody talked at their wedding of this world or that.

Lawrence prodded Heinemann to hurry with the publication of *The White Peacock* in order that his mother might see it before she died. They managed to get an advance copy to the house, but by that time she was probably too far gone to realize what it was. Nobody could be sure.

There are in existence photographs of Lawrence's best girls. Jessie's pictures, though they give an idea of her regular features, are probably not fair representation, because they lack that warmth of coloring so often mentioned by her contemporaries. But the cabinet photo of Louie that serves as frontispiece for *Lawrence in Love* is better, showing as it does Miss Burrows gently bending her head over a large rose at her bosom. She looks appealingly soft and sweet, though in time she became a successful headmistress, and that is usually not considered a very soft or sweet calling. Incidentally she must have had a slight mustache, for in one of his letters Lawrence scolded her lovingly for cutting it. He liked it, he said.

"You are like Canaan—you are rich & fruitful & glad," he wrote.

We can speculate that his mother's dying, for all the pain and guilt it aroused in his heart, must have seemed to him like the slow opening of prison gates seen from the blackness of a cell. But losing her would also leave him without ballast or support, and it is no wonder if, watching her die, his thoughts turned to marriage. To be sure, he had often harped on the subject in his talks with Jessie, but he had never actually come as close to taking the final step as he did now.

Louie's parents, who did not like him, argued that the betrothed couple was too young to marry, but the protest was unconvincing; she was twenty-three and he twenty-five. A more cogent objection was that the young people had no money, and Lawrence admitted that this was reasonable. He assured them that he did not intend to marry Louie until he had at least £100 in his pocket and the assurance of a job with £120 a year; he would try for a country school, he said, and save up.

True to what he said to McLeod, he wrote to all his other girl friends, as well as to Louie's father. At least we know that he told the news to Jessie, Helen, and also—though she was hardly a girl friend—Rachel Annand Taylor, the Scottish poet.

To Jessie he wrote, "I was in the train with Louie on Saturday and I suddenly asked her to marry me. I never meant to. But she accepted me and I shall stick to it. . . . Do you want me to say little, or nothing, or much? I'll say anything you like, only I can't help it, I'm made this way."

To Rachel Annand Taylor:

I have been to Leicester today, I have met a girl who has always been warm for me—like a sunny happy day—and I've gone and asked her to marry me: in the train, quite unpremeditated, between Rothley and Quorn—she lives at Quorn. When I think of her I feel happy with a sort of warm radiation —she is big and dark and handsome. . . . Louie—whom I wish I could marry the day after the funeral—she would never demand to drink me up and have me. She loves me—but it is a fine, warm, healthy, natural love—not like Jane Eyre, who is [Jessie], but like—say Rhoda Fleming or a commoner Anna Karenina. She will never plunge her hands through my blood and feel for my soul, and make me set my teeth and shiver and fight away.

Mrs. Lawrence died on December 8, and Lawrence went over to see Jessie and face the music the day before the funeral. She rebuked him for involving Louie in "the impasse" of their relationship—"You should not have drawn [Louie] into things. She has no idea of the real state of affairs"—at which he drew himself up haughtily and quoted a remark he was fond of using: "With *should* and *ought* I have nothing to do."

On the point of leaving, he said, "You know—I've always loved mother."

Jessie replied, "I know you have."

"I don't mean that," said Lawrence. "I've *loved* her, like a lover. That's why I could never love you."

As if to emphasize this statement he gave her the drafts of some poems he had just written, including "The Bride":

My love looks like a girl to-night,
  But she is old.
The plaits that lie along her pillow
  Are not gold. . . .

The friendship between Helen Corke and Jessie Chambers had gone from strength to strength. They wrote long letters to one another, and in October Helen had been to visit Jessie's family in the new farm, in Arno Vale near the mining village of Arnold northwest of Nottingham. It is thanks to her that we know details of the household, such as the fact that Jessie, now an assistant mistress in a Nottingham school, no longer worked in the kitchen; a younger sister did that, and neither sister nor mother would allow Jessie to touch housework. Though as a breadwinner she need not have felt guilty over her escape, she was still angered by the sight of her mother toiling away at rough domestic tasks. Two of the brothers worked on the land with their father, as in the old days; still they tracked in mud on the floor and took for granted the women's work indoors.

Helen's friendship was a lifesaver for Jessie, keeping her from complete despair. It gave her an outlet that she needed: there was nobody else in the world whom she could talk to about Lawrence. Also, Helen was in touch with him and saw him quite often, sometimes during the same day she saw Jessie. As she said herself, she made a bridge between them.

"I suppose you will have seen [Lawrence] by now," wrote Jessie in a letter to Helen, adding that she thought she ought not to talk about him at all because she was not strong enough. Of course she did continue to talk about him in spite of all pious resolutions, but she did not sit at home yearning and repining. She had her work at school.

Consistency was never Lawrence's strong point, and in spite of having made a break with Jessie he soon picked up the acquaintanceship again, writing to her occasionally and urging her to feel free to write to him. He felt in need of the old reassurance. A writer usually takes the gloomiest view possible of his reviews, and Lawrence was downcast by the notice of *The White Pea-cock* printed in the *Times Literary Supplement* for January 28, 1911, in which the book was brushed off briefly. The reviewer said that his natural descriptions were good, but there was no well-knit plot, the book was aimless, and much of the conversation was banal. The *Observer* critic was kinder: he said that though *The White Peacock* was strange and disturbing, nobody could deny that it had elements of greatness. Still, Lawrence was disappointed and frustrated. There was no mad rush on the part of the public to buy his book. He said disconsolately to Helen Corke, "I *did* think it would have given me a start."

It was natural, then, that he should turn again to Jessie's "long loyalty" and her stout belief in his genius. Louie's fond encouragement was not enough. It was not Louie who had nursed him along for the past ten years. When Louie resented the fact that Jessie had actually written to him he refused to take her complaint seriously. It was strange of her to be angry with Jessie, he wrote, especially as Jessie's was a harmless letter in reply, he believed, to some question of his. It certainly wasn't a love letter. He counseled Louie not to be jealous, because it is not a nice feeling. One wonders what she would have said if she had been able to read some of his letters to Jessie.

"At times I am afflicted by a perversity amounting to minor insanity," he confessed in one of them. "But the best man in me belongs to you. One me is yours, a fine, strong me. . . . I have great faith still that things will come right in the end."

This may not have meant what it sounds like, but naturally enough Jessie took it as a hint that the Louie entanglement was not, as she put it, irreparable. Brooding, she concluded that the mischief between herself and Lawrence dated back to that day when the twenty-year-old youth came from his mother to tell her that he did not love her as a man should love his wife. Yes, that was the critical point, and Mrs. Lawrence had been the villain. If only the son could be brought to realize it, even now he might throw off the spell and come untangled from the strings with which Mrs. Lawrence still strangled him from beyond her grave. ("Strangled" was a word Jessie often used in this context.) The theory seemed as clear as day to her, but she could not say such things straightforwardly to Lawrence. Instead, she wrote a short story embodying the incident and sent it to him under the pretense of asking for literary criticism. In reply, he tried for a sentence or two to maintain the same pose, but soon he broke down and talked directly:

"You say you died a death of me, but the death you died of me I must have died also, or you wouldn't have gone on caring about me. . . ." To us this seems obscure; perhaps Jessie, too, did not understand it, but she took comfort from the words that followed: "They tore me from you, the love of my life. . . . It was the slaughter of the foetus in the womb."

To Jessie it looked now more than ever as if they would one day be reunited, the Burrows engagement wiped out and forgotten, and her spirits recovered—until she heard that Louie was proudly showing off a copy of *The White Peacock* to her friends and telling them it was the work of her clever young man. Remembering how hard she herself had worked on the book, Jessie could not keep bitter thoughts out of her head.

Still, she was not alone. There was Helen to talk to and take her mind off her troubles, Helen to make her go on little excursions. They visited the South Downs and saw the town where Helen was born. They went to London often, to visit art galleries and concerts; Jessie adored music and particularly enjoyed this part of her cure. The great city that had once frightened her now became familiar. She and Helen read together an enormous number of books, including all ten volumes of the new novel *Jean-Christophe* that was making such a stir among literary people. What with one thing and another, though 1911 was a long dreary year for Jessie, it had its bright moments.

For Lawrence it was a decisive year. During the first months after Louie promised to marry him he wrote to her every day. If his letters grew slightly less ardent with the passage of time, he made up for the loss by retailing gossip, planning this and that, and talking about his work. He sent Louie his story "Odour of Chrysanthemums" so that she might tell him how good it was and also—of course—copy it out for him. He told her that he had heard from Agnes Holt, who was to be married soon; they must go and see her together, he said, because he liked her very much and he was sure Louie would, too.

"Somehow, I always feel sorry for her," he said. "She's not strong in health. Poor A!"

So much for an erstwhile fiancée. There is also in the letters a considerable amount of talk about his drawings, for Lawrence had the custom of copying pictures he liked, believing that in this way he could acquire the artist's technique. In fact, he was so fond of drawing that he had occasionally, as a boy, contemplated being an artist rather than a writer.

Louie and Lawrence went on a trip together during their Easter holidays, an experience that marked a watershed in the engagement. Lawrence was impatient to have full sexual relations with his beloved, but Louie refused. Lawrence had hoped for better things from her. She was ardent in temperament—at any rate, she *looked* ardent—where Jessie, he thought, was cold; yet here she was, pushing him away. He wrote a poem about it, "The Hands of the Betrothed":

> . . . yet if I lay my hand in her breast
> She puts me away, like a saleswoman whose mart is
> Endangered by the pilferer on his quest.

What was the matter with women, anyway? The fact was, Lawrence decided angrily, Louie was *immature*. He made up his mind to cool off a bit and see if that didn't bring her round. As soon as he got back to Croydon, on April 24, he wrote to her saying that he would send her only two or three letters a week from that day on, as he had to "push himself into correspondence." It was also a sensible resolve—he was at the same time working hard on *Sons and Lovers*—but he found the time to write to his sister Ada, complaining of his girl: "I never want Lou to understand how relentlessly tragic life is—not that. But I want her not to jar on me by gawkishness, and that she must learn. . . . When she is a bit older she'll be more understanding."

She would have seemed less gawkish, no doubt, if she had been willing to go to bed with him. He grew more and more irritated with the woman. In July he flew into a temper with her because she asked what he had done with the £ 10 he was paid for "Odour of Chrysanthemums." Did ten quid seem so much to her, he asked? Pah, it was nothing. Sarcastically he asked if he should make out an account of how he had spent it, and without waiting for an answer he proceeded to do so: he had sent some money to Eastwood, he gave something for Agnes Holt's wedding present, his shirts were patched and his shoes unpresentable, and when Ford invited him to the Reform Club he couldn't go because he hadn't got a decent suit.

"I don't chuck money about," he continued, "—ten quid doesn't seem to me a lot of money—but a scroddy bit.—I went to Dover yesterday alone—trainfare 2/6—tea 1/—oddments, 1/—. I suppose it *was* extravagant. No matter, it's done." By this time poor Louie, reading, must have been reduced to tears, but Lawrence's wrath still burned. If he didn't make a lot of money at once, he told her, he couldn't save; he had too many calls on it. "So beware—chuck me if you're going to be sick of my failures: but they may be successes."

Of course the quarrel blew over, but soon there was more friction over the summer holiday, which they planned to take in Prestatyn in Wales. Ada was going, and possibly some other Pagans, though that was not certain. Louie's parents, always suspicious, thought that she should not share such a holiday without an older person to chaperon her, and Lawrence was furious with Louie for failing to take a firm stand against them. Louie knew—who better?—that their fears were justified, but Lawrence would not forgive her, though he gave in. The vacationers found lodgings, in the end, with a Methodist parson and his wife, and Louie's virtue was safe. Afterward the parson's wife wrote to the Burrows parents to compliment them on their daughter, who, they said, had been very good while with them and a credit to her upbringing.

That September found Lawrence complaining of his fiancée to Helen Corke, and no doubt to other women as well. He said that he really loved Louie—that is, one of him did, the common, everyday, rather superficial Lawrence. The other one, however—the open-eyed, sad, critical, deep-seeing man—had to humble himself sorely to accept her standards. Having thus blown off steam, he wrote placidly to Louie announcing that he was expecting his brother George to come for a visit in October. During this visit Jessie and Helen, who had gone to a London theater, ran into the brothers in the audience. Lawrence did not mention the meeting to Louie, saying only that George's visit had tired him terribly, but Jessie noticed that he looked ill and unhappy, and she mentioned it on the following Sunday night, when she and George shared a railway carriage on the way back to Notts. George readily agreed that Bert wasn't at all well. He had nightmares, said George, from which he would wake up shouting that someone was trying to kill him.

And when, asked Jessie politely, did he think the couple were to be married?

"Married!" said Bert's brother contemptuously. "I don't *think*, I *know* they'll never get married!" He continued, saying that Bert had announced the engagement on a blooming postcard; what sort of behavior was that? To George it was clearly an indication that Bert didn't take the thing seriously (and, in the light of future events, he might have been right). Yes, said George to Jessie, he had met Louie. Bert had brought her over—a nice enough girl, but not right for Bert. Just because she was handy during their mother's last days and had been kind to her. . . . No, in George's opinion Bert had got the wrong girl.

Soon after the meeting in the theater Lawrence sent Jessie the manuscript, as far as he had completed it, of *Sons and Lovers*, or "Paul Morel," as he was still calling it. He said he wanted her opinion; it was clear that he was stuck, for it was only two thirds finished. Jessie, who read it immediately, was surprised at its badness. The writing was strained and unconvincing; probably, she said, because Lawrence himself was unconvinced. He was following an artificial story line, and she was sure he had been forcing himself. Knowing that the book was supposed to be an autobiographical novel, she was surprised by the way he had switched things around; the departures from the truth had hurt it badly. Even in telling the story of his mother's married life he sounded lackluster, though Jessie knew how lively the true version was. This manuscript was storybookish and not like Lawrence at all. For some reason, he had left out Ern and his Gypsy completely, though that story was a fascinating part of the family's real life. And she herself, "Miriam" in the book, had been transmuted into a foundling adopted by a bourgeois family; to what end? Lawrence had only just embarked on the chief part of the book, the struggle between Mrs. Morel and Miriam over Paul, when he ground to a halt.

Jessie wrote Lawrence that she was surprised to find so many changes from reality, since what had really happened was so much more arresting than his inventions. She said that she thought he should write it all again, this time as it actually was. She was sincere in this advice, as she wrote in her memoir; she genuinely believed that it would be a fine story if he did it properly—but she also hoped that, while he wrote it, Lawrence would free himself from his obsession with his Mrs. Lawrence. As he worked out the spiritual theme, reasoned Jessie, he would resolve his own conflict: "he would thereby walk into freedom, and cast off the trammelling past like an old skin."

It goes without saying that she did not mention this particular line of thought to Lawrence, but she stressed the other argument—the vitality he had sacrificed, which must be restored; the true plot waiting only to be put down on paper.

"He fell in absolutely with my suggestion," said Jessie, "and asked me to write what I could remember of our early days, because, as he truthfully said, my recollection of those days was so much clearer than his. I agreed to do so."

This exchange took place late in October or early in November at a time when Lawrence was still feeling ill and depressed. Writing to Louie on October 30, after having been with her for a day or two, he complained of the weather—it was raining like hell, he said. He also complained of their enforced chastity: ". . . the long slow drag of hours is very trying. I've now got to digest a great lot of dissatisfied love in my veins. It is very damnable, to have slowly to drink back again into oneself all the lava & fire of a passionate eruption." And he ended even more sourly:

> The most of the things, that just heave red hot to be said, I shove back. And that leaves nothing to be said. All this, you see, is very indelicate & immodest & all that . . . and I always want to subscribe to your code of manners, towards you— I know I fail sadly.
>
> Good-bye—just imagine all the things I don't say—they're there
>
> Goodbye D. H. Lawrence

This feeling is expressed in a poem sequence he wrote at the time, "Whether or Not," which is in the local dialect that Lawrence was experimenting with, after Thomas Hardy's example. Admittedly the story line has no obvious bearing on his own case—a village girl engaged to a policeman discovers that he had got his landlady into trouble, and she flies into a rage—but the young man's self-defense is very definitely applicable to Lawrence. The girl, Lizzie, bitterly says:

> An' me as 'as kep' my-sen
> Shut like a daisy bud,
> Clean an' new an' nice, so's when
> He wed he'd ha'e summat good!

How, she wonders, could he have given his "clean young

flesh" to a widow of forty-five with a swarthy skin? Lizzie storms off to confront the faithless Timothy and throws at him her wedding dress, which she declares the Widow Naylor needs more than she. The policeman, Lawrence-like, says it's no use to scold him, since what's done is done and he has no intention of marrying the widow. Besides, he says, his misstep is as much the girl's fault as his:

> . . . but let me tell thee
>   Hasna ter sent me whoam, when I
> Was a'most burstin' mad o' my-sen
>   An' walkin' in agony?
>
> After I'd kissed thee at night, Lizzie,
>   An' tha's laid against me, an' melted
> Into me, melted right into me, Lizzie,
>   Till I was verily swelted.

Naturally, continued Timmy, in that state he was easy prey for his landlady or anybody else who wanted his young flesh.

Writing the poem must have relieved the poet a little, but Louie remained unconvinced, her virtue unassailable. Still, life was not always as gloomy as he made out to Louie. He was beginning to win a certain amount of critical appreciation beyond the limits of the *English Review* and the staff's immediate friends. Edward Garnett, a critic and an editor with the publishing firm of Duckworth, noticed his work, thought well of it, and wrote to him to say so. Ford introduced the two and they became friends. Lawrence was made welcome at Garnett's house and there met his wife, Constance, the woman who translated Russian writers into English and presented the Western world with a whole new literature. The Garnetts lived in a country cottage, The Cearne, near Edenbridge in Kent, and Lawrence wrote of it enthusiastically to Ada: "a big cottage built in the 15th century style, and you'd think it was a fine old farmhouse. Everything old, thick blue earthenware, stone jugs for the beer, a great wood fire in the open hearth in the inglenook and all buried in the middle of a wood, hard to find."

Even being an intimate of the Garnetts, however, with visiting rights at The Cearne, did not really cheer Lawrence up. Helen Corke thought he had changed and not for the better. His life, she said, was "peculiarly disjointed . . . spiritually impoverished by the break with Jessie Chambers, complicated by his irresponsible engagement to marry, discouraged by the poor reception accorded his first novel [*The White Peacock*]." Miss Corke said that his pride was hurt because he had begun to realize the gulf between a schoolteacher who was also an artist and those young artists, who, though "often penniless themselves, yet lived within a charmed circle of influence and wealth." Lawrence was always feeling this difference at London literary parties. After such a gathering he would make fun of the other guests to Helen. She didn't care for his new tastes in literature—Flaubert, Maupassant, Baudelaire—or his new talk, which was probably an echo of smart people he met at the parties, disquisitions on such subjects as art for art's sake and the need for *form* in writing. At such moments Helen thought he sounded less like her old David and more like Ford. Then too, he was unpleasant about school and the people there. He took relish in showing up his headmaster, Smith, because Smith had forgotten his Latin. The erstwhile gentle David was becoming unkind. He referred to Eastwood as "that insipid Sodom," and somewhere he had picked up a tiresome habit of classifying people as "types." He once said to her, "You are not the wife or mother type, you must be *femme de plaisir*."

This was so crass, she wrote, that it only made her smile, but she felt that he had coarsened sadly. However, she continued to see him and knew, because he told her, that he was working very hard and fast on the second version of "Paul Morel," which Jessie had given advice on.

According to Helen Corke it was a shower of rain that brought catastrophe on Lawrence; he was caught in it one November evening on his way to visit the Garnetts, and when he arrived at the house soaking wet he neglected to change his clothing. As one who had always been delicate and subject to colds, this was recklessness itself, but Lawrence was probably in a reckless mood. As a result of the wetting—said Helen, at least—he came down with pneumonia. His sister Ada rushed to Croydon to nurse him, and he pulled through this second bout, but it was discovered during his convalescence that he had tuberculosis, though he would never admit it and, indeed, was never heard to pronounce the word. He realized, however, that it meant the end of his career as a teacher, for nobody with a history of TB was permitted to work in school.

Ada kept the anxious Louie informed of the progress of her patient, signing her letters "Your Sister" and generally keeping up the pretense that all was well between Bert and his girl. The last week in December Louie came to Croydon to be with him, and he wrote of her to Garnett, "My girl is here. She's big, and swarthy and passionate as a gypsy—but good, awfully good, churchy."

In fact Lawrence was thinking hard, and the conclusion he came to was that he must break the engagement. He had good reason: now that he couldn't teach the future was even less certain than it had been before, and—though one must not say it—he had got over wanting to marry Louie anyhow. But how was he to tell her? He and Ada talked it over and she told him severely, in the same words she must have used all those years ago when he was going to break with Jessie, that he must tell Louie now, in all fairness. But he shilly-shallied: it was not an easy thing to do. In January he went to Bournemouth for convalescence, and sent Louie postcards from there, and talked about the weather, and signed his letters affectionately. . . . It was *not* easy. At last, on the fourth of February when, after Garnett suggested it, he had moved to The Cearne to complete his convalescence, he wrote:

"I have been thinking what the doctor at Croydon & the doctor at Bournemouth both urged on me: that I ought not to marry, at least for a long time, if ever. . . . I will not drag on an engagement—so I ask you to dismiss me. I am afraid we are not well suited." His illness had changed him, he went on to say, and broken many of the old bonds that had held him. It was a miserable business, and the fault was all his.

Louie did not take her *congé* easily. She argued that the doctors and Lawrence were mistaken, and begged him to postpone making a decision, asking him to telegraph her that he would. Lawrence refused to change his mind or even to telegraph. He wrote again that it would be better to break the engagement as he didn't feel that he had the right sort of love to marry on, but if she wished he would meet her to say it in person. The more one reads of Lawrence's personal relationships the more it becomes clear that he actually enjoyed such encounters, which most people would travel miles to avoid.

In February, on the tenth, he wrote from Eastwood suggesting that Louie meet him on the following Tuesday in Nottingham for the final interview. "By a cursed irony, that is your birthday," he commented, but he couldn't make it Wednesday, he said, because he had an appointment with Mrs. Dax. One wonders if he was cutting off from Alice Dax too. It seems reasonable to suppose that he was, that the shock of discovering his tuberculosis infection meant a general severing of sentimental ties. As he himself had said, his illness had broken many of the old bonds.

We have yet another woman's word in support of this theory: Helen Corke, in a lecture given in Colchester in 1950, reported that she saw Lawrence for the last time on the day he returned from Bournemouth, February 3, 1912. They had the matter of *The Trespasser* to discuss—the promise not to publish the novel for five years after her lover's suicide. The five years were not up, but Duckworth wanted to publish the book soon, and Lawrence asked her to permit it.

They met by prearrangement for tea at Victoria Station in London, he on his way to Edenbridge and The Cearne, and Helen Corke to Croydon on the same train. She was immensely relieved to find him looking tanned and healthy. The business of *The*

*Trespasser* was quickly settled, with Helen consenting to early publication. "We were quite gay, tacitly avoiding anything controversial," she reported. Lawrence was glad that he did not have to go back to school. He was so charming, so unlike his recent unpleasant self, that Helen deliberately passed up her station at East Croydon and rode on with him as far as Woldingham. Nevertheless this was the end of their friendship. Lawrence had no further need of Helen, and she recognized this fact. "We said no formal goodbye, but I think we both realised that here our paths diverged," she admitted, "and it was unlikely they would approach again." She was not the type to delude herself.

The meeting between Louie and Lawrence came next, after Lawrence's convalescence of several weeks was over and he had left The Cearne. Louie had evidently come to the conclusion that the only thing she could salvage from the ruins was her pride. At any rate Lawrence wrote to Garnett after the meeting, "I saw Louie yesterday—she was rather ikey [snooty]. She had decided beforehand that she had made herself too cheap to me, therefore she thought she would become all at once expensive and desirable. Consequently she offended me at every verse end —thank God. If she'd been wistful, tender and passionate, I should have been a goner."

It is impossible not to be very sorry for Louise Burrows, faced with a feminine intelligence like Lawrence's. One feels that it was not a fair contest. She was outmatched from the start.

Ada gave support to her brother, writing to Louie on the sixteenth, three days after the Nottingham encounter, to point out that it was really kinder to break off an engagement that could never come to anything. Moreover, she said in effect, Louie was well out of it because Bert had changed very much since his illness, "and changed for the worse too I think," she added. "I've had a serious talk with him about it too—his flippant and really artificial manner gets on my nerves dreadfully. Perhaps he may get alright by and by but he's very strange now, I can tell you."

It will be remembered that the same artificial flippant manner was getting on Helen Corke's nerves even before Lawrence fell ill, so there is no reason to suppose that Ada was making it up just to persuade Louie to give in gracefully. Probably Ada did not realize that the change in her brother had already taken place before he got pneumonia. She had not seen him for some months previously.

Her letter ended with a burst of surely sincere comment: "You really deserve someone better than Bert Louie, I wouldn't marry a man like him, no, not if he were the only one on earth."

# 5

## *Jessie as Miriam: "The death-blow to our friendship"*

WHILE LAWRENCE was still in Croydon, ill but mending under his sister's watchful eye, he had had two visitors, Helen Corke and Jessie Chambers, who was visiting Helen and naturally came along to wish him well. Jessie was shocked by his wan appearance but glad to see that he was again interested in his work, for he asked her if she had yet finished her notes about their youthful days, which he needed for the new version of "Paul Morel." She had not, but she promised to hurry now and complete them while he was away growing stronger at Bournemouth. After getting back from Bournemouth, as we know, he went to The Cearne, and very soon afterward, like everyone else in the neighborhood, she heard that his engagement to Louie Burrows was broken. Such news always travels fast.

Lawrence returned to Eastwood early in February. He had been corresponding with Jessie and had arranged to meet her there rather than at Arno Vale to pick up her notes, because as he said he would feel embarrassed to meet her family after what they must certainly consider his desertion of their girl. That was all right with Jessie, especially as she couldn't get home anyway because the roads were blocked. Lawrence came to see her at her Eastwood lodgings, arriving on the doorstep with a box of chocolates for her, an uncharacteristic gesture that surprised and gratified her. His whole attitude, in fact, was so easy and friendly that she found herself wondering if the painful period of the past year had been real or just a bad dream. There he sat, talking about himself as always; there sat Jessie, listening to him as she always had, letting him talk himself out. She never took seriously his bitter, extreme assertions about people or things but accepted them as indications of his mood of the moment.

But she soon realized that Lawrence *had* changed, after all. He was more constantly acerbic and less hopeful, as if inside him a spring had broken. No doubt the knowledge of his ill health was responsible for his depression, and Jessie's heart ached for him. But in one respect he was no different—he had not grown less awkwardly discerning of her inmost thoughts. She knitted vigorously to conceal her agitation, until he said dryly, "There's nothing I admire like industry." After that, of course, Jessie had to put her knitting down.

At one moment he seemed so full of chagrin and grief over the catastrophe of his broken health and the crisis in his career that she had a strong impulse to cross the room and sit next to him. Just in time, however, she held herself back, because it seemed to her that she heard him clearly, though within herself, saying, Don't imagine that because Mother's dead you can claim me. So she stayed where she was, even when Lawrence made one of those leading remarks so typical of his dealings with women: "If we were to marry now you'd expect me to stay at home."

*If we were to marry now!* A girl less experienced would have rejoiced at the implicit promise, but Jessie knew better than to let hope bound ahead of her. She replied calmly that of course she would expect it, because home is the place one works in. His lure refused, Lawrence speedily retreated. He didn't want a home, he said fretfully; "I want to be free. I think I shall go abroad."

He had been thinking this idea over, he said, for some weeks. Through his Aunt Ada's husband, Fritz Krenkow, he thought he might possibly get work in Germany as a university lecturer, for Krenkow, though he was now a businessman, had an academic background and knew people over there who might help. Even at the worst, Lawrence could stay in Germany for a while with Krenkow's relatives, and then perhaps he could travel around Europe a little, taking a year away from England. Jessie thought this an excellent plan and said so, reflecting as she spoke that a year abroad would give him a chance to "come to some kind of peace with himself." However, after this exchange Lawrence still seemed deeply unsatisfied, sitting in gloomy silence, staring into the fire and looking so unhappy that her heart melted for him. If we took *Sons and Lovers* for a truthful guide, we might interpret this silent pause as the signal that Lawrence wanted Jessie to put her arms around him and claim him. Paul in the book longed desperately for this solution to his problems. But novels are tricky, and interpreters would do better to avoid them. Jessie *did* go over and take Lawrence's hand where it hung limply at his side, but the gesture solved nothing. Instead, he remarked that if after a year neither of them had found anyone else, they might get married. Not surprisingly, Jessie found herself revolted by such a prospect. If their love-making was in fact resumed, then or ever, she has told no one, not even Delavenay. It seems unlikely that it was.

However, Lawrence continued having relations with Alice Dax. She told a friend who was in her confidence that Lawrence at the time actually suggested that she leave her husband and child and go away with him, but she could not bring herself to do so. (She was probably already pregnant by that time.)

With Jessie's notes to help his memory, Lawrence started rewriting *Sons and Lovers* at high speed, handing the manuscript over to her as he finished it, twelve pages or so at a time. As she read the first installments she was delighted. He was closely following her advice, telling his mother's story as she had often heard it, putting in Ern and Gypsy and all.

"Here was all that spontaneous flow . . . that filled me with admiration," she wrote. She was now seeing a lot of Lawrence,

all the more easily because he went often to the Holbrooks'
cottage and chatted with May about himself, as he had done in
the old days. A friendship had developed between Lawrence and
Will—now Bill—Holbrook: the smashed stonecarving had been
forgotten, perhaps because Bill was no longer a stonemason but
a farmer. To the Holbrooks Lawrence complained amusingly of
Ada, who, on the grounds that she was the only female Lawrence left in Eastwood, had taken to bullying him. She was quite
ready to step into his mother's shoes, said Lawrence. If he went
into Nottingham for the evening she would ask him after his
return where he had been, whom he had seen, and what he had
done.

"[Ada] mustn't think she's mother," said Lawrence.

Eventually he even went to Arno Vale and faced Jessie's
parents. He told her beforehand that everything would be quite
all right after the first brush, but it wasn't, not quite. Mrs.
Chambers greeted him as she had always done, quietly making
him welcome, but Jessie's father, who may have suspected the
cause of Jessie's unhappiness, was not as he had been in the old
days. He now treated Lawrence as he did everyone else, cour-
teously enough but as if from a distance. There was no longer
that quality of special recognition that had characterized their
friendship in the past. But then, Jessie reminded herself, Lawrence himself was not as he had been in the old days. No longer
did he have a sunny disposition; he was spasmodic, restless, resentful that he had to be careful of his health, even at times
wistful. Once when he saw Jessie's brothers preparing to go out
on Sunday evening, he asked, "Are you going courting?"

They were startled and amused by the quaint question.
Later that evening, alone with Jessie, he dropped all pretense of
cheerfulness and began nagging her in the old way about her
frigidity.

"Except in relation to beauty or passion you never think of
sex," he said accusingly. Jessie did not try to defend herself but
was patient. It was the fault of his mother, she reminded herself
—always his mother, whose memory made him feel disloyal for

being with Jessie at all. As for her attitude toward sex, the unsatisfactory experience she had undergone with Lawrence was hardly likely to change that. It must have been a relief to her that he did not now attempt to start it all up again.

The novel grew, chapter by chapter. There are certain deviations from the true story even apart from those that were later to dismay Jessie, though as she rightly noted they did not interrupt the flow and the power. Paul Morel himself is Lawrence, but in the book he is not a writer; he is an artist. There is no character who resembles May Chambers Holbrook. Alice Dax is represented, though much disguised, in the person of Clara Dawes. Paul's stint at the stocking factory is drawn out for months, perhaps a year or two, though Lawrence worked in his factory for only a few weeks, and Paul's fellow workers, the factory girls, are gentle, though in reality they were rough harpies who terrified Lawrence by assaulting his modesty in the crudest manner. Of course Lawrence did not write everything as it really was, as it really happened—he would have been less of a genius to do so—but there was a grain of truth in almost all of it. That is why Jessie was so hurt, when the time came to read it, by his account of their experiments in sex:

> And after a week of love he said to his mother suddenly one Sunday night, just as they were going to bed:
> "I shan't go so much to Miriam's, mother."
> She was surprised, but she would not ask him anything.
> "You please yourself," she said.

Perhaps it was really like that and perhaps not. In matters of personal history poems are more trustworthy than novels, and we have one of Lawrence's about this frustration—"Last Words to Miriam,"—that could not be more specific:

> Yours is the sullen sorrow,
>     The disgrace is also mine;
> Your love was intense and thorough,
> Mine was the love of a growing flower
>     For the sunshine.

Some lines are especially significant, such as the following:

> You yielded, we threw the last cast,
>     And it was no good.
> You only endured, and it broke
>     My craftsman's nerve.
> No flesh responded to my stroke;
> So I failed to give you the last
>     Fine torture you did deserve.

Masculine pride assures the poet that since he has failed to burn his mistress's body free of its "deadness and dross," nobody else can do it either, and he ends:

> A mute, nearly beautiful thing
>     Is your face, that fills me with shame
> As I see it hardening;
> I should have been cruel enough to bring
>     You through the flame.

Though this is a good poem, one can hardly expect Jessie to have cared for it—if she ever read it, which seems likely. In any case, Lawrence's poem had not been written, much less printed, before he and his Miriam came to a parting of the ways over *Sons and Lovers,* which he had nearly finished before Easter. As I have said, Lawrence kept bringing pieces of it to Jessie as he wrote them, and Jessie read them eagerly at first, but with mounting dismay as the story unfolded. It was not so much the story of Paul's and Miriam's love-making that offended her: indeed, she had not reached that part of it when she became indignant over the portrayal of Miriam vis-à-vis Mrs. Morel. Jessie felt as if she were living the whole thing over again, even more cruelly. Mrs. Lawrence was resurrected, and Lawrence in these pages showed what he really thought of Jessie: *he was siding with his mother.*

For a while, Jessie lost grasp of the truth that this was a novel and not purely a recapitulation. There was a veil before her eyes; shock had robbed her of logic. That Lawrence could write the story like that seemed to her a clear case of betrayal, and that Mrs. Lawrence, the real one, lay dead in her grave could not alter the issue.

"His mother had to be supreme, and for the sake of that supremacy every disloyalty was permissible," she wrote.

With all her might she battled for self-control and managed to hang on to it, but when Lawrence asked her for her opinion of his work she was unable to express what she really thought. She was lost and wandering in a world of fiction that she could not distinguish from fact. She was living a nightmare.

"I could not appeal to Lawrence for justice as between his treatment of Mrs. Morel and Miriam," she wrote piteously, and it was true: a shred of sanity prevented her letting go to that extent. Nevertheless, something of this mental and emotional turmoil communicated itself to Lawrence, and he showed his awareness of it by staying away from Jessie. Still he continued to send the manuscript to her as it developed, and Jessie felt impelled to go on reading it. It was not always an ordeal. As long as the text didn't touch on Miriam versus Mrs. Morel she was all right, able to take a detached point of view. She could see, for example, that Clara Dawes was an adaptation of elements from three people, all of whom she knew, and she recognized that "The events related [i.e., connected with Clara] had no foundation in fact, whatever their psychological significance." Even in these harmless passages, however, she was not now happy with *Sons and Lovers,* as she had been with the opening chapters. The book was spoiled for her. Miriam and Mrs. Morel apart, many of the incidents struck her as cheap and commonplace, in spite of what she had to admit was the hard brilliance of Lawrence's writing. He finished the last chapter in March, 1912.

Jessie wrote that the shock of the book "gave the death-blow to our friendship." She felt as if she had died, that her life was merely illusion and that reality was only to be found in "the betrayal" she saw in *Sons and Lovers.* Throughout everything that had happened before, however painful, she had held on to the comforting belief that there was a bond between Lawrence and herself. But now his harsh treatment of her—Miriam, Jessie, what difference?—denied its existence. Still she had to understand what had occurred, and over and over she tried, analyzing Lawrence's behavior:

"He had to present a distorted picture of our association so that the martyr's halo might sit becomingly on his mother's brow." Yes, all right, she could even understand that, but how could he—how *could* he—have painted a recognizable portrait of their friendship, his and Jessie's, without crediting her with all she had done for him? He had left out "the years of devotion" —admittedly, "devotion that had been pure joy"—and that was like presenting *Hamlet* without the Prince of Denmark. One feels that even if Lawrence had been at her elbow, expostulating that he had not tried to reproduce those things, she could not have heard his voice: she was blinded and deafened. "I was hurt beyond all expression. I didn't know how to bear it." Jessie wrote this almost a score of years later, and we cannot doubt her words.

Worst of all was that from that time on Lawrence was no longer her chief concern. Jessie's occupation was gone.

She was not too shocked or blind or deaf, however, to appreciate her own irrationality. She reminded herself that it was only a novel, but those words meant nothing. She realized exactly what Lawrence would have said—"Of course it isn't the truth. It isn't meant for the truth. It's an adaptation from life, as all art must be. It *isn't* what I think of you; you know it isn't—" but none of this was any comfort. The very fact that he could so distort truth was inexpressibly painful. Emile Delavenay expresses Jessie's feelings as well as his own interpretation of Lawrence's actions in writing as he did:

It is as if he no longer wanted to love the girl he had so long been accustomed to trying not to want to love, and who, no doubt, recalled too vividly a period of his own development not particularly pleasant to remember. This period . . . he now feels he has put behind him. . . . It is not so much a distortion of Paul's feelings as of the actual character of Miriam: we no longer see her in herself, obeying the laws of her own internal evolution, nor even as Paul saw her at each step of their love, but instead with a deliberate hostility, a blend of bitterness, guilt and commiseration.

Delavenay expands this thesis to remind us that Lawrence now felt himself on the road to success and higher social standing, so he wished to rid himself of Jessie. But as he both loved and feared her, he presented Miriam statically, instead of living and developing as the real Jessie did. She—Miriam, that is—was

> concealed behind a more or less appropriate label, which provides Lawrence with an alibi [by which Delavenay probably means excuse] and assuages his sense of guilt. It is easier to throw off responsibilities towards a label than towards a living woman. Thus Miriam is shown either jealous of Paul or 'romantic in her soul'; moved by the 'will to power' as she 'drenches' Paul or her small brother with her love; stroking flowers with a selfish passion.

We remember Lawrence's remarks in his letter to Rachel Annand Taylor announcing his engagement to Louie Burrows, in which in a strange, irrelevant outburst he says that she would never demand "to drink him up and have him" like Jessie.

All the time Jessie was undergoing her hurt and sense of deprivation, there was the culprit demanding to know what she thought of his book. What was she to do about that? Never in all her life had she withheld her opinions and judgments on Lawrence's work, and she could not do it even now. She arranged by letter to meet him on a Sunday in March when she planned to spend the weekend with the Holbrooks. She knew he always felt at home with them, and they liked seeing him. Lawrence replied that he had to spend Saturday night in Staffordshire, but he would get to the cottage about noon. Jessie must have spent the whole morning, if not the preceding night, planning what to say to Lawrence, composing tongue-lashings to make him squirm and leave him speechless. The meek, long-suffering girl was stirred at last to rebellion—but though noon arrived, Lawrence did not. The afternoon wore on and still he did not come. It was like some travesty of that long-ago memorable day when Mrs. Lawrence held him back, filling his mind with poison before she let him go to Jessie, waiting at The Haggs.

Lawrence got to the cottage late that evening, tired out and looking like death after a frustrating day's travel from Staffordshire. Trains had been late and he had missed his connections. Serious talk had to be postponed until the following afternoon. Even next day Jessie had to hold her fire, since Lawrence had a headache and looked worse than ever—"far too much a sick man for me to dream of telling him all I thought and felt about his novel," wrote Jessie. Yet she knew him too well to believe he was trying to avoid a confrontation. He was afraid of what she might say, but he had to know all the same. With new cynicism, she told herself that he wouldn't want people saying afterward that he hadn't given her at least a chance to express herself. So they sat in uneasy silence before the fire, each waiting for the other to make a move, until he said at last, "Do you want to go out, or would you rather stay in?" Very politely she left the decision to him, and he opted for a walk, saying that he felt quite well enough for it. So they took their walk, Lawrence talking about early spring flowers until Jessie was ready to burst into tears because it seemed to her that springtime and spring flowers had gone out of her life forever. Lawrence saw her emotion as he always did and seized his chance, saying almost wistfully, "I thought perhaps you would have something to say about the writing."

The moment had come, but Jessie could not grasp it. She was cowardly. "I've put some notes in with the manuscript," she said.

Lawrence replied, "Oh, all right. I thought you might like to say something. That's all."

He seemed relieved but puzzled. He had expected fireworks and was ready for them; cold silence was something he was not prepared for. They returned to the cottage, and when it was time for Jessie to go to her parents' house, Lawrence as usual said he would walk part of the way with her. She was ready for this and asked May to come along too, so that Bert need not go back alone, she said. As Jessie was putting on her hat her eyes met Lawrence's intense stare in the mirror and she felt a strong revulsion. He seemed a total stranger. She gave him his manuscript done up in a parcel, and the three of them walked to the top of the hill, where Jessie said good-bye, mounted her bicycle, and rode off. May understood nothing of what was going on, but she told Jessie later that on the way back to the cottage, Lawrence said, "She's wild with me, isn't she? She's angry about something."

May, who knew nothing of the business, said that she didn't think so, but Lawrence insisted.

"She is, she's angry. Hasn't she told you about it?"

Jessie was to see Lawrence only twice more, though their communication continued for a while afterward. She happened to be at the station on Easter Monday, waiting for May, when she saw Lawrence with Ada and Clarke, Ada's fiancé, and had the chance to take a good look at him before he spotted her. He looked miserable, more so than she had ever seen him before, utterly lonely, utterly hopeless. Three weeks later Jessie and her father drove over to the Holbrook cottage and unexpectedly met Lawrence, who, it seemed, was spending the weekend there. This time Jessie thought he looked much better, as if the load on his spirits had lightened, but his attitude was odd; for once, she said, she saw him tongue-tied. Jessie offered him a lift in the trap when they started back, but he decided that he would stay with the Holbrooks. However, he drove part of the way with them, talking with determined cheerfulness of his plans to go to Germany in a few days. She thought he winced a little at Mr. Chambers's casual tone. When Jessie coolly asked him about his work, he said that he had written a play that might be produced in London. Before they reached Watnall hill he got out, shaking hands casually with both Chamberses. Looking back, Jessie saw him raise his hat in farewell as he always did. May reported afterward that he returned to their cottage in thoughtful mood and seemed subdued and gentle. Lying out on the field that afternoon with Holbrook, he suddenly said, "Bill, I like a *gushing* woman."

That he had found one was not clear for several weeks, and even then Jessie was the only member of the family who knew. As far as his friends were aware, Lawrence went off alone to Germany. He sent a postcard showing Trier Cathedral to Jessie, and in a week or so a letter from him announced that he was going through the novel. "I'm sorry it turned out as it has," he added. "You'll have to go on forgiving me."

A few weeks after this she got another letter addressed to her personally, slipped into another missive intended for the whole family. On her letter he had written characteristically, *"Pour vous seulement."* It contained what Jessie described as a hysterical announcement of the new attachment he had formed: he had run away with Frieda, the German wife of his former linguistics professor, Ernest Weekley of the University College of Nottingham. Jessie was to tell no one, he insisted; not May or anybody. Only Alice knew.

The news came as a shock, said Jessie, but she wasn't really surprised. Her deepest feeling was a sense of relief because she was, at last, really free. She had always felt a great responsibility toward Lawrence, and this was gone. But she was not happy about the matter—that would be too much to expect. Though freedom is good, life without Lawrence looked very bleak. She was stunned and miserable. Later she recounted how in her emptiness she tried to read and get her mind off Lawrence, but her attempts were fruitless until she happened on Dostoevsky's *The Brothers Karamazov*. Even that book failed to hold her attention at first, but the text broke through at last and gripped her. Nothing else interested her; she abandoned the novel "Eu-

nice Temple" that she had started writing in 1910 and revised
a year later, though Violet Hunt and Ford had thought it promising and wanted her to go ahead with it. How could she have
anything now to do with it or the *English Review?* Later she
was to destroy the manuscript.

Her friendship with Helen Corke survived, but Helen, who
did not yet know the facts, was puzzled that summer by Jessie's
behavior and could not understand what had happened to her.
Jessie's vitality had suddenly ebbed, thought Helen; her letters
lost all their old spontaneity and her conversation was strangely
ironical. She moved as if in an enemy world. She was actually
defensive. Why? That August the two young women went on a
holiday trip they had planned for months. By a coincidence
cruel to Jessie, it was in the Rhineland that they toured, but as
far as Jessie was concerned it could have been anywhere—
Africa, America, or whatever. She never looked at things or
tried to take in the beauty of their surroundings. Sunk in *The
Brothers Karamazov* she scarcely ever spoke, and Helen Corke,
neglected and bewildered, felt curiously alone throughout their
jaunt. Not until the following year did the reason become clear
to her.

In the spring of 1913 Jessie received from its publisher,
"with the compliments of the author," Lawrence's first book of
poems. She already knew most of them. Politely she wrote to
thank him and not long afterward got a letter along with the
proof sheets of *Sons and Lovers*, soon to be published. In the
letter Lawrence said that he felt Jessie should see the novel before publication and asked her to send the proofs on to Alice
Dax after she had looked at them; he supplied Mrs. Dax's address. He continued:

"This last year hasn't been all roses for me. I've had my ups
and downs out here with Frieda. But we mean to marry as soon
as the divorce is through." So far there was nothing unusual in
this; Lawrence had always talked about his personal affairs with
everybody, and there was no reason for him to change now.
Jessie read on until she reached the following passage:

"Frieda and I discuss you endlessly. We should like you to come out to us some time, if you would care to." He added quickly, "But we are leaving here in about a week, it's getting too hot for us, I mean the weather, not the place."

Jessie's feelings as she read these extraordinary words were so violently mixed that she nearly burst. The tone of the letter, she wrote, was so offensive—the offhand attempt to be casual and matter-of-fact yet to appeal to her sympathy—and to send her that book once more! She had no desire to read it again; she didn't think she could bear to. She was still staring at the letter and the proofs when May happened to drop in, and Jessie, completely unnerved for once, showed her the letter, something she would never have done in more normal times. May was at once furiously protective of her sister. How *dare* Bert write like that to Jessie? She must send the letter back immediately. No, certainly May would not read the book; let them forward it straight away to Mrs. Dax.

That was what Jessie did. The book went off to Alice Dax, and Lawrence's letter was posted back to him without a word of comment.

Presently we shall examine Frieda, who became Lawrence's wife and remained married to him, sometimes tempestuously, until he died. But for the moment let us see what happened to some of the women left behind.

Jessie eventually recovered, at least to some extent, from her trauma; that August she summoned up the energy to go alone to France and, through a friend's connections, live for a time on a French farm. She wrote to Helen Corke from there that she found existence different to some extent, yet not really far removed from life at The Haggs, and it was pleasant. She liked the people because they were "direct and genuine." Returning to England much the better for her trip, with her spirit quietened and with a renewed liking for country life, she made the acquaintance of a farmer's son, John R. Wood of Nottingham, whom in 1915 she married. After that, according to

Helen Corke, Jessie devoted herself to her home and her husband's interests, though as we know she also went in for socialism. The friendship between herself and Helen languished,
no doubt, as Helen remarked, because the need Jessie had once
felt for a link with Lawrence had vanished, taking with it the
chief reason for their meetings, but after Lawrence's death it
flared again for a little while. For one thing, both women were
soon engaged—with about half the literary world, seemingly—
in writing books about him.

Helen's essay entitled "Lawrence and Apocalypse," which
dealt with Lawrence's ideas on that part of the Bible, appeared
in 1933, and she sent a copy to Jessie, who replied at length,
thanking her with markedly muted praise and going on to say
that it was concerned with that aspect of Lawrence which she
had always found least interesting. As an artist dealing with the
immediate and concrete, she said, he was superb, but when he
essayed to be a thinker she found him superficial and unconvincing—and quite soon a bore. Lawrence's concern was not
really with Revelation, she declared, but to find some means
of escape from the narrow prison of his own ego; to do that
he was prepared to assault the cosmos. She could never read his
almost delirious denunciations of what he pretended to look on as
Christianity without seeing a caged panther lashing himself into a
fury, trying to find some way out of his prison.

Jessie said that she didn't propose to write a book about
him, yet she knew an aspect of his life unknown to anyone else,
and so she meant to leave a simple historical record of this,
which some day might be a help to a biographer who had a
genuine desire to understand Lawrence. We may suppose that
Emile Delavenay persuaded her to look on him as such a biographer, and, of course, in the end she did not wait for posterity
but published the record in her lifetime.

Continuing her letter to Helen, Jessie described an extra-
sensory impression that she had experienced during Lawrence's
last illness. They were not in touch, nor had been since the re-

turn of his letter in 1913, but for some eighteen months before his death she felt acutely drawn to him at times and thought that once she heard his voice saying, "Can you remember only the pain and none of the joy?"

His voice was full of reproach, and she made haste to tell him that she did remember the joy. Later, in a strange confused way, the voice said, "What has it all been about?"

The next morning, busy with her housework, she was suddenly conscious that the room was filled with his presence, and for a moment she seemed to see him as he had been in the early days, with a little cap on the back of his head. The momentary presence was so full of joy that she concluded that it was an earnest of real meeting in the near future. She even said to herself, 'Now *I know* we're going to meet.' On the following day she saw the notice of his death in the paper.

It was Jessie's conviction that he had broken out of prison before he died; she judged this from his last poems. But of his imprisonment through most of his adult life she had no doubt. His Golden Age had been during the years leading up to the age of nineteen or so, before his fatal self-division manifested itself and ruined his work. The letter was signed "Jessie Wood," instead of the old "Muriel," and Helen, already indignant at much of its content, took this as merely another sign of how very far apart the friends had grown. For herself she refused to accept Jessie's interpretation of Lawrence's schizophrenia, but she saw no point in arguing. Jessie's book, *D. H. Lawrence: A Personal Record,* came out two years later.

In 1940 Helen Corke happened to be staying near Nottingham. Suddenly possessed by many memories, she obeyed an impulse and wrote to Jessie suggesting a meeting, to which Jessie replied naming a certain café in the town where they could have tea. Helen, who arrived first, nearly failed to recognize her friend in the bent, heavy figure that slowly approached. Jessie said that she was recovering from a nervous breakdown which had left her deaf; one wonders what sort of nervous breakdown could have had such a bizarre effect, but certainly the deafness was a fact, and Helen found it almost impossible to converse in the noisy restaurant, where she had to shout to make herself understood. Not that it seemed to matter, for Jessie preferred to carry the burden herself, uttering a stream of complaints. She had become sour and would talk of nothing but the heinousness of the commercial literary world, specifically the American publishers who had published her book without her consent, and the stupid British public that had not welcomed it as enthusiastically as it merited.

She was so unlike the old Jessie Chambers that Helen, appalled by the change wrought by time and illness, found herself unable to feel anything for the woman but pity. Unfortunately Jessie sensed this and fired up, as furious with Helen Corke as if she saw in her the whole hostile world of money-grubbing publishers. In the end, turning her face away, she left, unreconciled. Altogether it was a thoroughly unhappy experience for Miss Corke.

Jessie died in 1944. In 1953, replying to an inquiry from Edward Nehls, who was then preparing his biography, her widower, John Wood, wrote rather brusquely that he had never met Lawrence and was not very interested in him or his work— "neither am I sympathetically inclined," he said. Shortly after the First World War, he added, his wife had burnt all letters and manuscripts in her possession.

Louise Burrows, like Helen Corke, remained ignorant for some time of Lawrence's elopement. To her, too, he sent a postcard—in fact, *two* postcards—from Germany, and she obtained his address from Ada and wrote to him for his birthday. Soon afterward, in November, 1912, he wrote telling her about Frieda: "I am living here with a lady whom I love. . . . We have been together as man and wife for six months, nearly, now, and I hope we shall always remain man and wife."

Remembering how he had written to Louie about the advice of his doctors and so on, he apologized for having deceived her, if he had done so—and he admitted that this was possible. At any rate, he said, he was sorry and saw no point in continuing their correspondence. But Louie had been hit hard and could not cut off relations so abruptly. She wrote once more, and the reply she got to that letter must have discouraged her, at least for some time. The editor of her papers thinks that she did write again, however, in the February following, when Lawrence was traveling about, because she asked Ada for his address. If she did write to him, however, she got no reply.

Louie was abandoned to the doubtful comfort of her family's recriminations and her own grief, which was real and intense. She seems to have turned all her energy thereafter to work. She became head of the Quorn school and remained in that position until 1924, when she became headmistress of a new school in Leicestershire, and there she remained for the rest of her working life. Those who knew her, according to James Boulton in the introduction to *Lawrence in Love*, remember her as a cultured woman of strong character and great decisiveness. Once, for example, she reacted sharply to a schoolmaster's declaration that manhood was humiliated by the appointment of women as school inspectors and vigorously denounced this male chauvinist outburst.

Whatever would have happened to these ideas if she had married Lawrence? In any case she never forgot him. When the news arrived in 1930 of his death in Vence, Louie decided that she must go there and look at his grave. This was more than eighteen years after they had parted, and at least one of her friends expostulated with her, but Louie insisted and had her way. Frieda's daughter Barbara, who was with her mother when Lawrence died, recalled having seen "a tall dark woman" at the cemetery soon after the funeral. It was probably Louie, for she afterward wrote to Ada that she had been there. Realizing that she had been seen, the stranger went away. Later, Louie left flowers on the grave mound.

She paid a second visit to the grave at some undetermined date. Sir Herbert Read, who met her on one or another of these occasions, reported that she had obviously never renounced her love and devotion for Lawrence. He added that she appeared to be dejected and unhappy, and seemed to feel she had been badly treated by Lawrence, which does not seem an unreasonable opinion for Louie to hold.

Her interests had always lain in music and art. Later she took to astrology, spiritualism, and archaeology, which esoteric studies no doubt lent to her literary style a certain eccentricity. In 1933 H. G. Wells received a letter from her which said that she and Lawrence had been "betrothed," as she put it, from November, 1910, to February, 1912—a fact that, as we know, is incontrovertible—and she went on to say that Wells's *Bulpington of Blup*, recently published, was in many ways hers and Lawrence's story. Naturally, this irritated Wells, for authors never like being told that someone else has supplied them with ideas. He wrote on the margin of the letter, "*File*. This lady is a mythomaniac."

In 1940, at the age of fifty-two, Louie, who was still living with her family at Quorn, married Mr. Frederick Heath and retired from schoolmistressing the following year. Until her death in 1962 she held on to whatever mementos of Lawrence she possessed and let no one else see his letters. Her friends understood that she meant to write a book about him, but she never did.

For obvious reasons the story of Alice Dax is not well documented, but in a letter dated 23 January 1935, which she wrote to Frieda Lawrence after reading the latter's book, "*Not I, But the Wind . . . ,*" we learn that her affair with Lawrence continued up to the eve of his elopement. Evidently Lawrence had at some time introduced the two ladies, and their relations were cordial.

The "Wind" nearly broke my heart with sadness and with gladness and other conflicting emotions. And I was grateful to you—really grateful [wrote Alice].

I had always been glad that he met you, even from the day after the event, when he told me about you, and I knew that he would leave me. I was never *meet* for him and what he liked was not the me I *was*, but the me I might-have-been—the potential me which would never have struggled to life but for his help and influence. I thank him always for my life though I know it cost him pains and disappointments. I fear that he never even enjoyed morphia with me [Lawrence called the relief of casual sex rather than of deeper feelings "morphia"]— always it carried an irritant—we were never, except for one short memorable hour, whole: it was from that hour that I began to see the light of life.

Mrs. Dax said that, unlike Frieda, she had never been able to quarrel with Lawrence because she was afraid of losing him, while he probably felt equally unsure of her; when he was very angry at her he would simply walk away from her. She continued:

He needed *you.* I remember so well his words: "You would like Frieda—she is direct and free, but I don't know how you would get on together" and his voice tailed off into "I wonder," whilst his mind compared us and his eyes left me in no doubt. You had, without doubt, all the things that he needed, and his sensitive soul knew it without an inventory.

Mrs. Dax wrote at length about herself and her life as a child. They were poor, and her mother suffered through the behavior of Alice's father. Privately, the child swore vengeance on all men, but after marrying Henry Dax—whom she grabbed as soon as he offered, for fear nobody else would propose to her—she became softer. Henry did not, after all, have a bad time with his wife. Lawrence must have suffered far more, she feared.

"Alas! I loved him," confessed Mrs. Dax to Lawrence's widow. Her feelings had been very mixed, she confessed, after her lover's elopement. She was glad of his happiness when he

wrote to her from Lake Garda "in the richness of fulfilment"—
he must have written from Garda to all his girl friends at the
same time: Louie, Jessie, Helen, the lot—but she envied Frieda
bitterly just the same.

"How I resented his snobbery and his happiness whilst I
was suffering in body and sick in soul, carrying an unwanted
child which would never have been conceived but for an
unendurable passion which only *he* had roused and my husband
had slaked."

# 6

# Frieda: "The most wonderful woman in all England"

"BILL, I like a *gushing* woman."

Frieda was in Lawrence's mind when he said this, and he did not misrepresent her. Gushing was a characteristic of German women, especially those as healthy and life-loving as Frieda Weekley. Fair, good-looking, fresh-faced, strapping, she was about the same height as Lawrence, who was five feet nine inches tall. (In his novels Lawrence sometimes referred to the fictional characters modeled on himself as "little," but five feet nine is a reasonable height; it was his slight build that diminished him in his own eyes.) Unlike Lawrence, Frieda, who was cheerfully indolent, put on weight easily, a tendency that does not seem to have distressed either Lawrence or herself.

Frieda was one of three children, all daughters, of Baron Friedrich von Richthofen, a regular army officer until, at the age of twenty-five, he was wounded in the right hand. This took place toward the end of the Franco-Prussian War, and Von Richthofen had to resign his commission and leave the army. In compensation he was given a post in the civil administration of Metz, in the territory of Elsass-Lothringen—Alsace-Lorraine—recently taken over by Germany. Frieda, the second daughter, was born in Metz in 1879. She was often to mention her pedigree with pride, sometimes ruefully, as when she referred to herself as "a poor baroness," but always seriously. As these things are judged the Richthofens were not an ancient family, and Else, Frieda's elder sister, laughed at her for boasting of it, but Frieda evidently used the thought of her blue blood as a cushion against hard facts such as that Friedrich's branch of the family was poor, that he constantly made matters worse by gambling, and that the girls had no dowries to tempt eligible suitors. The situation was difficult, but at least Frieda, like all children of the German aristocracy, had a title; she was a baroness, and as Lawrence once quoted to the mystified Jessie, "How that glittering taketh me!" It took young Frieda too.

The baron's gambling was the cause of quarrels between him and his wife, a member of a Black Forest family that was originally French. The girls often overheard such dissension and tended to side with their father; he was a fond parent and they loved him. Playfully he sometimes said to them, "I don't mind whom my daughters marry, as long as they don't marry a Jew, an Englishman, or a gambler." It was a rich family joke that they should all have gone against his wishes in this matter: Else married the Jewish professor Edgar Jaffe, both Frieda's husbands were English, and Johanna or "Nusch," the family beauty, married a gambler.

As a child Frieda was a tomboy, hard for the nuns to manage—for she and her sisters, like many other Protestant girls in Metz, attended a convent school. She was reasonably intelligent in class, though not like Else, who was brilliant. Five years older than Frieda, Else was interested in sociology and politics. But Frieda and Nusch were ordinary girls, taken up with watching the officers who paraded the streets in smart uniform, ogled the Baron's daughters in church, and, in small numbers, with proper introductions, called at his house to drink tea and look appraisingly at the maidens. At the age of sixteen Frieda fell in love with a distant cousin and was kissed a few times in the moonlit garden. Not long afterward she fell more seriously in love with a lieutenant who would gladly have married her if only she had had money. As it was, he could not afford the poor baroness, and they parted.

Each girl was given a year's polish at a boarding school in the Black Forest run by two maiden ladies named Blass, and this period marked the end of formal schooling for Frieda and her younger sister. Else, however, had elected to go on to the university. Frieda emerged from the Blass sisters' school eighteen years old and a debutante; a photograph taken at this time shows her with a mischievous, lopsided grin on her wide mouth. She was then sent for a season in Berlin, staying with her bachelor uncle Oswald von Richthofen, Undersecretary to the Foreign Ministry, whose widowed sisters kept house for him in the Tiergarten. Frieda's biographer Robert Lucas described the Berlin of 1897 as a huge bundle of nervous energy, of vitality and ambition, speculation and fraud, hard work and robust efficiency. Of course the new architecture was hideous, but Berlin nevertheless attracted artists from all over Europe. For a time, until the censor banned them, the public could see plays by Hauptmann, Ibsen, and Tolstoy. The galleries exhibited paintings by exciting young moderns. What with theater, opera, carriage drives in the Grunewald woods, cafés, racing, and the occasional court ball, Frieda had a wonderful time. Once when Nusch too was in Berlin and the sisters attended a court ball together, the Kaiser himself asked who they were and commented, when he got the answer, that Herr Undersecretary had very beautiful nieces. The girls did not care for the Kaiser, but it was undeniably flattering.

Meanwhile Else attained the distinction of being one of the first females ever admitted to the University of Heidelberg, where she worked under Professor Max Weber and wrote her doctoral thesis on Germany's new social-security laws. Through her, Frieda met the few German intellectuals she could include in her list of acquaintances during girlhood, but she collected Ernest Weekley, a professor from the University College of Nottingham, all by herself. She met him during a visit to the Blasses in the Black Forest, where Ernest was enjoying the first holiday he had ever permitted himself in all his industrious life. Fourteen years older than Frieda, Weekley came of a poor family that lived on the outskirts of London. His father was a civil servant in the lower echelons in the city. The Weekleys were an honest, pious lot, all eleven of them—Ernest was one of nine children—and he grew up with a strong sense of duty. He was intelligent and made the most of the chance given him by a family connection, a clergyman with a good boarding school, to attend it without paying fees.

As soon as he could, when he was seventeen, Ernest won a post as schoolteacher. While he taught he worked with all his might to get a degree from London University through correspondence courses, and when he had succeeded in this aim he went on to the University of Berne, where for a year he studied German subjects. His interest in languages now firmly fixed, he forged along on the scholar's path to Cambridge (Middle English and modern languages), and to the Sorbonne, and then held a post as lecturer in English at Freiburg University. Finally, at the beginning of 1898, he was offered a professor's chair at Nottingham. It was a great day for Ernest Weekley when he got the news. All his efforts had been crowned, and he thought that life could hardly be better. He needed nothing to complete his bliss but a wife, and he fell in love with Frieda at first sight. Besides, what could be more fitting for him, with his interest in linguistics, than to marry a German girl?

The attraction Ernest held for Frieda is not so easily explained. At thirty-three he must have seemed old to her nineteen-year-old eyes, and though he was good-looking in an ascetic way, he had not the animal attraction of the young officers of Metz. Perhaps it was this very difference that she liked. Certainly she appreciated his sterling qualities, his capacity for hard work on behalf of his family, his kindliness and intelligence. At any rate, when in due course he proposed she accepted him, and her parents approved of the engagement. They had never hoped that any of their daughters, without money as they were, would make what the world considered a brilliant match, and an English professor was a respectable person. Frieda, they thought, had chosen sensibly. So in 1899 she was married to Ernest, and he took her to live in Nottingham.

Like almost everyone embroiled in Lawrence's life, Frieda has been eloquent on the subject of her emotions. Several times, under various guises of fiction, she recounted the lamentable story of her wedding night when Ernest, shy in matters of sex, left her alone in the hotel room to prepare for bed while he went downstairs, as he awkwardly explained, for a drink. Frieda was undressing when she noticed a huge, old-fashioned wardrobe at the side of the room. On a sudden impulse she climbed to the top of it and sat there half dressed, legs dangling, stifling her giggles in anticipation of Ernest's reaction at finding her gone. She would wait a bit to enjoy the joke and then say "Boo!" But when he did appear and stared blankly around at emptiness, he looked so crestfallen that her heart misgave her and she called to him. He looked even more frightened when he saw where she was. Of course she climbed down quickly, but he still seemed shocked. And their first experience of love-making was a miserable disappointment, because Ernest seemed to know just as little about that as he did about jokes. After he fell asleep she stood for a long time at the window and contemplated jumping out. But no, reflected the baroness, only housemaids jump out of windows. She went meekly back to bed, hating Ernest.

In time she got over hating him. She even got used to living in Nottingham, though, like Ernest, it was not terribly amusing. For one thing, she hadn't enough to do. Other Nottingham women liked to follow a rigid routine in housework—Monday washday, Tuesday ironing day, and the rest of the week for cleaning room by room. Meals were fixed, too: the joint appeared on Sunday to reappear cold or as a mince on Tuesday, and so on. Not that Frieda did any of these chores herself; the Weekleys had a cook and another woman to clean and launder. Madam was expected to supervise, that was all, and it is only fair to say that the arrangement suited her well enough.

In June, 1900, the Weekleys' first baby, a boy they named Montague, was born. For the occasion Baroness von Richthofen came over from Metz and brought with her a German nurse-maid. Two daughters, Elsa and Barbara, arrived in turn, and for those years, in the bustle and flurry of successful motherhood, Frieda was happy. Besides, Ernest wasn't around enough to irritate her, as his activities increased year by year. He held classes all day every weekday, and three times a week he went out in the evening to teach at a workers' institute. On Saturdays he went to Cambridge. In whatever spare time he could squeeze from this heroic program he indulged himself by studying Italian, a hobby in which Frieda joined. He also wrote textbooks for students of French. In future years he was to publish two books that became famous among philologists, *The Romance of Words* and *The Romance of Names*.

He encouraged Frieda to academic pastimes too, until she edited a couple of books in a series called Little German Classics. As she wrote to her sisters, it was a job that at least exercised her rusty brain and earned a little money. Else, who had by now married Dr. Jaffe, approved of such activity, but Nusch, the wife of a staff officer, laughed at Frieda's metamorphosis into a highbrow. Nusch had become worldly, even dissipated. When she visited the Weekleys in Nottingham she was astonished that Frieda, who had been such a madcap as a girl, was apparently content with her lot as a dowdy housewife in a second-rate English city. "Are you really satisfied in your life?" she asked.

The question started Frieda thinking uneasily. *Was* she really satisfied? Probably not, now that she came to think of it: life was boring, but what else was there for her to do? She had no reason to cut loose from Ernest, no burning ambition or any particular desire for anything different. But she *was* bored; she admitted it to herself. In the end she reverted to a cure she was often to use later, the excitement of sexual infidelity. There was a prosperous lace manufacturer in town, a man named Will Dowson, whose wife was active in the cause for woman's suffrage and left him much to himself. He owned that rare novelty, a motorcar, and he admired Frieda. The two of them dropped into the habit of taking long drives in the country and soon embarked on an affair that amused Frieda, though it did not impress her to any great extent. She said in her memoirs that Will made her feel "alive again," that was all. No twinge of conscience troubled her, but she was careful that Ernest should not suspect anything.

Frequently she took the children to Germany to see their grandparents, but in 1907 she went alone to Metz, spent a few days there, and then joined Else in Munich. Else was visiting a school friend, Friedel Gross, wife of an Austrian psychologist and analyst named Otto Gross, whose father was the famous criminologist Hans Gross. One of Freud's brightest pupils, Otto had taken off in his own direction and evolved a quite different philosophy. He maintained that the world could only be saved by sexual revolution, an abandonment of the Western ideal of monogamy and family life. Women had been victimized, said Gross; women must rise up and take their proper place as mistresses of civilization. Away with the trammels of conventional morality! As men had done before, women should choose their men at will; the bourgeois family must be destroyed, and with it the bourgeois notion of marital fidelity. These theories of Gross's were the foundation of the new "erotic movement" that for a time had an effect on all of Western civilization.

One of Otto's disciples, at least temporarily, was Frieda's older sister, Else Jaffe. Nobody had ever pretended that Else's marriage was one of love, but it was convenient for both partners. Now Else was convinced for the moment by Otto's ideas, and she entered into a relationship with him. As a result she too became pregnant, but Friedel, who had always loved and admired her, did not resent the situation too much for domestic peace. Friedel herself did not feel like going out, however, so when Frieda Weekley arrived in Munich it was Otto who took the Von Richthofen sisters around, showing them the night life of the Schwabing district, Munich's Bohemian center and Otto Gross's favorite stamping ground. Frieda thoroughly enjoyed Schwabing, which was such a change from Nottingham; she loved the taverns and clubs and endless café talk. Soon she was in love with Otto and he with her. According to his philosophy, which soon became hers, there was no reason they should not go to bed together, nor was there any reason why either Friedel or Else should complain if they did. Everybody ought to do exactly as he or she wished; the only sin was possessiveness. And so, though Else and Friedel and another young woman of their circle were all pregnant by Otto Gross, Frieda considered Else unreasonable for objecting to the liaison. The sisters quarreled.

"Our last meeting in Heidelberg was completely in the style of 'Brünnhild and Krimhild,'" Frieda wrote to Otto; it had been "dramatic but not good." The quarrel finished when Else abandoned Otto, as she soon did; she, like Friedel, bore him a son, and both infants were named Peter. But for some time Else was furious with her little sister and remonstrated strongly when she heard that Frieda was considering leaving Ernest and bringing the children to Germany in order to set up a masterless household in accordance with Otto's ideal pattern. Else wrote to Frieda expostulating. Couldn't she see that Otto had ruined his wife's life? Couldn't she see that he was unable to constrain himself even for a quarter of an hour? (As a matter of fact, Otto was a cocaine and opium addict, habits not conducive to self-restraint in any direction.)

"As a 'lover' he's incomparable," wrote Else, "but a person doesn't consist of that alone. God, it's useless to say anything. You are under that tremendous power of suggestion that emanates from him and which I myself have felt."

She went on to say that Ernest Weekley's love for Frieda was far greater than Otto's, and she begged Frieda to go back to her husband. In spite of such urging, Frieda was strongly tempted to stay. Otto knew far more about love-making than did Ernest or Will Dowson, but that wasn't his whole attraction; she was fascinated by his brilliance. However, something

—possibly an instinctive caution—held her back from leaving Ernest and entering openly into Otto's crazy world. Though the affair was known to everybody in the Schwabing circle, Weekley never heard of it. As with Will Dowson, she kept the romance within bounds as far as England was concerned—though, as her biographer Martin Green points out, she seems to have spread the gospel after she got home, taking lovers and creating "a little Schwabing" in Nottingham. She must have missed Otto—but there were still the children and all the inertia of marriage.

For a long time Gross wrote her passionate love letters which she treasured, assuring her that she was a goddess. In one outburst of admiration he reminded her that she had chosen him, not he her, and for this she was glorious. Often in the same letter he would complain bitterly about Else because she had left him and taken a new lover he did not at all like, but most of the time he talked about Frieda and how wonderful she was. He wrote:

> I am grateful that you exist and that I have been privileged to know you. . . . It is like a miracle, like a greeting from the future that you have come to me. Now I know what men will be like who will no longer be tainted by all the things I hate and combat. I know it through you, the only human being today that has remained free from all the false shame and sham Christianity and false democracy, free from all the accumulated bunk, remained free through your own strength.
>
> How did you accomplish this, you golden child, with your laughter and your love, banishing from your soul all the curse and dirt of two thousand sombre years?

He begged her to come back to Germany, but Frieda resisted. "How could she leave her children?" she wrote about this period in her old age, in one of the fictionalized memoirs she sometimes produced. "They were so small! She could not burden him with them. He lived for his vision."

Well, not exactly. Frieda does not seem to have known of Otto's narcotics addiction, which indirectly killed him in 1920 when he lay out of doors all night. In her memory he remained a guiding star, and she retained from the experience more than a smattering of knowledge about Freud, sex, and psychoanalysis. Otto had convinced her that her sexual behavior, however society might condemn it, was right in principle. She was Woman Triumphant. Sex was right, sex was *healthy*, and she, Frieda, was a goddess of the new order.

So though in England Mrs. Weekley apparently resumed her conventional everyday existence, inwardly she was convinced that Otto Gross had awakened her forever from a somnambulist's trance. Every day she thought of him and the lessons he had taught her. She was being made over, she reflected.

"Being born and reborn is no joke," she wrote, "and being born into your own intrinsic self, that separates and singles you out from all the rest—it's a painful process." Apart from this great private adventure in self-exploration, however, her life did not seem to have changed to any great extent. She was still a Nottingham housewife, though to be sure she was now a more prosperous one; Ernest's hard work was paying dividends in recognition and increased income. The Weekleys enlarged their scale of spending, moving to a bigger house in suburban Mapperley and even buying the new status symbol, a motorcar of their own.

Five years had passed since the Munich adventure, and Frieda reflected sadly that she was now thirty-two, a middle-aged woman. It was spring in 1912, and Easter was approaching. Late in March Ernest remarked casually that he had asked a former student from his night classes, a young genius, he called him, to lunch. The ex-student was asking his advice, Ernest told Frieda, about getting a job as lecturer in a German university.

"I want to be free. I think I should go abroad."

Having said this to Jessie, and with the latest draft of *Sons and Lovers* finished and submitted to Heinemann, Lawrence had made up his mind to do something constructive about the plan. Hence his luncheon appointment with Professor Weekley, the only member of the college staff, he told Jessie, for whom he had genuine admiration.

"He's my favourite Prof.," he once said to her, and again, "He really *is* a gentleman. He's quite elegant. He leans back in his chair and points to the blackboard, too elegant to get on his feet. And he addresses us as 'gentlemen.' He's sarcastic, of course." But there was never any personal contact. Lawrence merely admired this professor from a distance as a scholar and a gentleman.

So it was to Ernest Weekley, as well as others at the college, that Lawrence now applied for advice on getting work in Germany. Ernest invited him home to lunch to talk the matter over, and there in the Mapperley house Lawrence met Weekley's wife.

Frieda made an immediate impression on the young man as she greeted him and asked him to sit down to wait for Weekley. He told her later that he fell in love with her at sight. His biographer Harry T. Moore used his imagination in describing the encounter: Frieda, said Moore, was an altogether different kind of woman from any Lawrence had ever known.

"There was more blaze about her than about English-women: she had the assured Continental manner and a throaty, strange-accented voice, and she could range in a moment from sophisticated poise into childish eagerness." Then there was her appearance. "Physically, she was a magnificent blonde tall animal, with high cheekbones and green 'Tartar' eyes flecked with brown."

From Frieda's memoirs we know what she saw. In a well-known passage she indicated that to her, at least, the twenty-six-year-old Lawrence seemed tall—"a long thin figure, quick straight legs, light, sure movements."

They had half an hour before busy Ernest arrived. Outside the French windows the children played on the lawn, and inside Lawrence talked. He talked about women, how terrible they are and how much he was involved with them and how he was finished forever with trying to understand the creatures. Frieda thought it an extraordinary outburst. She wrote that she had never in her life heard anything like it—though, as we know, Rachel Annand Taylor had, and had been equally startled. This was a regular gambit with Lawrence: his line, as a later generation would have called it. Frieda was impressed.

"I laughed," she admitted, "yet I could tell he had tried very hard, and had cared."

She felt sympathetic to this youth who had suffered so much, especially when he spoke with such emotion of his mother. Ah, the Oedipus complex! Frieda, who considered herself an expert on Sigmund Freud, sat up and spoke the magic name, which delighted Lawrence. Hadn't he just finished a book on the same thing? It was exciting to discover that this handsome woman knew all about such matters. As Frieda recalled: "understanding leaped through our words."

The belated arrival of Ernest did little to interrupt the flow between wife and guest. Lawrence's reason for having requested the interview seems to have been brushed aside; his hostess concentrated on a dialogue with the young man, while Ernest communed with his thoughts. The meal over, Weekley excused himself and dashed off to study or lecture, while Frieda and Lawrence continued talking. Hours passed. They had afternoon tea, darkness fell, the children disappeared from the lawn, and still they talked. At last the young genius took his leave. Uplifted, transported, he set out on the eight-mile walk to Eastwood, and when he got there five hours later he sat down at once and wrote to Frieda, saying, "You are the most wonderful woman in all England."

Frieda replied, gratified but modestly demurring, and Lawrence replied in turn.

On the afternoon of Easter Sunday, April 7, he came to call. Ernest was away and the maids had the day off; only Frieda and the children were at home. The children were out of doors in the chilly sunlight, hunting for eggs in the garden. Frieda attempted to make tea for Lawrence, an unusual gesture for her, so much so that she didn't know how to turn on the gas to boil the water. Horrified by such hamhandedness in a woman, Lawrence scolded her. She was surprised and charmed.

"Such a direct critic!" she mused. "It was something my High and Mightiness was very little accustomed to." Yet, she wrote in her memoirs, he really understood her: "From the first he saw through me like glass, saw how hard I was trying to keep up a cheerful front." Ernest didn't understand like that; only Lawrence did, and she was to have faith in his uncanny comprehension for the rest of her life.

"What I cannot understand is how he could have loved me and wanted me at that time," she wrote. "I certainly did have what he called 'sex in the head'; a theory of loving men. My real self was frightened and shrank from contact like a wild thing."

Lawrence often accused women of having "sex in the head."

A few days later, Frieda and her two small daughters went into the country with Lawrence on an expedition to the Holbrook farm. On the way they paused at a brook with a stone bridge over it, and the frolicking children quieted down to watch Lawrence as he made paper boats and set them adrift on the brook's current and showed them how to sail daisy heads downstream. He and the little girls were completely wrapped up in their game, and Frieda, looking at the three bent heads, felt a sudden rush of emotion and realized that she loved Lawrence. Years later the younger girl, Barby, recounted how she and Elsa and her mother had started out for a walk when they met "a tall, pale, cross-looking young man" whom her mother obviously knew, who took them to a place called Holbrook's Farm. The farmer, Mr. Holbrook, showed the children over the place and gave them a ride on a horse. Barbara Barr, as she grew up to be, remembered the ride because the horse reared while she was sitting on it, and Mr. Holbrook caught her as she fell off.

After tea the Weekleys went home, but Lawrence stayed

on for the night with the Holbrooks and was there next day when Jessie and her father made that unexpected visit—the last time Jessie and Bert ever met.

Afterward, as Frieda said accurately, "things happened quickly." Lawrence called at the Weekley house on another Sunday and again found Ernest away. True to her accepted pattern, Frieda suggested to her new young man that he spend the night with her, but the collier's son had his own kind of morality, vastly different from hers. He said sternly, "No, I will not stay in your husband's house while he is away." Instead, he had a far more radical plan. He said that Frieda must tell Ernest "the truth" about Lawrence and herself, after which the lovers would go away together. His proposals alarmed Frieda. If she acted on them it would mean the end of the life she had known for so long; it would mean misery for Ernest and separation from her children, at least temporarily—for on that point Frieda's sanguine temperament did not permit her to despair. On the other hand, Lawrence declared that if she did not accept his terms he would walk out of her life there and then. She believed him, partly because his attitude was so deliciously flattering. She reflected that few men would stake everything on love as Lawrence was doing; few men would take such a gamble for a woman's sake. That it was her gamble as well added to the excitement. She agreed to do as he said.

For a time, however, she did nothing more, and Lawrence waited in great agitation, traveling about from Eastwood to Leicester as he prepared to go and writing to Frieda constantly. "I feel so horrid and helpless," he scribbled in his Eastwood lodgings in April. "I know it all sickens you, and you are almost at the end of the tether. And what was decent yesterday will perhaps be frightfully indecent today. But it's like being ill: there's nothing to do but shut one's teeth and look at the wall and wait."

On April 17 he wrote to Edward Garnett that he would probably be in town the next week, and so would Mrs. Weekley. "She is ripping," he added; "—she's the finest woman I've ever met—you must above all things meet her. . . . She is the daughter of Baron von Richthofen, of the ancient and famous house of Richthofen—but she's splendid, she is really. How damnably I mix things up. Mrs. Weekley is perfectly unconventional, but really good—in the best sense. I'll bet you've never met anybody like her, by a long chalk. You *must* see her next week. I wonder if she'd come to the Cearne, if you asked us. Oh, but she is the woman of a lifetime."

Frieda did go to The Cearne, and Garnett for a long time afterward was the lovers' best friend.

The day of reckoning approached when Frieda would have to tell Ernest; it couldn't be put off any longer. She and Lawrence made up a timetable fixed on the fact that Baron von Richthofen was to celebrate the fiftieth anniversary of his entry into the army on May 4, 1912. All the members of his family were expected to gather at that date at Metz, and Frieda had planned for weeks to go to Germany for the occasion. On the eve of her departure she went into Ernest's study and began making her confession. It was incomplete even then; she could not bring herself to speak of Lawrence. What she did was tell her husband of her past infidelities. Aghast, Weekley at first refused to believe any of it, but when Frieda went on to give him names—Will Dowson, Otto Gross—and dates as well, the unfortunate man was at last convinced. Horror and indignation took over. He called his wife biblical names, and Frieda wept. Elsa and Barbara, playing outside the study door, stared after her in childish wonder as she swept past them and up the stairs, sobbing. Next morning she eloped with Lawrence.

All her plans were worked out. Monty and Ernest had left the house before she finished packing. Monty, she was sure, would be all right with the German girl to look after him, because he was nearly twelve. But she took Elsa and Barby to London, to the house of Ernest's parents, and after telling them some hastily cooked-up story she left them there. Her maternal duty done, she hurried to meet Lawrence at Charing Cross Station where he was waiting with all his worldly wealth in his pocket—eleven pounds. They went by night boat to Ostend and arrived at Metz on the fourth of May, just in time for the family party.

Needless to say, Frieda did not take her lover home. He signed in at the local hotel while she reported to her parents; the house was full to overflowing with relatives, and nobody thought it strange that she should decide to live at the hotel. Though Lawrence's presence must be a secret from her father and mother, Frieda immediately told her sisters about the situation and presented Lawrence to them. They were sympathetic, as she had known they would be. Else was always ready to help people in revolt against convention, and Nusch, who had never approved of the Weekley ménage, was more than willing to like Lawrence. Both sisters pronounced him gentlemanly and trustworthy—unlike Otto Gross, Else must have thought.

It was not clear how long Frieda expected to keep her secret, but as cable after cable arrived from Ernest her parents naturally realized that some mischief was afoot and decided that the couple was quarreling. Tactfully, they refrained from speaking of it, but Metz is not a large town and the locals began to notice the silent Englishman—silent because he couldn't speak German—who took such long walks by himself. In fact, Lawrence was miserable; he felt neglected and he hated Germany. Everything was at sixes and sevens, he complained on the rare occasions that he saw Frieda. He had hoped to rewrite parts of his novel, but he couldn't get down to work. Only three days after their arrival he was telling her that the situation was insupportable. They had planned a week's blissful honeymoon in Metz, but here half the week had already gone by and he had hardly seen her. In lieu of working on the novel he wrote a letter to Ernest, which Ernest cannily kept and two years later produced during the divorce hearing. It was a remarkable missive. Lawrence reminded his erstwhile professor that he, Ernest, was not alone in suffering; there were three persons in the unhappy situation. Admittedly, said Lawrence, he couldn't compare his own sufferings with those of an abandoned husband, but one feels that he considered himself very ill-used, notwithstanding. Candidly, he wrote:

> It is really torture to be in this position. I am here as a distant friend, and you can imagine the thousand lies it all entails. Mrs. Weekley hates it, but it had to be. I love your wife, and she loves me. I am not frivolous or impertinent. Mrs. Weekley is afraid of being stunted and not allowed to grow, so she must live her own life. Women in their natures are like giantesses; they will break through everything and go on with their own lives. . . . Mrs. Weekley must live largely and abundantly: it is her nature. To me it means the future. I feel as if my effort to live was all for her. Cannot we all forgive something?

Oddly enough, this effusion impressed Ernest favorably, and he wrote to Frieda about it. "I bear him no ill-will and hope you will be happy with him. But have some pity on me. . . . Let me know at once that you agree to a divorce. . . . You have loved me once—help me now—but quickly."

The poor man could not maintain a consistent attitude: on the matter of divorce, for example, he changed his mind again and again. More than once he begged Frieda to return to him. Once he wrote that if she could assure him that she had not been unfaithful to him quite recently, it would be possible to get back together. On this occasion Lawrence made her reply by cable, QUITE RECENTLY, which settled things for a while—but not forever.

One day while the lovers were visiting the town fortifications a sentinel heard them talking English and promptly arrested Lawrence on suspicion of being a British spy. Frieda had to call on her father for help, which meant telling him everything. The Baron was in a rage but controlled himself sufficiently to get Lawrence out of the toils of the law and even acquiesced when the Baroness invited the interloper to tea. It was a very stiff tea party, but the Richthofens were at least courteous. Next day Lawrence left Metz and went to Trier, fifty miles away, to wait and let matters simmer down. Alone there and at peace, he actually began to forgive Germany for his earlier discomfort. Frieda followed him a few days later, but she did not stay long. There was a quarrel, and Lawrence went on to Waldbröl in the Rhineland, where he had arranged to visit his Aunt Ada's relatives, the Krenkows.

"It's really very nice here," he wrote to Frieda about May 13, all anger evidently forgotten; "—Hannah is very bright and so decent with me. Her husband is 'a very good man'—uninteresting. She never loved him—married him because she was thirty and time going by. Already she's quite fond of me—but do not mind, she is perfectly honourable—the last word of respectability."

The next day he wrote Frieda the first of several remarkable letters discussing their future together, which apparently he wanted to postpone. Among other things, he said:

> I am very well, but, like you, I feel shaky. Shall we not leave our meeting till we are better? Here, in a little while, I shall be solid again. . . . Let us have firm ground where we next go. Quakiness and uncertainty are the death of us. . . .
>
> Look, my dear, now that the suspense is going over, we can wait ever a bit religiously for one another. My next coming to you is solemn, intrinsically—I am solemn over it—not sad, oh no—but it is my marriage, after all, and a great thing—not a thing to be snatched and clumsily handled.

On May 15 he wrote about how necessary it was to have a stable foundation. He followed a discussion of finances with another comment:

> Can't you feel how certainly I love you and how certainly we shall be married? Only let us wait just a short time, to get strong again. Two shaken, rather sick people together would be a bad start. A little waiting, let us have, because I love you. Or does the waiting make you worse?—no, not when it is only a time of preparation. Do you know, like the old knights, I

seem to want a certain time to prepare myself—a sort of vigil with myself. . . . Give me till next weekend, at least. If you love me, you will understand.

Frieda did not understand, not at all. Lawrence seemed to her to be shilly-shallying, nor did she appreciate all that talk about a knightly vigil. If he needed a stimulus, she reflected, she was ready to administer it. Look out, she implied in her answering letter; if Lawrence didn't want her there were others who did, and she named one of them, an admirer in Metz.

Lawrence refused, as always, to rise to such bait. He still maintained that she must give him time. As for his rival, he said merely, "If you want H——, or anybody, have him. . . . But I don't believe even *you* are at your best, when you are using H—— as a dose of morphia—he's not much else to you. But sometimes one needs a dose of morphia. I've had many a one. So you know best."

He was not so complaisant in his next letter. "You fling H—— in my teeth. I shall say Hannah is getting fonder and fonder of me. She gives *me* the best in the house. So there!"

A few days later he wrote to Edward Garnett, "My cousin Hannah is newly married—and wishes she weren't. She's getting in love with me. Why is it women *will* fall in love with me."

The sparring with Frieda lasted only a little longer. She had already moved on to Munich to wait for him there, and on May 24 he too went to the city and met her. Together they went to Beuerberg, twenty-five miles to the south, and had their honeymoon at last. It was a happy one.

"Frieda and I began our life together in Beuerberg on the Isartal," Lawrence wrote to a friend years later, "—and how lovely it was!"

After having worried and rationalized for months over his sexual failure with Jessie, and perhaps other women too, he must have been vastly reassured because he was astonishingly all right with Frieda. He felt he had found the one woman in the world for him, as she had found the one man for her.

# 7

## *Ivy: "Stunned and shaken"*

· ELSE JAFFE was estranged from her husband and had become the mistress of Professor Max Weber. She now borrowed from Weber a kind of summer-resort apartment that he owned in the village of Icking on the Isar and lent it to Lawrence and Frieda to stay in. It was a romantic four-room dwelling perched over the local general store, with a balcony that overlooked the river and the mountains beyond. There the lovers lived quietly. Frieda, who always liked to stay in bed, would lie there in a haze of well-being, listening to Lawrence trying to talk Bavarian German with the proprietress of the store until he brought her her breakfast. Nothing bothered her. Even, as she later remembered, when she spilled coffee on the pillow, she only turned the pillow over. The two of them would talk and talk as if they had a lifetime to catch up on each other's lives: Frieda reminisced about her childhood in the pretty house in Metz with its gardens, and Lawrence told her of life as a working-class child, his mother, and his father working in the pit. It seemed romantic to Frieda, who in her sentimental way made up an exaggerated picture of her darling's sufferings. Such terrible poverty! Her heart melted at the very thought of it. He would never have been so desperately ill that time he told her about, she believed, if his mother had been able to care for him and feed him properly. So their days passed.

"I love Frieda so much, I don't like to talk about it," wrote Lawrence to Sallie Hopkin, the wife of his old Eastwood friend Willie Hopkin, who had been in his confidence from the beginning. But he did talk about it, in letters to Garnett and in poetry. Soon he was training his beloved in the way she should go, trying to teach her tidiness and economy and cooking. The lessons did not mar their happiness; Frieda enjoyed being bullied over housework. But in one matter she proved intractable. She *would* grieve for her children, and nothing Lawrence did or said could cure her of this unreasonable habit. Her early conviction had been that Ernest would let her have them at least part of the time—anything else was not to be imagined. But as letters continued to go back and forth between Germany and England and Ernest got over the first numbing shock, his attitude hardened. He was still hot and cold about divorce, but on the subject of the children he was adamant. Frieda was to have nothing to do with them, he said, and unfortunately for her, under the law as it then stood, she hadn't a leg to stand on because she was the offending party. It would be unfair to accuse Weekley of inordinate spite in this matter. Most people at that time would have agreed that the influence of an immoral mother must be avoided.

Frieda, of course, was not a woman to take such things coolly. When she felt like weeping she wept, and every time she thought of the children there were tears, which maddened Lawrence. Whenever she wept he railed at her so brutally that onlookers were shocked. Sometimes he seemed to feel that it served her right to lose the children, that she *ought* to suffer for running away with him. In letters to Garnett he boasted that he would not stand for such nonsense:

"She lies on the floor in misery—and then is fearfully angry with me because I won't say 'Stay for my sake.' I say 'decide what you want most, to live with me and share my rotten

chances, or go back to security, and your children—decide for
*yourself*—choose for yourself.' And then she almost hates me,
because I won't say 'I love you—stay with me whatever happens.' " On a melodramatic note, he continued, "I *do* love her.
If she left me, I do not think I should be alive six months hence.
And she won't leave me, I think. God, how I love her—and
the agony of it."

No doubt it *was* agonizing for both actors in this melo-
drama, but they must have enjoyed themselves too, and Frieda's
memoirs give a kinder picture of Lawrence than does his own
account. When, in her vivid phrase, "my grief for my children
would return red hot," Lawrence sometimes said consolingly,
"Don't be sad." If she continued to cry, however, his mood
suddenly changed and he shouted, "You don't care a damn about
those brats really, and they don't care about you." Of this out-
rageous statement Frieda commented wisely, "Perhaps he, who
had loved his mother so much, felt, somewhere, it was almost
impossible for a mother to leave her children." It was indeed
hard to condone such an action, she admitted. "But I was so
sure: 'This bond is for ever, nothing in heaven or earth can
break it. I must wait, I must wait!' "

Baron von Richthofen wrote angrily to his stubborn daughter. He felt humiliated by her behavior—traveling about like a
barmaid, he said—and Frieda was sorry for him, but nothing
shook her determination; the bond was for ever.

In Icking, Lawrence received reviews of his novel *The
Trespasser,* which had been published by Duckworth within a
few days, as it happened, of his elopement. The plot—Helen
Corke's love story—elicited an amount of shocked criticism,
and Frieda and Lawrence drew defiant amusement from this.
What would such people say if their own story were known?
On the whole, however, the reaction was favorable, and there
were kind words for Lawrence's style. He cheered up until he
heard that Heinemann, who had published *The White Peacock*
and had a kind of option on his work, did not want to bring

out *Sons and Lovers* because, he said, it was dirty. Lawrence was furiously indignant. But Edward Garnett, as reader for Duckworth, recommended that the book be taken up by that firm, and so matters were arranged. Garnett wrote a list of suggestions for slight changes here and there, and Lawrence accepted them.

Shortly before he and Frieda left Icking they had an un-expected visitor: Frieda's mother, who dropped in without notice on her way to Munich, expressly to give Lawrence a piece of her mind. Who did he think he was, she asked, to expect a baroness to clean his boots and empty out his slops? No decent man would expect a highborn lady to live like a barmaid. The Baroness then took her leave and marched back to the railway station, but Lawrence accompanied her and put her onto the train so politely that when she got to Munich she told Else that Frieda's man was a lovable and trustworthy person.

On August 5, Lawrence and Frieda set out on a long-planned journey on foot across the Tyrolean Alps to Lake Garda in Italy. This was quite an adventure. Though he was an accomplished walker, Lawrence had never climbed mountains, and Frieda was even less experienced. They were heavily laden, ready for all emergencies with their rucksacks, provisions, and stove. The first night out they spent at an inn, but after that they had to take whatever shelter they could find: haylofts, shepherds' huts, and even, once, a room over a pigsty. They paused at Mayrhofen in the Zillertal for a few days' rest at an inn, and they were joined, by prearrangement, by Edward Garnett's son, David, whose nickname was—and is—Bunny. At the end of August the trek was resumed, Bunny staying with them part of the way.

Frieda stood up well to all the trials they encountered, cold and fatigue and uncertainty and general discomfort, until just at the end. She and Lawrence had arrived at Trient, or Trento, near Lombardy and Lake Garda, their destination. They had to stay undercover that night, and Lawrence, always care-

ful in his management of money, selected a cheap hotel. Frieda
was so disgusted by the dirty sheets on the bed and the nauseat-
ingly filthy toilet outside that she disappeared the next morning,
and Lawrence eventually found her huddled on a stone bench
next to a memorial to Dante, sobbing her heart out.

On September 7 they took the train to Riva, an Austrian
garrison town on the shore of Lake Garda, stepping out of the
station into a scene of leisured elegance that was bewildering to
the dirty, disheveled wanderers. Officers in light trousers and
pale-blue jackets—chocolate soldiers, Lawrence called them
sneeringly—strolled by the lakeside with fashionable ladies.
And there they stood, said Frieda: "two tramps with rucksacks!" She was wearing a badly rumpled cotton dress and a
wilted panama hat on which the colored ribbon had run; Lawrence's trousers, "Miriam's trousers" they called them because
he had bought them in company with Jessie, were frayed. Never
mind. Baths in a lodging house worked wonders for their morale,
and even better was to find their trunks which had been sent on
by rail along with Nusch's contributions, some smart gowns
and hats. The travelers changed their clothes and hurried out to
peacock with the rest of Riva.

But they were still short of money until the post brought
a wonderful surprise, fifty pounds in notes, Duckworth's advance on *Sons and Lovers*. Fifty pounds! Why, they were rich!
Lawrence immediately decided not to try for a job in Germany,
because free-lancing seemed such a reasonable way to live, so
he and Frieda left Riva and moved to Gargnano, farther around
the lake in Italy, where they set up housekeeping in the Villa
Igéa. From there Lawrence wrote to all those of his friends,
Jessie included, who might not yet have heard the news of
Frieda, telling them the story and assuring them that he wished
to marry his mistress as soon as possible. Frieda wrote notes of
a similar sort, to Will Dowson among others, and Will replied
gallantly, "If you had to run away, why did you not do it with
me?"

Carelessly, Frieda used his letter as a bookmark when she was reading *Anna Karenina* and forgot all about it. On finishing the book she sent it to Ernest, hoping that the story might help him to understand how a married woman, in certain circumstances, might reasonably run off with a lover. Ernest opened the book, found Dowson's letter, read it, and maliciously posted it straight back to Lawrence in Gargnano, no doubt precipitating a quarrel between Lawrence and Frieda. In spite of his professed indifference, Lawrence was always jealous and had already accused Frieda of betraying him with a woodcutter with whom she spent several hours on an island in the Isar— and he might well have been right.

For her part, Frieda was jealous of Mrs. Lawrence's influence, even though the lady was dead, but she tried hard to understand her lover's feelings on the subject. In an early letter to Edward Garnett she had spoken enthusiastically of Mrs. Lawrence, saying that Lawrence's mother must have been a darling. But at the same time she resented the strength of Lawrence's attachment to his mother. It was all very well to label it an Oedipus complex, but labels do not settle these matters.

Rewriting *Sons and Lovers* in accordance with Garnett's suggestions, Lawrence discussed the work with Frieda, showing her what he wrote as he went along and asking her opinion. In her memoirs she said, "I lived and suffered that book, and wrote bits of it when he would ask me: 'What do you think my mother felt like then?' I had to go deeply into the character of Miriam and all the others." So it was no mere phrase Lawrence used when he wrote that infamous letter to Jessie; he and Frieda did indeed discuss her endlessly. The trouble from Jessie's point of view was that it was not so much Jessie they discussed as Miriam.

Forced as he was to write the deathbed scenes about Mrs. Lawrence all over again, Lawrence suffered grievously; according to Frieda he was really ill. But the exercise made him see the relationship more clearly than he had done before. Significantly, he commented to his companion, "If my mother had lived I could never have loved you, she wouldn't have let me go."

All in all, Frieda did not care much for *Sons and Lovers*. She soon tired of Lawrence's filial piety, and when she came on a poem he had written to his mother in his notebook, she scribbled rudely on the page, counseling "the little boy" to go back to his mother's apron strings and have done. She also wrote what she described as a skit on Lawrence's work, entitled "Paul Morel, or His Mother's Darling," the humor of which escaped Lawrence, and she wrote to Edward Garnett about *Sons and Lovers* soon after he had received the new version, "The novel is a failure, but you must feel something at the back of it struggling, trying to come out."

Some failure, we would say today, but Frieda never changed her mind about it. Years later, commenting on Lawrence's complicated attachment to his mother, his widow could write that she thought he had got over it at last, "only, this fierce and overpowerful love had harmed the boy who was not strong enough to bear it." She added, "In his heart of hearts I think he always dreaded women, felt that they were in the end more powerful than men."

This is a discerning statement. Frieda knew what she was talking about. Most of their fights boiled down in the end to the question, on Lawrence's part, as to which of them was dominant. Unlike Gross, he was always talking about submission. The woman, he insisted, should be submissive to the man, and he claimed that they would never be at peace until Frieda admitted this and knuckled down to him. It was her wicked will, he said, that made her defy him—yet in truth she didn't defy him very often. She was not a passionate defender of woman's rights, and philosophical concepts did not obsess her. Most of the time it didn't matter to her who was in command, but when it came to a dispute over something she really cared about—usually the children—she would dig in her heels, and then there was trouble.

During the Gargnano period, between quarrels, Lawrence did a tremendous lot of work. When *Sons and Lovers* had been rewritten to Garnett's satisfaction and was scheduled to appear in the spring of 1913, he turned his attention to a variety of projects. A collection of his poems had already come out; now he organized the new ones he had been writing about himself and Frieda, which were ultimately published under the title *Look! We Have Come Through!* He also planned two new novels, of which one was to be *The Lost Girl;* the other he called "The Sisters." This latter title in the end became two books, *The Rainbow* and *Women in Love.* In addition he tried his hand at playwriting and started a romance based on the life of Robert Burns, but the book was never finished.

No matter what work he did he was never too busy to fight with Frieda. The disagreements were usually sparked by her reactions to the latest news about or from Ernest Weekley. When she heard nothing she could cheer herself up by entertaining new hopes of divorce or at least of permission to see the children, but then another letter would dash her spirits and send her into the depths of despair again. Lawrence would lash out at her, and she would weep, and this made him even angrier. Probably the worst time she experienced was when Ernest sent her an ultimatum: if she did not come home, he said, it was the end; the children would no longer have a mother and she would never see them again. In the same envelope he enclosed a photograph of the little girls. It almost broke Frieda's heart. But, as she said, nothing shook her determination to stay where she was:

"I could not leave [Lawrence] any more, he needed me more than they did. But I was like a cat without her kittens, and always in my mind was the care, 'Now if they came where would I put them to sleep?' "

It was not a problem she was likely to face in the near future. Ernest was selling or had sold the Mapperley house, had discharged the German girl, and had moved the children to London. There, in a house in Chiswick he bought for the purpose, they lived with his parents and a few other relations, while he stayed in lodgings in Nottingham, near his work.

The Christmas season drew near with all its sentimental meaning for German Frieda, and she found her unhappiness increasingly hard to bear. Sometimes Lawrence ill-temperedly urged her to leave him and go back to England. For a time she did contemplate a quick trip, at least, to London, where she could linger in the vicinity of the children's schools and perhaps catch a glimpse of them. However, she did not go, and on Christmas Day Lawrence wrote to Sallie Hopkin:

> We've had such a hard time pegging through this autumn —the children, Weekley and ourselves. If two people start clean of trouble, without children and other husbands between 'em, it's hard for them to get simple and close to each other— but when it's like this—oh Lord, it takes it out of you. But we've done wonders, really. . . . Once you've known what love *can* be, there's no disappointment any more, and no despair. If the skies tumble down like a smashed saucer, it couldn't break what's between Frieda and me.

Lawrence often referred in this manner to the relationship between his mistress and himself, as if he were sending dispatches from the front in a war. It was a disconcerting mannerism.

On the twenty-ninth of December he told Garnett that Frieda meant to go back to England at Easter to see the children, because at one time Ernest had promised that she might. Whether his promise would continue to hold good was a moot question, but they would try. Lawrence meant to go along too. On January 12, 1913, again in a letter to Garnett, he sounded more confident of the situation:

"The divorce will come off, I think, for sure," he wrote. He was evidently thinking now of getting a teaching job in England—perhaps in the country, he speculated, but he had his doubts even so. "I don't want to bury Frieda alive. Wherever I go with her, we shall have to fall into the intelligent, as it were, upper classes." What he added is mildly astonishing:

I could get along with anybody, by myself, because, as Frieda says, I am common, and as you say, 1/5 Cockney. I find a servant maid more interesting as a rule than a Violet Hunt or a Grace Rhys. After all, I was brought up among them. But Frieda is a lady, and I hate her when she talks to the common people. She is not a bit stuck-up, really more humble than I am, but she makes the *de haut en bas* of class distinction felt— even with my sister. It is as she was bred and fed, and can't be otherwise. So, that really cuts out a country school. I mustn't take her to England to bury her alive.

Burying Frieda alive, it will be remembered, was a crime of which he tacitly accused Ernest Weekley.

At last came encouraging indications that this same Weekley had begun divorce proceedings. To the invaluable Edward Garnett Lawrence wrote that they would probably need a lawyer; could Garnett suggest anybody? Garnett could and did; as luck would have it, his own brother Robert would fill the bill. The case was scheduled to come up just after Easter, said Lawrence, and if all went well that meant that he and Frieda could be married six months afterward. Since there seemed small chance that she could see the children before then, the lovers would remain abroad until August. On March 4 came a sign that things really were moving, when what Lawrence described as "a mangy old gentleman" arrived at the Villa Igéa and politely handed a document to each of the guilty pair, explaining that he came from the English consul's office in Verona. As soon as he had gone Lawrence read his summons.

"It says in bald language that I have 'habitually committed adultery,' " he wrote merrily to a friend in England. "—What a nasty habit!"

At the end of March they moved away from Gargnano. Richard Aldington once commented disapprovingly that the Lawrences in the course of their life together spent a lot of money unnecessarily on trips that did not seem to him to have much point. At this stage, for example, their money was running out; it seemed feckless to Aldington that they should have continued to move about as they did. But Lawrence renewed himself when he changed his domicile. Evidently he needed the stimulus it gave him; certainly he was always in a better temper than usual after a move. This time the object of their peregrination was not far away: San Gaudenzio, up in the hills near the lake shore, where a friend of the Garnetts named Mrs. Cyriax was staying, in a peasant's house. Here at San Gaudenzio, of course, the Italians called Lawrence "Lorenzo," a name which was to stick to him the rest of his life.

Then, by way of Verona, they went to Irschenhausen in Bavaria, not far from Icking, to stay in a chalet borrowed from Edgar Jaffe. Perhaps they thought that the magic of their honeymoon days would be recaptured there, but it wasn't, quite. Lawrence regretted Italy and decided that the militant spirit of Germany was unpleasant—as no doubt in 1913 it was. And Frieda's sights were set on London and the children; she had not accepted Lawrence's plan of waiting until August to go to England.

Just before Lawrence and Frieda left Italy they had got the surprising news that Garnett had received a manuscript from Jessie Chambers, an autobiographical novel that he thought interesting. He wondered if Lawrence would care to see it. Indeed he would, said Lawrence; he might write to Jessie himself and suggest that she send him a copy, though come to think of it he hadn't heard from her recently. Now, in Irschenhausen in April, he mentioned the manuscript again to Garnett: he hadn't seen it, and he would like Garnett to send it on. In this letter he sounds nervous and defensive, which indicates that the editor had given him a hint of what to expect.

It's all very well for Miss Chambers to be spiritual—perhaps she can bring it off—I can't. She bottled me up till I was going to burst. But as long as the cork sat tight (herself the cork) there was spiritual calm. When the cork was blown out, and Mr Lawrence foamed, Miriam said 'This yeastiness I disown: it was not so in my day,' God bless her, she always looked down on me—spiritually. But it hurt when she sent a letter of mine back: quite an inoffensive letter, I think. And look, she is bitterly ashamed of having had me—as if I had dropped her spiritual plumage in the mud. Call that love! Ah well.

So Edward Garnett sent Jessie's manuscript. It was now entitled "The Rathe Primrose" instead of "Eunice Temple"; Jessie had used the nom de plume "Eunice Temple" to sign it with. Though she destroyed her manuscript eventually, when she wrote her book on Lawrence she kept Eunice Temple's initials and signed it "E.T."

Lawrence and Frieda both read her novel as soon as it arrived, as Lawrence reported to Garnett on May 19, 1913. "We got Miss Chambers' novel. I should scarcely recognise her —she never used to *say* anything. But it isn't bad, and it made me so miserable I had hardly the energy to walk out of the house for two days."

"Miriam's novel is very lovable, I think," was Frieda's verdict, "and one does feel sorry for her, but it's a faded photograph of *Sons and Lovers*, she has never understood anything out of herself, no inner activity, but she does make one ache!" In the end the novel was never published.

In his letter Lawrence announced that he and Frieda would be coming to England for a short visit in a fortnight's time, early in June, since Frieda felt that they must make a move soon about the children. "The idea is that Frieda sees her son Monty at St. Paul's School, talks to him, arranges to see the little girls, keeps everything quiet from the father. Then the children shall say to their father, 'We want to see our mother in Germany.'" He didn't like the idea of setting children between parents, he said, but there seemed nothing else for it.

*Sons and Lovers* came out just before the Lawrences got to England. It met with the approval of most reviewers, a fact that made Lawrence's return pleasant—even though in the end that first edition lost money. In time, as history shows, the novel went on from strength to strength, and even then the more perspicacious of the critics realized its virtues. In years to come Lawrence's was to be the best-known Oedipus complex in the literary world. He had the advantage, too, of being a man of working-class origins. The working classes mattered a good deal to guilt-ridden British intellectuals, and Lawrence was just in time to benefit from that sentiment.

London seemed a far warmer, more hospitable place than they remembered it, and Lawrence, if not quite a lion, was at least a lion cub. For a while they stayed at The Cearne, where Bunny Garnett got very angry at Lawrence for his manner of sounding off at Frieda. Then they took up residence in rented quarters in Kingsgate, a little resort on the east coast not too far from London. Being near London was of course very important for Frieda. She put no faith in orderly legal processes that might, some time in the future, allow her to see her children; she set out at once on independent action. Knowing only that they were living somewhere in Chiswick, she walked up and down the streets of that district hoping that she would be lucky enough to run into members of the family. Such stubbornness paid off: one day she spotted in a certain house, in a couple of upstairs windows, curtains that she had herself selected for the house at Mapperley. Frieda promptly walked into the house through the unlocked back door. She saw nobody on the ground floor, so she followed the sound of voices upstairs and found Elsa and Barby in the nursery, eating their evening meal with Ernest's mother and aunt. Everyone stared in amazement as Frieda appeared at the door. Barby in later life recollected her as "a terrifying apparition." After all, she explained, for the past year they had been told, over and over, that their mother was a bad woman, and here she was. Aunt and grandmother, as soon as they got over the first shock, leaped to their feet in great excitement "and hurled abuse at her, as if she were the embodiment of evil," wrote Barbara Barr. "I am sorry to say that we children joined in. Frieda fled, shocked and humiliated."

Frieda's own memories were kinder. She never told about

this encounter; instead she recounted that she had met the little girls in the street, no doubt on a later date, when they were on their way to school, and that they danced around her in delight, crying, "Mama, you are back, when are you coming home?" Frieda told them that she couldn't come back, that they must come to her; they would all have to wait. She tried to meet with them again in the same way, this time with Lawrence standing some way off, but the children had obviously been told that they must not speak to her any more, "and only little white faces looked at me as if I were an evil ghost." It was hard to bear, Frieda admitted, the more so because the incident sent Lawrence into a helpless rage. But with Monty she had better luck. Knowing that the thirteen-year-old boy was at St. Paul's, she took with her a little army of accomplices, Bunny Garnett and Lawrence and Katherine Mansfield, of whom more later. She and Bunny strolled up and down outside the school's front door until Monty appeared in company with a group of other boys. Deftly extracting him from his fellows, she whisked him to a nearby teashop with Katherine and regaled him with goodies. Monty was to remember Katherine as a fascinating young lady with a charming and rather mysterious smile. Later, however, when Katherine tried to carry a message to him from Frieda, the authorities sent out word that he was not to be interviewed by anybody, so that door too was closed. It was as far as Frieda's campaign went in 1913.

Katherine Mansfield, three years Lawrence's junior, was a New Zealander whose real name was Kathleen Beauchamp. She was the daughter of Sir Harold Beauchamp, president of the Bank of New Zealand. Good-looking in an unusual way, with high cheekbones, and wearing her dark hair bobbed, with bangs —a style years ahead of its time—she determined to cut loose from her background and had succeeded rather violently in her ambition. At the time she met Lawrence and Frieda she had not yet begun to publish the short stories that later won her acclaim; nevertheless she had already led, at the age of twenty-five, a varied and somewhat painful life. She had been married briefly and then left her husband, but he would not consent to a divorce. Her father made her an allowance of a hundred pounds or so a year. Her acquaintance with Lawrence and Frieda began by mail when they were in Italy; she and her companion, John Middleton Murry, were publishing a little magazine at the time, and they wrote asking Lawrence to write for it. The magazine died a natural death, but the Murrys, as everyone called them, immediately started another.

Murry was a year younger than Katherine. In his auto-biography he has told of his background; he came of a poor family in London. He was a bright boy, however, who got scholarships and achieved a good education. Having grown up, as he said, between two worlds, he found himself adrift for a time, unable to fit in anywhere. It was evident, however, that he could write and had a gift for criticism. When he and Katherine came together he found protection and encouragement under her wing. Lawrence and Frieda and the Murrys quickly discovered how much they had in common, what with implacable husbands and all that, and quickly became good friends. At the beginning, however, there were misunderstandings. The Murrys assumed that Frieda and Lawrence were rich, possibly because they always assumed this of other people; it is a variety of purse pride that is not unknown. The Lawrences made the same mistake about the Murrys, and the truth did not come out until one Sunday when the Murrys, who had been invited down to Kingsgate, did not put in an appearance. Their defection puzzled Lawrence until another guest, Sir Edward Marsh, explained it casually by saying that they probably hadn't the money for their railway tickets. Marsh, who wrote poetry and published anthologies of modern poems by other writers, understood such difficulties because he dealt with many young poets, but Lawrence was amazed and scandalized. He wrote to Murry asking why on earth they hadn't simply explained their predicament and borrowed a pound from himself. He wasn't that hard up, he protested.

At any rate the friendship quickly ripened into intimacy. Frieda wrote of Katherine, "I thought her so exquisite and complete, with her fine brown hair, delicate skin, and brown eyes which we later called her 'gu-gu' eyes. She was a perfect friend and tried her best to help me with the children. She went to see them, talked to them and took them letters from me. I loved her like a younger sister."

The Murrys were not at all gregarious and often lamented this quality in the Lawrences, but they did have some friends, one of whom became equally attached to Lawrence and Frieda: an Irish barrister, Gordon Campbell. Lawrence pronounced him a most delightful man, and he was a hospitable one too, for he often let them stay in his flat when they found it inconvenient to return to Kent. But it was through Marsh that they met Herbert Asquith, second son of the prime minister, and his wife, Lady Cynthia, who had taken a summer house at Broadstairs not far from Kingsgate.

Lady Cynthia was utterly charmed by Lawrence. "Except the mere facts that he wrote poetry, was the son of a coal-miner, and had a tendency to consumption, we at that time knew nothing whatever about Lawrence," she wrote in an autobiographical book; "but the moment a slender, lithe figure stepped lightly into the room, we both realised almost with the shock of a collision that something new and startling had come into our lives." She liked Frieda too: "Exuberant, warm, burgeoning, she radiated health, strength and generosity of nature," she said, and the Asquiths' friend Professor Walter Raleigh agreed, calling her "a first-rate poet's wife." Herbert and Lady Cynthia had the Lawrences over quite often for dinner, and their pleasure in this social success—Lady Cynthia was the daughter of a Scottish earl—would have been complete if only Lawrence had not felt guilty at introducing Frieda as his wife. What would all these charming, grand people say when they found out the truth? Honesty compelled him to write and confess to Eddie Marsh, but nothing very terrible ever happened as a result. In the meantime, there it was: time after time they went to Broadstairs.

"We have had a good time down here (now and then)," Lawrence wrote to Garnett at the end of July. "The Asquiths have been awfully nice—so were Sir Walter Raleigh (Lady Raleigh invited us to Oxford—I suppose we still look innocent) —and Lord Elco (Mrs. Asquith's people.) Frieda is quite set up at this contact with the aristocracy—of course I am quite superior."

He was uncertain as to how to address Lady Cynthia, who had only recently come into the right to the title, but he was more than impressed by her beauty and intelligence. Moore says that she became to him a kind of ideally worshiped dream woman: in his writings and possibly even his paintings he indirectly made love to her. His letters to her sparkle in the collection like especially brilliant jewels. One knows that he worked over them as he did over none of the others—except possibly some of his letters to Lady Ottoline Morrell in years to come.

As the weeks went on it became obvious that Frieda and Lawrence had been overly hopeful about the divorce; Ernest Weekley backed water again and did not start proceedings as they had hoped. So they gave up the battle for that year and at the end of July went back to Irschenhausen for some weeks. Lawrence wrote to Willie Hopkin that Frieda was "getting better of her trouble about the children, for the time being, at least," and he was right: Frieda had seen them, after all, and the future did not look quite so bleak. Some day, she knew, the divorce would take place. Meantime she settled down to enjoy the company of her relatives. Lawrence was writing this letter on Frieda's birthday, and he described the celebration and her little niece and nephews, all dressed up and carrying gifts of flowers and sweets and perfume, "walking in procession up the path through the meadow" to where Frieda stood on the veranda, dressed in Bavarian peasant's costume, to receive them. Seven-year-old Peter "recited some birthday verses, and Frieda blew on a mouth organ." Lawrence had a hard time suppressing his laughter. It was quite a day, he admitted.

To Lady Cynthia he wrote, "We live in a little wooden house (but genuine Dürer engravings and Persian rugs) in a corner of a pine forest. But it rains—oh, Lord!—the rain positively stands up on end. Sometimes one sees the deer jumping up and down to get the wet out of their jackets, and the squirrels simply hang on by their tails, like washing." Apparently fearing that the Dürer engravings and Persian rugs might not impress the lady enough, he went on to explain, "It's Frieda's brother-in-law's house. He's staying here now and then. He's a professor of Political Economy, among other things."

The stay in Germany came to an end and the Lawrences moved as they had planned to Lerici, near Fiascherino, where they found a pink villa that Lawrence declared perfect, overlooking the Gulf of Spezia. There they settled down, Lawrence exulting at the cheapness of life, and from there he wrote a characteristic letter to Murry, scolding him and laying down the law generally. Murry had replied to Lawrence's suggestion that he and Katherine come out and live with the Lawrences, pointing out that he could not afford to live abroad: he was a writer, a critic, he said, and he had to be in London where the work was. To Lawrence's suggestion that Katherine had enough money for both of them, he had said he couldn't, he wouldn't, think of living on her. Lawrence pooh-poohed these scruples. When Jack—i.e., Murry—talked like that, said Lawrence, it simply meant that he didn't trust Katherine's love.

"It looks to me as if you two, far from growing nearer, are snapping the bonds that hold you together, one after another," wrote Lawrence. A preacher at heart, he was never happier than in the role of family counselor. "I suppose you must both of you consult your own hearts, honestly. She must see if she really *wants* you, wants to keep you and to have no other man all her life. . . . She must say, 'Could I live in a little place in Italy, with Jack, and be lonely, have rather a bare life, but be happy?' If she could, then take her money."

Lawrence wrote on and on, repeating the message, hammering it in, and working up to a grand crescendo: "If you want things to come right—if you are ill and exhausted, then take her money to the last penny, and let her do her own housework. Then she'll know you love her. . . . But, you fool, you squander yourself, not for *her*, but to provide her with petty luxuries she doesn't really want. You insult her. A woman unsatisfied must have luxuries. But a woman who loves a man would sleep on a board."

After sending the letter off, Lawrence apparently worried that he had gone too far; he half expected never to hear from Murry again. Jack, however, was pleased. He recognized in that furious letter, he said, a warm affection. "Lawrence loved men, and he kindled love in them," said Murry. "I had never felt for a man before what his letter made me feel for him. It was a new thing, a unique thing, in my experience; and it was to remain unique."

Most of the time Frieda was happy at Fiascherino, but though she was not sleeping on a board there were bad moments. One rough day she grew angry with Lawrence for going out in their little rowboat and putting himself, as she thought, in danger. She thought of Shelley, who had met his death nearby, and shouted from the shore, "If you can't be a real poet, you'll drown like one, anyhow." Yet it was Frieda who came near to upsetting the same boat another time when she and Lawrence were both in it and had a fight.

There was also an unpleasantness when Mitchell Kennerley, who was publishing *Sons and Lovers* in America, sent them what turned out to be a bad check for £25. The Lawrences could not afford such disappointments; they were hard up at

Fiascherino. But there were compensations. Many Americans and English people lived in the vicinity, and they had read Lawrence's work and made a gratifying fuss of him. He boasted in a letter that he and Frieda were always out to tea or having visitors. It was pleasant to learn that he was becoming a cult figure among the young writers of England, according to reports from one of them, Miss Ivy Low in Hampstead.

Ivy had not one but two Freudian psychologists in her family, her aunt, Barbara Low, and Barbara's brother-in-law, Dr. David Eder. Ivy's uncle David, said Barbara Low, was *the* pioneer for making Freud's theories known in England. Because of this, Ivy knew more than the average young Englishwoman about Freud, and when she read *Sons and Lovers* she was stirred to great enthusiasm. She read it in one sitting, all night in her bachelor flat, and next morning she bought half a dozen postcards and wrote a message on each: "Discovered a genius!" or "Be sure to read *Sons and Lovers!*" or "This is a book about the Oedipus complex!" These she sent to various friends, among whom was Viola Meynell of the literary Meynell family. Between them the two girls worked up quite a number of people who admired D. H. Lawrence above all other modern writers. Ivy wrote that they adopted him as their creed; no adverse criticism of their idol escaped scathing comment. She wrote to Lawrence in what she later called a "youthfully pompous" vein, using such sentences as "We of the younger generation believe you are the only English writer who represents our aspirations."

The flattered Lawrence replied, and a lively exchange of letters followed. Ivy noticed one odd thing: that he always used crested paper and invariably put a little note next to the crest which said, "Don't let the crest upset you—my wife's father was a baron, and we're just using up old note paper." Even a fervent admirer like Ivy could perceive something odd behind this gesture, especially when it was repeated the third time. Nevertheless when in spring, 1914, the genius invited her to visit

Frieda and himself in Italy she was in a seventh heaven of joyful excitement.

"It was early spring," she wrote. "I was twenty-five. I had written a book. I had written two books—one of them had been banned. I had left home and found myself one of the most attractive small apartments in London. And here I was, setting off to the romantic land of Italy to visit the greatest living English author. Surely I was the happiest girl in the world!"

The famous pair met her at the train. Ivy thought Frieda pretty but observed that she had the limpest hand ever taken in her own. Ivy never did come to like Frieda, and one feels that Frieda returned the compliment with interest. Lawrence, however, seemed much impressed; he stepped back to stare at her and said, "Why, the girl's a swell!"

From her letters he had somehow got the impression that she was "a poor little city typist whom he must take care not to frighten with his wife's grandeur." But here stood Ivy, smiling and confident and wearing an embroidered blouse that only an intellectual of a certain type could have appreciated.

"Frieda was very beautiful, very central European, but not elegant in the way London and New York women are elegant," commented Ivy shrewdly. "She was picturesque in her fair way, and a bit sloppy and arty. Embroidered Rumanian blouses were right up her alley." One feels that even if Frieda had expected to like the visitor—and that limp handshake is no proof of it—she did not maintain such an attitude very long.

Things did not start out well, because Lawrence asked Ivy if she thought he looked like a working-class man, and she innocently said that she did. He was offended, and she longed to tell him what she considered the truth: "I loved you the moment I saw you. I thought you were a darling." Of course she could not and did not say it: anyway, she confided many years later to a friend, it wasn't really true: a virgin, as she was at the time, couldn't love anybody. As a fan of Lawrence's she naturally felt that she must make an effort to get him, but she never honestly wanted him. He wasn't virile. She hazarded a guess that he could be potent only with Frieda, a fact that she thought would explain his lifelong tie with what she looked on as a false, honey-sweet—well, a gushing—woman. Be that as it may, at the time Ivy Low certainly did have a schoolgirl crush on Lawrence, and the first week of the visit was the happiest time she had ever known. Lawrence looked at her admiringly, with his soul in his eyes. Both he and Frieda listened raptly as she talked, and—unlike all her friends at home—actually let her finish her sentences.

And Lawrence had such a charming way of talking about himself, asking her advice and confiding in her. He actually begged her to walk with him on his errands. Frieda, still sweet-tempered that week, remarked that the last thing she saw was the pair of them going down the path with their heads together, and when they came back the first thing she saw was their jaws moving.

Then, all of a sudden, everything changed, and whatever Ivy said or did was wrong. When Lawrence urged her to go with him to Lerici he went on to say, "I'd rather go for a walk with old Lisa (the servant's half-wit mother) than alone," and Frieda added, in explanation, "Lawrence can't bear walking alone! He'd ask the dullest person in the world, just so's not to walk alone."

Lawrence began picking on Ivy, searching out her defects one by one, along with quite a few she had never suspected in herself. He said she had no sense of rhythm, "which meant apparently that walking in an unknown town I did not know instinctively where Lawrence was going to turn," she wrote. "He seemed to take a delight in turning unexpectedly, so that, in my eagerness to follow him, I bumped into him." Furthermore, he told Ivy that she was thoroughly selfish and unhelpful as a guest, without any evident wish to look after him. She never went into the kitchen when dinner was cooking to see if she could help; she never offered to darn his socks.

But, protested poor Ivy, she had merely taken her cue from Frieda, who never lifted a finger about the house. How was she to know that Lawrence *wanted* help? She had never dared.

Frieda, Lawrence explained, was different: it was enough for Frieda just to exist. (In time, he seems to have changed his mind about that and made her work, but this was in the early days of love.)

One criticism followed another. Lawrence kept at it, picking his guest to pieces. He didn't like her piano playing, though he himself couldn't play at all; he thought her ideas on religion were valueless; he mocked her feelings of friendship with Viola Meynell—it was all the worse, said poor Ivy, after that deliriously happy week at the beginning. She saw herself clearly at last, she felt: she was not "charming and original," as at first she was led to believe, but was "fidgety, garrulous, clumsy and absurd." Not that Lawrence used a sledge hammer to make these points. He did it delicately. After an afternoon when people called on them, he mocked her way of speaking so amusingly that even she had to laugh.

One thing that might have comforted her, but probably didn't, was that she saw the Lawrences giving the same treatment to other people who came into their orbit. At first they would be sweet, attentive, and flattering. Then when the visitors were gone they both, but Lawrence with greater talent, tore the clothes off the poor strangers' backs.

By the end of six weeks, said Ivy, they had had enough of each other and she went back to England. Yet when she got on the train she wept and wept, while Lawrence, waving good-bye with one hand, wiped his eyes with the other. Ivy arrived home "stunned and shaken. Not only had I lost confidence in myself," she wrote, "—I was sure I would never write again, and that this was a good thing—but I was discontented with all my friends."

It seems clear enough what happened. Frieda grew jealous of Ivy, and Lawrence, to appease her, sacrificed the girl. It was Ivy's bad luck that nobody could outdo him in malicious, sly destruction of this sort, and we can hardly blame her if she was bitter in retrospect. When the Lawrences went back to London, she said, Lawrence's snobbery made him rather beastly to her. He was anxious to keep her out of the new circle of interesting people he and Frieda had entered. He discovered that Ivy was, after all, just a rather ill-bred little Jew girl—her words—and acquaintance with her did him no particular good, so that was that.

In later years when Ivy Low was Madame Maxim Litvinoff, wife of the Russian Ambassador, things were different; at one time he thought of asking her to help him go to Russia. But on this matter Ivy is silent.

# 8

## *Lady Ottoline: "All this soul-mush"*

THAT SPRING Lawrence and Frieda quarreled as much
as ever, perhaps more than ever, about Ernest and the children
—so much so, in fact, that the biographer Harry T. Moore
ventured an opinion that the writer put more energy into
establishing his relationship with his mistress than into his work.
Nevertheless Lawrence was able to tell Murry on April 3 that
he was two thirds finished with his novel "The Sisters" and
that he thought it beautiful. Perhaps I should not use the word
"nevertheless," since with Lawrence everything he experienced
went straight into his writing, and he certainly put Frieda into
that novel, colored stockings and all. He was very sure of the
excellence of "The Sisters," and when Garnett declared that
he was disappointed in it, the author rejected all his criticisms,
retorting that the editor was merely looking for more on the
lines of *Sons and Lovers*. He would not get it, said Lawrence
defiantly; writers, he implied, or at least himself, must change
and keep changing, and his new book was so unlike the last that
it was written in almost a different language, which was how it
should be. He said he was not going to write ever again in the
old style and pointed out that he had even changed while
writing two versions of the book under discussion.

"Before, I could not get my soul into it," he said. "That

was because of the struggle and resistance between Frieda and me. Now you will find her and me in the novel, I think, and the work is both of us." But things are not quite so clear-cut, because in the earlier writing he was basing his female character on Louie Burrows. When this didn't work, inevitably the newer image of Frieda pushed out Louie.

Suddenly there arrived a piece of news that they had almost stopped expecting: Frieda was a free woman; the divorce had come through on May 28, 1914. It changed everything. As soon as possible they gave up the Italian villa temporarily, as they believed, and departed. Frieda's parents had moved to Baden-Baden, where her father lay seriously ill, and it was decided that she should go to visit them for a fortnight while Lawrence again crossed the mountains on foot, this time northward. They met in London soon after the first of June and moved in with Gordon Campbell in Kensington because his wife and child were in Ireland.

"Finally," wrote Frieda casually, "I and Lawrence got married at a registrar's office in Kensington. Campbell and Murry went with us." So also did Katherine, but Eddie Marsh, who was invited, couldn't get there. "It was quite a simple and not undignified ceremony," continued Frieda. "I didn't care whether I was married or not, it didn't seem to make any difference, but I think Lawrence was glad that we were respectable married people."

The marriage took place July 13. In retrospect Frieda recollected that the First World War had started almost immediately afterward, but in fact it was nearly three weeks before England and Germany were fighting; Lawrence heard the news as he returned from a walking tour. Frieda as the wife of an Englishman—actually, two Englishmen—was not considered an enemy, but she was under considerable mental and emotional strain, cut off as she was from all the Von Richthofens, and her sentiments were sadly torn. As for Lawrence, the very fact of the war affronted him and most of his

friends. They were all unhappy and indignant. According to
Bunny Garnett in his book *Flowers of the Forest,* hostilities
had been instituted a mere week or so when something most
unpleasant happened to the Lawrences. Bunny, glad to hear
that they were in town, quickly invited them to dinner in his
duplex apartment with a college friend of his—Bunny was a
scientist at that time. There was a bottle of wine, the food
was appreciated, and Frieda let down her hair and talked frankly
about her feelings as a German and her experiences at Court
when she was a girl. She told her listeners that she had never liked
the Kaiser and felt that Germany's militaristic spirit was mostly
his doing. On the other hand, she said, she loved her relatives
and much admired two of her young Von Richthofen cousins
who had just joined the German air force. The whole thing was
difficult. There was Nusch, for instance, her beloved younger
sister, married to a staff officer. She knew that people in England were angry with her for being German; she was always
being snubbed. It was hard, said Frieda.

The two young men listened, sympathized, and agreed that
it was difficult. Lawrence relaxed, and it was altogether a pleasant evening. As the Lawrences left, Bunny's friend leaned over
the stair railing to call in guttural accents, within hearing of
the tenants below, *"Auf Wiedersehen, gnädige Baronin!"* and
Frieda laughed and answered in German.

A few days later a couple of detectives came to see Bunny
to make inquiries about his friends. Detectives came again and
then again, until after the third such visit he protested, and then
it stopped. But, as he said, this was only the start of the persecu-
tion the Lawrences had to undergo.

Among Ivy Low's intimate friends was a Scottish writer
named Catherine Jackson, later Catherine Carswell, a pretty
young woman who had lent her best clothes to Ivy for that
memorable visit to Fiascherino. Like her friend, she lived in
Hampstead. Separated from her husband, she was soon to be

divorced and remarried. She agreed with Ivy that Lawrence was a great writer and had said so in a favorable review in the *Glasgow Herald*. Therefore when Ivy and Viola Meynell brought Lawrence and Frieda to Catherine's house for a first meeting, they were predisposed to like each other. Catherine was immediately charmed by Lawrence and continued under his spell for the rest of his life. There has never been any hint of amorous love between them; rather, her feelings for him approached idolatry, as is evident in the biography she wrote, *The Savage Pilgrimage*, after his death. In that book she admitted that her first impression of Frieda was not so favorable. Mrs. Lawrence's beauty had been extolled at great length, but Catherine couldn't see it; Frieda struck her as "a typical German *Frau* of the blonde, gushing type," dressed in an unbecomingly tight checked coat and skirt that did not do justice to her "finely-cut, rather angry Prussian features." Later she was to change her mind about Frieda's beauty: "Frieda has a nose like a puss fox, so fine and tremulous about the nostrils, and her eyes might be the eyes of a lioness into lady. It was not for nothing that Lawrence's mind often ran upon poachers, —and gamekeepers." That first day, however, she was more impressed by Lawrence, who had a "swift and flamelike quality . . . a fine, rare beauty . . . deep-set jewel-like eyes," and so on.

There was a characteristic exchange between the couple when Catherine asked Lawrence what Katherine Mansfield was like, and Frieda cut in before he could reply.

" 'So pretty she is, such lovely legs!' she shouted.

"But Lawrence broke in violently, if not so loudly with, 'If you *like* the legs of a principal boy in the pantomime!' "

It is a typical Lawrence remark, not only because it is catty, showing what Catherine described as "a flick of spinsterish tartness that he always had," but because, though no stranger would have guessed it, he was speaking of a good friend.

After tea the whole party strolled down Finchley Road with the Lawrences, seeing them to their bus, Catherine with

Lawrence at the head. They passed the graveyard and she found herself talking to this comparative stranger about her child buried there, quite as if she had known him all her life. Later she gave him the manuscript of her novel to read, and he applied himself to it so promptly that it was still June when he wrote to her:

"I must tell you I am in the middle of reading your novel. You have very often a simply *beastly* style, indirect and round-about and stiff-kneed and stupid. And your stuff is abominably muddled—you'll simply have to write it all again." Fortunately, at this point the lady did not pause to cut her throat, but read on. "But it is fascinatingly interesting. Nearly all of it is *marvellously* good. It is only so incoherent. But you can *easily* pull it together." There was more of the same, very encouraging, especially as he declared that he would finish reading the manuscript in a day or two and they must have a long discussion about it. He was as good as his word, writing the next day to announce that he had finished reading the manuscript, and wanted her to spend the afternoon with him talking it over. Of course she accepted eagerly.

"Anything livelier than Lawrence in such a situation—anyone more emphatic or less portentous it is impossible to imagine," Catherine wrote. "Though he sat quiet and teacher-like beside you at the table, you had the impression that he was darting about in the air like a humming-bird—a humming-bird with a very sharp beak. At the same time he was humanly charming."

Frieda seems not to have resented Catherine as she did Ivy, but the Murrys were stoutly opposed to any enlargement of their cozy circle, sometimes in a way that embarrassed Lawrence. One July day, because he insisted on it, Murry and Katherine agreed to come on a picnic with him to meet Catherine Jackson in Hampstead, bringing with them Gordon Campbell. Obediently they accompanied him by tube to the station in Hampstead, got out, and were following him reluctantly up Holly Bush Hill, when suddenly somebody (Ivy Low) cried

piercingly, "Lawrence!" and a young lady in what looked like
a kimono came running down the hill, arms outstretched in
greeting.

"Good God!" said Campbell.

"I won't have *that!*" said Katherine, and with one accord
the three friends ran down the hill, around the corner, and out
of sight. They never saw Catherine Jackson at all. Afterward
Lawrence scolded them heatedly for making him look like a
fool and was not appeased when Katherine explained that "she
simply had a horror of effusiveness" and "could not bear things
that rushed at her." The Murrys continued to resist Lawrence's
gregarious nature, but he nonetheless persistently made welcome
such people as Dr. David Eder, who was fascinated by his
evident understanding of the Freudian theory and spent hours
discussing psychoanalysis with him in Campbell's drawing room.
Murry would sit there too, vainly—as he said—trying to make
sense of it all, and after Eder had gone Lawrence would scold
him for his skepticism. Murry of all people, said Lawrence,
would profit from a study of Freud, because he had the wrong
attitude toward sex; he didn't take it seriously enough.

So that summer, in spite of the war and the Murrys' disapproval, the Lawrences' circle enlarged considerably. For one
thing, Lawrence made the acquaintance of Amy Lowell, who
was visiting the country; they talked about forming a new
poetry group. For another, the Lawrences and the Murrys were
all invited to a grand dinner party at the H. G. Wellses', for
which Lawrence insisted on wearing his first dress suit. Though
Murry tried to dissuade him because, he said, Lawrence looked
awful in the suit, Lawrence was determined to do the correct
thing. Murry was exasperated with Frieda for not siding with
him. Couldn't she see that her husband looked silly? But then,
Murry told himself resignedly, Frieda was always "completely
preoccupied with her own appearance" and paid no attention to
Lawrence's; "yet oddly enough, she would submit herself entirely to be dressed by him, and he did it well."

At the party the Murrys decided to make a joke of the whole business, but Lawrence refused to fall in with their mood. All evening he was as stiff as his own shirt front and collar: he became as puritanical as he looked, and frowned on Katherine's ill-timed gaiety. Not surprisingly, nobody in the party enjoyed it very much, and on the way home, said Murry, "Lawrence was apocalyptic in his denunciation of Wells—even though Wells had been very decent to him at the party. Tactlessly, Katherine made matters worse by mentioning that two or three ladies who usually gushed over Lawrence had neglected him that evening because they were so busy gushing over Wells. At this, Lawrence's anger "fairly boiled over," said Murry, as if he realized he had let himself down.

As the war intruded more and more on life, London seemed too small for comfort to the Lawrences and they moved into the country, into what Bunny Garnett called "a horrid little cottage," "The Triangle" near Chesham, Bucks, where lived their friends Gilbert Cannan and his wife, Mary. Cramped and damp and ugly, The Triangle had a bad effect on Lawrence's health. He wrote to Catherine in October that he had been "seedy" and had grown a beard which he thought made him hideous, but he was keeping it because it was "warm and complete, and such a clothing to one's nakedness." (He wore it the rest of his life.) Small as the cottage was, the Lawrences did not stop inviting people to stay with them. Catherine went down and visited them once, and more frequently they saw Lawrence's friend S. S. Koteliansky, a Russian who had come to England on a scholarship in economics but spent much of his time translating the great Russian novelists.

The Murrys were not long in following their leader. They took another very small cottage about two miles from The Triangle and spent many an evening with their friends. Murry said that, though he was fascinated by Lawrence, he could not understand the latter's attitude in many matters. He had really been shocked by Lawrence's suggestion that he himself live on

Katherine's allowance, and "I was still more shocked the first time I witnessed one of his bursts of physical fury against his wife," he said. "It was (I thought) utterly wrong; worse than wrong, it was mysterious and incomprehensible. Quite how mysterious and incomprehensible it was to me will be understood only by those who know—through her letters—the nature of my relation with Katherine Mansfield. Here were two utterly different conceptions and experiences of the relation between a man and woman. It did not seem that they could belong to the same world." Except for one or two estrangements, said Murry, he and Katherine had a simple, happy sexual relationship, and anything complicated and stormy, like that of the Lawrences, seemed to him abnormal.

Not that Lawrence was always attacking his wife. Most of the time all of them, Lawrences and Murrys and Koteliansky, spent pleasant hours in The Triangle, Lawrence cooking the meals and everybody joining in with plans for the Utopia they hoped to create away from wartime England, possibly on some island. Katherine gave the name "Rananim" to this imagined settlement, taking the word from one of the Hebrew chants Kot often sang. Most of the time it was like that—Frieda described it too, in happy memory—but there were those bad times now and then, as witness an anecdote Leonard Woolf heard from Kot. The contretemps took place, said Kot, during his first visit to The Triangle, when he was lunching with the Lawrences and had not yet met the Murrys. At the table Frieda spoke of her children and began lamenting her loss of them, whereupon Kot took it upon himself to rebuke her, reminding her that she had, after all, made her choice: she had left the children in order to marry Lawrence.

"You must choose either your children or Lawrence," he said severely, "and if you choose Lawrence, you must stop complaining about the children."

What Lawrence contributed to this conversation, if anything, is not on record. He must have been pleased by Kot's speech, however. Frieda was silent, and after lunch she left the men together and disappeared. They sat by the fire talking, while outside rain poured down. Suddenly the door opened to admit a young woman who was sopping wet, her skirts tucked up, her feet in rubber boots. She said, "Lorenzo, Frieda has asked me to come and tell you that she will not come back."

Lawrence shouted, "Damn the woman, tell her I never want to see her again."

The young woman, who was of course Katherine Mansfield, turned around without another word, walked out into the rain, and vanished. It was the first time Koteliansky had ever seen her, but it was not to be the last; they became great friends.

Is this, or is it not, a version of another story that Murry told? According to this the Murrys were both at The Triangle one evening for supper, though Kot was not, and one of them innocently mentioned the Weekley children, at which Frieda began to cry. Lawrence turned white with fury—a frightening sight with his white face and red beard, said Murry—and shouted at her that she must get out of the house at once; she could have half of all the money he owned, he said, but she must leave that very minute. He rushed upstairs to the bedroom and rushed back again, money in his hands. This he put on the table and with shaking fingers counted out in two portions. There, he said; take it and get out, out, out!

Frieda put on her hat and coat and moved toward the door, then paused in tears while Murry endeavored, finally successfully, to calm the frantic Lawrence. Was Lawrence serious in his frenzy? Probably, for the moment. No doubt Frieda reflected philosophically that geniuses were all like that, or perhaps she blamed it on the war's effect on his spirits. Murry, however, worked it out on more metaphysical lines, comparing his and Katherine's relationship with that existing between Lawrence and Frieda. He decided that he and Katherine were, and regarded themselves as, distinct beings, whereas Lawrence seemed to merge himself in impersonal Woman and often regarded his wife "as a sort of prophetess and instrument of that 'blood-conscious-ness' " he talked so much about. Murry was making a shrewd guess here, or perhaps Lawrence had tried once or twice to explain the theories of Otto Gross to him. Lawrence did take over much of Gross's philosophy, at least what he understood it to be from Frieda's no doubt mangled interpretation. He did not go all the way with it, of course. He often said sternly that married people should be faithful to one another, and, as we know, he kept a sharp eye on his private Woman, to make sure that there would be no more Schwabing-type adventures.

Early in December he wrote Kot a letter in which he seems to refer to that lunch at which the guest scolded his hostess so frankly. He explained that he was accompanying Frieda to Nottingham; she was going there to pin down Ernest, if possible, on the subject of the children. Lawrence said he didn't think she would want to go alone, and added, "You mustn't judge her lightly. There is another quality in woman that you do not know, so you can't estimate it. You don't know that a woman is not a man with different sex. She is a different world. You do not understand that enough. Your world is all of one hemisphere." Which sounds like another echo of Otto Gross.

They did go to Nottingham, but Frieda went alone to see Ernest. It was an unsatisfactory interview, from the moment he leaped up and cried, "You—I hoped never to see you again," to the last exchange, when he declared himself totally inflexible. The children didn't want to see Frieda, he declared, and she was not to have them. There seemed nothing more that she could do, at least for the time being, so she left.

Early in 1915 the Lawrences were able to give up The Triangle and move to better quarters in Greatham, Sussex, where Viola Meynell had lent them her new house. Wilfrid, head of the large Meynell clan—the Patriarch, Bunny Garnett called him—had created a sort of Meynell village at Greatham with a house for each branch of the family. The advantages of a larger, prettier, far more comfortable establishment were augmented for Lawrence by the fact that Viola could and did type his latest work in progress. (Frieda never did any typing for her husband, because, she said, she hated to type, and Lawrence didn't think people should do things they didn't enjoy. In time, however, she learned other useful arts—cooking, cleaning, and such.) Another good thing about the Meynell house was that the Lawrences now had more to offer those guests who were so important to them. Even before they moved Lawrence was sending out invitations for the future to Lady Cynthia, E. M. Forster—a new acquaintance—another new acquaintance, Lady Ottoline Morrell, and Barbara Low, Ivy's aunt, who, like her relative Dr. Eder, was a psychiatrist. With Miss Low Lawrence had a close friendship for a while, closer perhaps than Frieda would have approved of had she known, but soon, with a characteristic switch of feeling, he turned against her and wrote of her in an unkindly spirit to correspondents as "the Jewish magpie."

The friendship with Lady Ottoline, like so many of Lawrence's sentimental connections, also ran into trouble eventually, but for nearly a year it flourished. It has been said that Lawrence was no great lover but rather a flirt. It is probably as good a description as any—at least a lot of ladies could bear witness that it was true—and his friendship, or whatever it was, with Lady Ottoline seems to have been of this nature.

Ottoline Cavendish-Bentinck, half sister to the Duke of Portland, was by her own account a shy, awkward girl, intensely religious, and a misfit in the stuffy, conventional life of her relatives until she married Philip Morrell, who went into politics and became a Liberal M.P. Ottoline would have been considered ugly if she had not been determined to go her own way in matters of dress as well as surroundings. She easily, and carelessly, lent herself to caricature. Nevertheless, with her dashing style she was known as a beauty. She loved the things she found beautiful in colors especially, but also in textures, shapes—in short, the arts; she therefore loved artists, and surrounded herself with them, as well as with anybody whose intellect she admired. Very tall, with what her lover Bertrand Russell described as a horse face, she wore whatever she liked—strange colors, sweeping skirts, shawls, enormous hats. She was painted by Augustus John and other contemporaries and became a leader in the world of art, literature, and general culture as well as fashion. The Morrells' house in Bedford Square was a gathering place for smart, slightly offbeat London, and she was proud of the conversation that went on there. (Cynthia Asquith, she said rather cattily, didn't fit in at *all*.) Philip Morrell accepted, if unhappily, his wife's affair with Bertrand Russell, but she was discreet about it.

When Lady Ottoline read *The White Peacock* and *Sons and Lovers*, she recognized with delight the Nottinghamshire in which she had spent much of her childhood. Of course her position then was widely different from that of little Bert Lawrence, but after she met him—as she determinedly did, as soon as she could—the contrast only gave a piquancy to their friendship. Ottoline was charmed with Lawrence, first as a real live member of the working classes and then for himself. For his part, Lawrence's pride was tickled at hobnobbing with a woman so far above him socially. He was particularly gratified because she was a Bentinck, of the grand family he, like all the others in the mining community, had heard so much of in his youth, and Lady Ottoline was flattered in exactly the same degree when he assured her that her people were well thought of by the miners.

Lawrence's first letter to his new conquest, dated January 3, 1915, from The Triangle, exhibits a method of approach that is typical:

> I was glad you wrote and told me you like my stories. One wants the appreciation of the few. . . . We should like very much to come and see you again. When we come to town we shall come to lunch with you. I shall let you know. We don't come very often, because of the poverty. I shake down the thermometer of my wealth, and find it just nearly at zero. But I like to be poor.

Lady Ottoline wrote that he gave one the impression of someone who had been undernourished in youth, making his body fragile and his mind too active. After the Lawrences moved to the Meynell cottage she went to visit them several times and noted that "except that one night I could not sleep on account of the cold, I was extraordinarily happy and at ease." She added:

When we met, we at once went back to our memories of Nottinghamshire. . . . He talked of the lovely wild commons, of Sherwood Forest, of the dark pit villages, of the lives of the colliers and their wives, and of all those scenes which he has described so vividly in his early books—scenes which were a part of his own life. He talked to me in the Nottinghamshire dialect which I loved to hear again. He also liked to talk of my family in Nottinghamshire, for he had a romantic feeling for them.

It was not long after their first meeting, on February 1, that Lawrence was writing to Lady Ottoline that he had plans for her: none other than to make her head of Rananim or something similar.

I want you to form the nucleus of a new community which shall start a new life amongst us—a life in which the only riches is integrity of character. So that each one may fulfill his own nature and deep desires to the utmost, but wherein tho', the ultimate satisfaction and joy is in the completeness of us all as one. Let us be good all together, instead of just in the privacy of our chambers, let us know that the intrinsic part of all of us is the best part, the believing part, the passionate, generous part.

This is the prophet Lawrence speaking; he always fell into that strained, messianic style when the spirit entered him. But however it sounds to us, he impressed Ottoline and she introduced him to Russell, who for a time was equally taken by Lawrence's ideas. Lawrence wrote a long letter to the future Earl Russell about his philosophy, and what he and Ottoline and Russell could do to save the world. More letters passed

between them, until at last Russell invited Lawrence to spend a
week end at Cambridge, where he himself held a chair in
philosophy, on the sixth and seventh of March.

Cambridge was the center, at least one of the two centers,
of British scholarship, and many learned men were there—
G. E. Moore the philosopher, John Maynard Keynes, and a lot
more. Lawrence had just finished *The Rainbow* and had plenty
of time on his hands, but he was dubious about going to Cambridge and walking into a whole cageful of lions. He was, after
all, a miner's son whose education had been garnered at workers' night classes or at best through provincial scholarships. It
was all very well to preach to Lady Cynthia and Lady Ottoline, or to innocent youngsters like the Murrys, but Cambridge?
Little things worried him; he wrote asking Ottoline if he should
take an evening suit.

He went to Cambridge, and Bertrand Russell did the
honors. He dined with great men but did not even try to talk
with them as equals. Perhaps what bothered him was that he
couldn't hold forth in soliloquy as he was used to doing in
small parties where everyone held him in reverence; that wasn't
the Cambridge style. After he got home he told Frieda scathingly that the men there walked up and down the room talking
of things like the Balkan situation, things they knew nothing
about. He did not dare to put them right on all these things, he
didn't know how, and his failure rankled. But the worst of the
weekend by far was Sunday breakfast, to which Russell had
invited Maynard Keynes.

In later years the famous economist recalled Lawrence's
behavior, which was awkward in the extreme. He was morose
from the beginning, and continued to be, uttering very little
while the others talked except for "indefinite expressions of
irritable dissent." Throughout the morning he sat crouched on
the sofa with his head hanging, which sounds exactly like the
position assumed by young Bert back in Eastwood when his
father joined the family at tea. Trying to explain this extraordinary behavior, Keynes hazarded the guess that Lawrence was

jealous of Lady Ottoline's other world of Cambridge, and may also have resented its hold on Bunny Garnett, who had many friends there. In any case, he said, Lawrence was generally antagonistic to the ambience of Cambridge and looked at the people there unfairly, through "ignorant, jealous, irritable, hostile eyes."

Lawrence, for his part, told Russell afterward that Cambridge made him feel "very black and down" and said he could not stand "its smell of rottenness, its marsh-stagnancy. . . . How can so sick people rise up?" he asked rhetorically. "They must die first." The week end did not bring an end to the Lawrence-Russell friendship—not yet, but it was not to survive much longer.

The Morrells decided to leave London on account of Ottoline's health, because she suffered various vaguely explained attacks; they bought a country house, Garsington Manor near Oxford, and gave up Bedford Square. Ottoline offered to provide a cottage on the grounds for the Lawrences; Philip was to fix up a house that was already there and only needed a certain amount of remodeling. She was so generous, wrote Lawrence to Russell, that he hesitated to accept. Did Bertie think she could afford it? It turned out that she couldn't; at least, she and Philip were not willing to do as much to the house as Frieda demanded. Frieda was making things very difficult generally; she was jealous of Ottoline. So nothing came of the plan, but the Lawrences spent a good deal of time as guests at Garsington nevertheless.

It is easy to understand why Frieda behaved in such a recalcitrant manner, if one understands her nature at all. Ottoline was a rival to her on special grounds. It was Frieda's title that had such glamour for Lawrence, but Ottoline was higher born than herself. Also, Ottoline dared to like Lawrence a lot. She made a great fuss of him, she puffed him up, and the more she did this, the worse Frieda behaved. At every opportunity she asserted herself, interposing herself between Lorenzo and the outside grasping world and shouting down any temptation he might have been offered to stray away from her. She considered herself challenged by Ottoline and promptly accepted the challenge, even to attempting to lure away from her rival the more or less official lover, Bertrand Russell. There, however, she didn't get very far.

Lawrence *was* hard to live with at that time, even for Lawrence. He wrote a lot of exhortatory sermons to both his titled ladies, Ottoline and Cynthia, and bursts of temper came thick and fast. On April 19 he wrote at length to Lady Ottoline complaining of a visit just paid him and Frieda at Greatham by Bunny Garnett and two other youths. To listen to those young men, he said, really made him furious; they talked endlessly, said nothing, and made him dream, he said, of beetles, and he described a dream in which he met and conquered a horrible beetle; it was all the fault of those guests. He wrote in similar vein to Bunny, who was so angry at this attempt to censor his friends that he broke off with the Lawrences, even though, he said, he still loved Frieda. Such unreasonable frenzies of Lawrentian irritation were possibly due to an attack of ill health. The beetle anger lasted several days, for on the twentieth he spoke of the whole outrage yet again in a letter to Kot and also said that they would probably not have the Garsington cottage after all and he was glad of it, as he preferred to live in some little place where he could be by himself.

"Thank heaven we shall get out of the Lady Ottoline cottage," he said, farther on in the letter. "I cannot have such a place like a log on my ankle. God protects me, and keeps me free. Let us think of some place to which we can betake ourselves."

The reader may reflect that nobody, after all, was *forcing* Lawrence to accept the cottage, but he was in one of his most illogical moods. They were just at the end of the Greatham stay, late in July, when Frieda got the news that her father had died.

"You didn't expect to keep your father all your life?" was all England's chief exponent of the Oedipus complex had to offer in comfort.

At the end of the month the Lawrences moved to 1 Byron Villas, in Hampstead, where Frieda hoped she could see the children more easily. And she did see them at least twice, because Lady Ottoline persuaded Ernest to permit the meetings. Even his stubborn temper could not hold out against a lady of such high degree. The Weekley children were probably in Lawrence's mind when he wrote to Lady Cynthia about the position of women in the ideal society he planned:

> And women shall not vote equally with men, but for different things. Women *must* govern such things as the feeding and housing of the race. And if a system works up to a Dictator who controls the greater industrial side of the national life, it must work up to a Dictatrix who controls the things relating to private life. And the women shall have absolutely equal voices with regard to marriage, custody of children, etc.

Lawrence and Frieda went often that summer of 1915 to Garsington, where guests were expected to help to get the house and grounds into shape, decorating the walls and planting the garden. At these tasks Lawrence shone, constructing a kind of lower-class rose arbor hardly in keeping with the larger grandeurs of Garsington, though Ottoline praised and retained it for his sake. But Frieda was not happy, and she made the people around well aware of this.

As biographer Robert Lucas explains, "She had the feeling of being treated as a mere chattel of her husband, especially when her exuberant hostess tried to tell her how to handle 'a genius, a being dropped straight from the sky.' To tell her, Frieda, how to handle Lawrence!" Her reaction to this, of course, was to beat her breast gorilla fashion and proclaim to the world that she, too, was important, in her own right. She raised hell with Lorenzo until he must have been sorry he ever went to Garsington. "She once told Philip Morrell (according to his daughter) that she would not have minded if Lawrence had had an ordinary affair with Lady Ottoline, but what she could not stand was 'all this soul-mush!' "

In her memoirs Frieda was more circumspect. "She was a great influence in Lawrence's life," she said of Lady Ottoline. "Her profound culture, her beautiful home, 'Garsington,' her social power, all meant much to Lawrence. I felt in those days: 'Perhaps I ought to leave Lawrence to her influence; what might they not do together for England? I am powerless, and a Hun, and a nobody.' "

With all due respect, I don't think we ought to take Frieda literally on this point. It seems unlikely that she really felt that way. Hadn't she Otto Gross's assurance that she was unique, the love goddess? She showed much more self-confidence in the spring of 1916, when the friendship between Lawrence and Bertrand Russell ran into trouble and ground to a halt. They had planned to collaborate on a series of lectures, but they could not see eye to eye on so many things that it was no use. Russell took exception to Lawrence's developing creed of "blood-consciousness," and Lawrence attacked Russell on his brand of pacifism, accusing him of really loving the war. For a time Russell was so shattered by this statement, he later told Lawrence, that he contemplated suicide. But Frieda liked Russell, and for a time they corresponded in a friendly manner even after he broke with Lawrence. She wrote of his formidable intellect:

"It's rather jolly, it's your form of *'Wille zur Macht,'* I should always be frightened of your intellect, I feel it against women, at present anyhow." Of Germany, she told Russell that, apart from Prussianism, it had got "something good and a new ideal to give to itself and the world—if nations would only, only allow each other's best characteristics to come out and take and learn from each other— It's all so tight now these little nations, so unembracing— All the people are so ugly now, but the other is there, in the nations and in the individuals." Frieda had her own way of looking at things, but she did not always allow for the attitude of others. When her son Monty came to see her, resplendent in uniform, she shocked him severely by urging him to let her hide him in the woods where the authorities couldn't get hold of him, and she reacted in the same way in 1917, when she heard that Lady Cynthia's husband was in the army. Why couldn't Cynthia get him out? "What is the good of being the Prime Minister's son?" she asked.

As the war continued, Lawrence determined to get out of England. Though travel was not easy on the Continent, it could be accomplished: Katherine Mansfield, for instance, temporarily estranged from Murry, had gone to meet a new lover in the south of France and promptly came back when the affair turned sour. Then both she and Murry went again to France, to Bandol. But Lawrence was not inclined toward France. Why shouldn't he and Frieda really strike out in the new world of America, well away from the war? America, a pioneer land, would be the best setting for Rananim, come to think of it—Florida sounded promising—but they would need documents to get out of England. In the halcyon days before the war people had not needed passports to travel in Europe, and Lawrence didn't have one. Frieda did, but it would have been dangerous to use because it carried the damaging information that she was born in Metz. So both of them needed passports, and Lawrence appealed to Lady Cynthia for help. She knew a lot of people in prestigious positions, and she was kind and painstaking. Thanks to her efforts, by the end of October the Lawrences had their passports.

Then disaster struck. Lawrence's new novel, *The Rainbow*, came out in the early days of November and all copies were immediately seized by the police on the grounds of indecency. I am not writing primarily about Lawrence's work, so we need not go deeply into the reasons for such official action, except to remind ourselves that what is called the climate of opinion was against him for his outspokenness. Richard Aldington blamed the suppression on politics; Lawrence would never have suffered, he said, if it had not been for his pacifist ideas, and this too may be true. Whatever the root of the trouble, there it was: *The Rainbow* was condemned and in disgrace. Lawrence was staggered. His first impulse was to get out of the damned country as quickly as possible. On November 6 he asked Eddie Marsh for a loan in order to do this, and Marsh promptly sent him far more money than he had requested. Lady Ottoline and Philip Morrell added to the sum and persuaded others, including George Bernard Shaw, to contribute. Lawrence booked passage for Frieda and himself on a ship sailing from Liverpool on November 24.

"I want you to go and stay with Ottoline," he wrote to Cynthia Asquith, in what was supposed to be a parting valedictory. To be sure, the ladies were not good friends nor likely to be, but this made no difference to him.

When I say she is *quite* unreal, that is wrong of me. There is an unformed reality in her, very deep. I think she is a big woman. But of course her whole effort has been spent in getting away from her tradition, etc. Now she is exhausted. She has, in some sense, got away; but she has not got anywhere. She feels it bitterly. It is a bitter thing, only to have destroyed, not to have created. But she is pretty well spent now. Yet she still understands that there is the beyond. She is like an old, tragic queen who knows that her life has been spent in conflict with a kingdom that was not worth her life. Her life is in a way lost, yet not lost. She has not found the reality, because it was not to be found until she had pulled the temple down. But she has, for herself, pulled the temple down, even if she lies exhausted in the ruins. It is more than remaining safe in the temple.

Ottoline Morrell was only forty-two at the time, hardly an "old, tragic queen"; what had she done to merit all this? Nothing, perhaps, but serve as an unwitting model for Hermione Roddice, a sinister character in Lawrence's next novel, *Women in Love*. But the letter was not all about her; Lawrence had much to say about Cynthia herself.

"I want you to reserve to yourself, always, the choice,

whether you too shall come to America also, at any time. You
have your children. Probably you will have to rescue them from
their decadence, this collapsing life." He promised to write her
all about America, where he would try to start a new school,
"a new germ of a new creation, there: I believe it exists there
already. . . . Your husband should have left this decomposing
life. There was nowhere to go. Perhaps now he is beaten." And
so on. Lady Cynthia, at least, was not beaten, said Lawrence.

"I know America is bad," he wrote the next day to another
woman friend, "but I think it has a future. I think there is no
future for England: only a decline and fall." Well, of course,
now that they had branded his book as indecent. But Philip
Morrell, husband of that "tragic queen," was going to ask a
question about the affair in the House, so there was a shred of
hope left for England's future. It was down for December 1,
so the Lawrences decided to give up their November booking
and see what happened. Other friends had rallied round—
Catherine Jackson, now Catherine Carswell, wrote glowingly of
*The Rainbow* in the *Glasgow Herald,* and was promptly fired
as a result—and the Authors' Society promised to take up the
case and fight for him. The fight never materialized, nor did
Philip Morrell's parliamentary question have any appreciable
effect on the case, so Lawrence began looking for another ship.
Meantime, once more the Lawrences were guests at Garsington, and Lawrence busied himself there recruiting for Rananim.
He got a firm promise from young Aldous Huxley to come out
to Florida and help build a brave new world, and Philip Heseltine was definitely interested. Heseltine, the composer who was
to make his name as Peter Warlock, also offered practical help:
he said that his good friend, the composer Delius, owned land
in Florida and might be induced to let Lawrence have it for his
colony. However, Delius when asked put a damper on the idea,
saying that the Florida climate would be very bad for Lawrence's health.

Yet another Garsington guest, a Muslim named Suhra-

wardy, professed an interest in the American Utopia, but in the
end none of these near-initiates proved faithful. It remained for
Brett, and Brett alone, to carry out the intentions of the Master.

Brett—the Honorable Dorothy E. Brett, to give her formal
title—was a painter who trained at the Slade School of Art.
Daughter of Lord Esher and sister of the Ranee of Sarawak,
she had left home to make a life for herself. Because she was
very deaf, she had to carry an ear trumpet everywhere and was
painfully shy as a result. For a time she shared a flat with Dora
Carrington—always called Carrington because she hated her
first name—the girl who fell so incongruously and permanently
in love with Lytton Strachey but who was first the adored and
pursued of a young painter named Mark Gertler. It was Gertler
who introduced Brett to Lawrence.

"He plagued and plagued me," wrote Brett, addressing the
dead Lawrence as if he still lived; "it was his insisting that I
meet you that overcame my shyness and brought your invitation to tea." She and Gertler went to Byron Villas and sat there
before the fire with Lawrence, discussing Ottoline, "our mutual friend and enemy," as Brett called her.

> I, terribly shy, in agonies of nervousness; you gentle, gently
> coaxing me out of my shyness. . . . We sit drinking tea, tear-
> ing poor [Ottoline] to pieces. We pull her feathers out in
> handfuls until I stop, aghast, and try to be merciful, saying,
> "We will leave her just one feather." You laugh at that a high,
> tinkling laugh, mischievous, saying, "We will leave her just
> one draggled feather in her tail, the poor plucked hen!"

They met only twice more before the Lawrences left
London, but Brett remembered Lawrence with ardent fondness.
So, one supposes, did Lady Ottoline.

"Are you putting Ottoline in your book?" Dame Rebecca
West asked this writer some time ago.

I said, "Why, she wasn't in love with Lawrence, was she?"

"*Was* she not!" said Dame Rebecca.

# 9

## H. D.: "Cerebral contact"

FRIEDA'S OPINION of *The Rainbow* affair was earnestly defensive.

> He [Lawrence] was sex-mad, they said. Little even now do people realize what men like Lawrence do for the body of life, what he did to rescue the fallen angel of sex. Sex had fallen in the gutter, it had to be pulled out. . . . "I'll never write another word I mean," he said in his bitterness; "they aren't fit for it," and for a time the flame in him was quenched. . . .
>
> The best were treated so during the war. And in those dark days I had a bad time. Naturally, I came in for all Lawrence's tortured, irritable moods. His sweetness had disappeared and he turned against me as well as the rest for the time being. It all made him ill. There was not even a little hope or gaiety anywhere. . . . [He] didn't like the little flat and he didn't like me or anybody else.

Until December 19 Lawrence seems to have been fairly sure of going to Florida with the people, his "young recruits" as he called them, collected mainly from Garsington. Though Delius's reply put an end to his hopes there, he soon heard of another place at Fort Myers not far from Delius's estate. Determined to get to Florida somehow, he booked passages for Frieda and himself on a tramp steamer sailing for the West Indies on the twentieth, confident of company even though

Murry refused to accompany him and so did Bertrand Russell, whom Lawrence had invited to be president of Rananim. What put an end to all these plans was the last-minute discovery that Lawrence, or any other Englishman for that matter, could not now leave the country without proof of official exemption from military service. Lawrence was so keen to escape from England that he tried briefly to obtain this exemption. He actually went to take a medical examination at a center in London, though usually he dreaded what doctors might find out about his health; above all, the specter of tuberculosis must not be mentioned, but Lawrence invariably felt it hovering near in medical reports. That day at the center, after waiting in line for two hours, his resolve evidently melted away, leaving him to be overtaken once again by the old terror. Reporting later on his behavior, however, he did not admit this but said only that he suddenly had the feeling that being there in the waiting line was an utter travesty of action, and so he simply walked out. For the time being, nobody in authority seems to have questioned this act of default.

As a stopgap—for Lawrence was confident that they would ultimately get to Florida—he and Frieda went to Cornwall, to Padstow, where Murry had managed to borrow a farmhouse for them until the end of February.

"This is the first move to Florida," he wrote to Kot, and in a letter to Katherine Mansfield, who was in France grieving for her brother lost in the war, he said:

> We have met one or two young people, just one or two, who have the germ of the new life in them. . . . I want it now that we live together. When you come back, I want you and Murry to live with us, or near us, in unanimity; not these separations. Let us all live together and create a new world. If it is too difficult in England, because here all is destruction and dying and corruption, let us go away to Florida: soon. But let us go *together*, and keep together, several of us, as being of one spirit. Let it be a union in the unconsciousness, not in the consciousness.

Lawrence was off once more on another of his messianic sprees.

He wrote again to Katherine but less urgently. She and Jack were to come if they wished; there was to be "no more questioning and quibbling and trying to do anything with the world. The world is gone, extinguished, like the lights of last night's Café Royal—gone for ever."

He wrote many lengthy letters to Lady Ottoline, full of thanks for the comforts she was sending him in a steady stream: woolen garments, strengthening foods. In some of the letters are hints of trouble between Frieda and Ottoline. For example, Frieda was sorry, said Lawrence, that she had written such a cross letter to Ottoline, but she was angry at the time because two young men visiting at Padstow, Philip Heseltine and Dikran Kouyoumdjian (Michael Arlen, as he was to be known), had been telling her things that Lady Ottoline had said about her.

"But she is not really cross," wrote Lawrence untruthfully. "Perhaps the way we behave to one another, she and I, makes everybody believe that there is real incompatibility between us. But you know that really we are married to each other—I know you know it." Yes, Ottoline knew it. She knew it, but she deprecated it. What a shame, that a conceited termagant like Frieda could make dear little Lawrence run around looking like a whipped dog!

Heseltine and Arlen were not the only gossips at Padstow. In another letter Lawrence expatiated at length to Lady Ottoline about Heseltine's love life, which was evidently complicated. Discussing the young composer's double amours with obvious relish, he came to the conclusion that the future Peter Warlock was a dual person, who might always have two separate things, "the real blood connection and the real conscious or spiritual connection." For such people, said Lawrence gravely, he believed that two wives were necessary. Monogamy was "for those who are whole and clear, all in one stroke. But for those whose stroke [whatever that means] is broken into two different directions, there should be two fulfillments." He wished

Lady Ottoline to have no doubt about his own oneness, however:

"For myself, thank God, I feel myself becoming more and more unified, more and more a oneness. And Frieda and I become more and more truly married—for which I thank Heaven. It has been such a fight. But it is coming right. And then we can all three be real friends. Then we shall be really happy, all of us, in our relation."

How much Lady Ottoline looked forward to this consummation is not stated, but even while Lawrence thus happily wrote to her, he was creating that unpleasant character Hermione Roddice in his new novel—who looked remarkably like Lady Ottoline, who had Ottoline's distinctive looks and her individual way of talking, who even wore Ottoline's clothes. In *Women in Love*, Hermione-Ottoline has an affair with a Lawrence character named Birkin, who jilts her. At her great house Breadalby, the vengeful Hermione-Ottoline hits Birkin-Lawrence over the head with a paperweight, nearly stunning him—but Lawrence did not write about that as yet because it hadn't yet happened in real life. It was going to, though the wielder of vengeance was not really Ottoline but Frieda. At any rate, Hermione was taking shape in the novel, while in his letters Lawrence talked on and on of the bright future of friendship between Ottoline, Frieda, and himself. It is very hard at times to understand novelists.

Then Lawrence had an attack of ill health which so worried Frieda that she asked Bertrand Russell to come down to the country and relieve her of some of the responsibility of nursing a genius. She may well have had other plans for him too. Whether or not Russell suspected her intentions he did not come, and Lawrence, recovered without his help, embarked enthusiastically on a plan to form a publishing company that was to produce a few select works, beginning with the suppressed *Rainbow*, in partnership with Heseltine and the Murrys. He wrote about all this to the Murrys, who were living happily and quietly at Bandol in the south of France, each writing a book. They were indignant. There was Lawrence again, they told each other, making new friends and trying to drag them into relationships they didn't need or want. Why should they welcome a total stranger into their midst and start a publishing company with this Heseltine? They wrote of their sentiments to Lawrence, and he replied persuasively and soothingly. They were sure to like Heseltine, he said; besides, Heseltine had money for the project. (Which was news to him, Heseltine remarked when he read the letter years later; at that time he hadn't a penny of his own.)

The Murrys remained unsoothed, and everybody's temper was riled for a time, but after the Lawrences moved from Padstow at the end of February, into a cottage at Zennor near St. Ives, Lawrence resumed his campaign to get the Murrys back so that they might, all together (though perhaps, after all, without Heseltine) build a new heaven and new earth. Near the Lawrence cottage, Tregerthen, was another that he was sure would suit the Murrys splendidly. The Murrys were not so sure; Bandol suited them. It was lovely and they were truly happy there, but Lawrence kept on coaxing. The other cottage had a tower in it, he wrote, that he already called Katherine's tower. Frieda too wrote to them, with all the persuasion at her command, until at last the Murrys submitted. Katherine was in tears at leaving Bandol, but she left.

"I see Katherine Mansfield and Murry arriving sitting on a cart," remembered Frieda fondly, "high up on all the goods and chattels, coming down the lane to Tregerthen. Like an emigrant Katherine looked. . . . It was great fun buying very nicely made furniture for a few shillings in St. Ives, with the Murrys."

According to her account life was happy in the incipient Rananim of Cornwall—"days of complete harmony," she described it. But things could not have been so completely harmonious, with Katherine sorrowing for Bandol and Lawrence's temper very uncertain. Often he quarreled not only with Frieda but very sharply with Murry too. With Frieda, however, his outbursts became more and more extreme—and they had been bad enough before, as witness the evidence of Eleanor Farjeon, the writer. Miss Farjeon was one of the Meynells' many friends who had known the Lawrences at Greatham; she too did some of Lawrence's typing, and like most women she was completely charmed by him when he felt charming. She loved his way of brightening the cottage with gaily painted jars and bottles:

> He made the simplicities of cottage life delightful, basting the mutton and stirring the onion sauce with the happy concentration of a child who is doing something it likes. [Evidently Frieda was not yet trying her hand at housekeeping.] His uncontrolled irritabilities astonished me at first, but I soon realized one must know Lawrence all-of-a-piece or not at all. Nobody held back so little of himself, no matter in what company, or cared so little for the embarrassments he caused. I did not like this side of him, but I accepted it equally with the things in him which stimulated and fascinated me.

In a letter to Nehls she enlarged on this passage:

> It is impossible to think of Lawrence without being re-stimulated to talk, his effect continues; I had no idolatrous illusions about him, I valued him greatly, and enjoyed his company, and his gift of entertaining and penetrating talk as I have enjoyed few other men's—until his company became unbearable, because of some atrocious outburst against Frieda. One had to remember that a volcano is not really responsible for its own eruptions; when something produced an eruption, you got it red-hot. . . . It is understandable that not everybody will risk the red-hot lava for the sake of the mountain. I myself could not have pitched my tent at its base for long spells of time together.

The Murrys, however, did try for a time at least to stay on the mountain slope. Katherine was never, from the very beginning, willing to try wholeheartedly. "I shall *never* like this place," she declared to Murry during their first night at

Zennor, and within three weeks she was writing to Kot, who was now her good friend and confidant, "I am very much alone here. It is not really a nice place. It is so full of huge stones, but now that I am writing I do not care, for the time. It is so very temporary. It may all be over next month; in fact, it will be. I don't belong to anybody here."

Much of the trouble, according to Murry in his memoirs, was that there was a kind of tug of war between Katherine and Lawrence, with him as the bone of contention. If he turned toward Lawrence in obedience to the latter's wishes, Katherine felt neglected, and this in turn affected Jack and made him miserable. But Lawrence would not see or acknowledge that this was so, said Murry. He went on: "His relation to Frieda left room, and perhaps need, for a relation with a man of something of the kind and quality of my relation with Katherine; and he wanted this relation with me."

This is very much the idea expressed by the Lawrence-character Birkin at the end of *Women in Love* and, more explicitly, in the Prologue to that book, which the publisher refused to use:

> All the time, he recognized that, although he was always drawn to women, feeling more at home with a woman than with a man, yet it was for men that he felt the hot, flushing roused attraction which a man is supposed to feel for the other sex. Although nearly all his living interchange went on with one woman or another, although he was always terribly intimate with at least one woman, and practically never intimate with a man, yet the male physique had a fascination for him, and for the female physique he felt only a fondness, a sort of sacred love, as for a sister.

At the end of the book Birkin, grieving over the death of Gerald Crich, is questioned by his accepted lover Ursula, who with a natural asperity asks why she is not enough for him. He replies that she is enough, as far as a woman is concerned, "But I wanted a man friend, as eternal as you and I are eternal."

Ursula repeats the question: Why isn't she enough? For, after all, he is enough for *her*. Birkin says that to make his life really complete, really happy, he wants eternal union with a man too, another kind of love. When Ursula calls his desire a perversity, he says, "Yet I wanted it."

Murry elsewhere denied that Lawrence felt a homosexual attraction for him, although if that was not his meaning it is hard to guess just what he did intend readers to believe. Similarly he tried to appear uncommitted in his account of a quarrel he had with Lawrence over Lawrence's desire for what he called *Blutbrüderschaft*, blood brotherhood. Lawrence said he wanted a ceremony to confirm this relationship. What ritual he had in mind is not explained: it was probably some kind of schoolboy business with both men drawing blood from cuts in their fingers and letting the streams mingle. But whatever it would have been, Murry, averring that he feared some sort of pagan theatricals among the Cornish rocks, evaded it.

"If I love you, and you know I love you, isn't that enough?" he asked Lawrence, upon which Lawrence flew into a fury and shouted, "I hate your love, I *hate* it." And once in the night when everyone should have been asleep Murry heard Lawrence next door shouting to Frieda that Jack was killing him; that he was an obscene bug, sucking Lawrence's life away. As we know, it was a bad sign when Lawrence had nightmares about insects.

His clashes with Frieda were frightening, said Murry. He described a scene that has since become famous: one night Murry and Katherine were sitting in their own living room when they heard Frieda shrieking. She rushed in crying, "He'll kill me!" and Lawrence rushed in after her to chase her around and around the Murrys' table, shouting "I'll *kill* her, I'll *kill* her!"

As Murry described it, he and Katherine were too numb to do anything. They simply sat where they were, though Murry just managed to save a lamp from destruction. Suddenly Lawrence collapsed into a chair by the fire, his frenzy gone. Frieda went back to the Lawrence cottage, and after a while so did Lawrence, pale and unsteady. In the morning the Murrys approached the other house with slow, reluctant steps, apprehensive of what they might find. But there sat Lawrence and Frieda side by side, apparently perfectly happy as Lawrence trimmed a hat for his wife.

To be fair, said Jack, it wasn't always Lawrence who started the argument. Sometimes Frieda, in a gentle, innocent voice, would make a dogmatic statement that was just as offensive to Lawrence as if she hadn't been quoting him in an earlier mood. Up blew the volcano, and another dramatic scene ensued. Frieda was certainly doing it deliberately.

Murry swore that he had no idea in those days that he and Katherine were the models for Gerald and Gudrun in *Women in Love*, though when he later read the book with this knowledge in mind, he could see clearly that they were.

>    Lawrence believed, or tried to believe, that the relation between Katherine and me was false and deadly; and that the relation between Frieda and himself was real and life-giving: but that his relation with Frieda needed to be completed by a new relation between himself and me, which I evaded [he wrote]. . . . The foundation of it all is the relation between Lawrence and Frieda. That is, as it were, the ultimate reality. That foundation secure, Lawrence needs or desires a further relation with me, in which Katherine is temporarily but totally ignored. By virtue of this "mystical" relation with Lawrence, I participate in this pre-mental reality, the "dark sources" of my being come alive. From this changed personality, I, in turn, enter a new relation with Katherine.

Though Murry and Katherine did not understand just what was going on—indeed, who could?—they did know they weren't happy at Zennor. Katherine said that for one thing she was tired of Lawrence's sex obsession, and she suggested sarcastically that he change the name of his cottage to "The Phallus." She wrote to Kot, "I don't know which disgusts me more. When they are loving and playing with each other or when they are roaring at each other and he is pulling out Frieda's hair and saying 'I'll cut your bloody throat, you bitch.' " (It will be seen that Koteliansky allowed Katherine to criticize his idol as much as she pleased, though he never permitted Frieda so much latitude.)

It could not go on. One day when the Murrys and Lawrences went on an excursion to Marazion, in a more southerly district of Cornwall, Katherine saw an escape route. Marazion was warmer than Tregerthen, she observed, and much more cheerful with its increased greenery and fewer rocks, so she and Jack would move there. Accordingly, Jack found them a cottage at Mylor, and the Murrys packed their belongings and departed.

Though Frieda later said that she was often lonely after they left, the Lawrences were not completely deserted. Catherine Carswell paid them a visit and found them laughing and quite ready to recount to her one of their most recent and violent quarrels. They had been very angry, they told her, but the row came to an end and Lawrence at least was ready to forget all about it. Indeed, he felt refreshed. He went into the kitchen, humming, and set to work washing up. But Frieda's wrath had not yet simmered down, and when she saw her husband so cheerfully standing there at the sink, his back to her, she suddenly grabbed a soup plate and broke it over his head. This incident became part of the Lawrence saga and also, as has been said, found its way in altered form into *Women in Love*, though there the woman who hit the man over the head was Hermione, and her weapon was not a humble kitchen plate but a stylish lump of lapis lazuli. Why lapis? Because Ottoline had once given Lawrence such a piece of lapis lazuli; we know this because he handed it over to another woman friend later with the remark that "the Ott" bored him.

During Catherine's visit she incurred her host's displeasure by going into the sitting room after a book when garbed only in an ankle-length petticoat and long-sleeved woolen vest. As she reminds us, Lawrence was of working-class origin, and was being true to his class when he evinced distaste of anything that could be regarded as indecent, even long petticoats and vests.

"It would indeed be easy to call him prudish," Catherine admitted.

He disapproved, he said, of people appearing in their under-clothes. No doubt, if I had not privately believed my *négligé* to be attractive as well as decent, I might neither have ventured to appear in it nor have felt so much abashed as I did by Law-rence's remark. So, essentially, Lawrence was right after all! How more than horrified he was—furious—when from his flat in Florence, looking across the Arno, he was compelled to overlook also a stretch of mud and shingle which the Flor-entine "gamins" found a convenient spot for the relief of nature. He hated the domestic dog on account of its too public habits. In such respects Lawrence was no advocate of what is often, but wrongly, called "the natural." Still less was he an apostle of the nude.

There were other visitors too to Tregerthen: Barbara Low; the poet Dollie Radford, who was a friend of the Lawrences; and even, once or twice, Jack Murry, before he was snatched up into the war effort and had to go to London. Once Frieda went to London herself, without Lawrence because they couldn't both afford it, for an official meeting with her daugh-ters, which is to say Ernest had consented to it this time. She took them to dinner and gave each of them ten shillings; then they went to the opera. But Elsa said to Barby in the ladies' room during the intermission, "You are not to *like* Mama, you know, just because we have got ten shillings," and later Ernest sent the money back.

Near the cottage a young composer named Cecil Gray

lived in a house called Bosigran Castle. Gray had a bad heart and had been exempted from military service. The three exiles became friendly and remained on intimate terms until the Lawrences left Cornwall. Gray was able to help them in various ways, but ultimately he turned violently against Lawrence for reasons that will shortly be explained. Lawrence did not depend exclusively on him for companionship in any event; he made friends with the Hocking family who farmed the land around the village. They seemed to fascinate him. He went more and more often to the farmhouse, much as he had gone to The Haggs when he was a boy living in Eastwood; and just as Lydia Lawrence resented it in those days, Frieda now found it a grievance when he spent so much time away from her. Once or twice she too went to see the Hockings, but it wasn't a success. The farm people were somewhat in awe of the great lady. Frieda did not suffer in silence; she complained to Lawrence that she was lonely, but he would not stay at home. He loved to help the men at their work in the fields, making hay with them, showing them how sheaves were stacked in Nottinghamshire, and learning how to raise vegetables in Cornish earth, in the plot he dug near the cottage. His particular friend in the family was William Henry Hocking.

"He could talk by the hour with William Henry, the farmer's elder son, ruddy and handsome," wrote Frieda. "In those days Lawrence seemed to turn against me, perhaps on account of the bit of German in me. I felt utterly alone there, on that wild Cornish moor, in the little granite cottage. Often Lawrence would leave me in the evenings, and go over to the farm, where he'd spend his time talking to William Henry and giving French lessons to Stanley, the younger son." In the empty silence she brooded about Germany and all the young men dying in the war. "And then Lawrence would come home and want to quarrel with me, as if he were angry with me because I too felt sad and hopeless and helpless."

At the end of June the authorities caught up with Lawrence: they sent him an official order to present himself for medical examination. This time it was impossible to run away. He was lucky to have avoided the critical moment as long as he had; almost all the men of military age known to the Lawrences had been drawn into the war in one way or another, whether or not they objected. Murry was at the War Ministry, doing a desk job. Bunny Garnett and many of his friends worked on the land as conscientious objectors. Herbert Asquith was an army officer, and so was Richard Aldington. It really did seem to be Lawrence's turn. He and Frieda walked to Penzance so that he could report on the stated date; then Frieda returned to Tregerthen and Lawrence was sent on to Bodmin. There he had to remain for a time, undergoing the discomforts of boot-camp life with other men and suffering the indignity of having to strip naked before the examiners. He was there only two days, but for the rest of his life those two days loomed up in Lawrence's memory like a nightmare. In his description of the experience in *Kangaroo* one feels that much of the mental torture he underwent lay in the fact that he, the son of Lydia Lawrence, had to appear naked before the doctors; he imagined that they were sniggering at him.

Poor thing, said Frieda, how glad he was to get back to her! For it goes without saying that he was rejected as unfit for military service, and though the army officers said something about finding useful war work in some other line than theirs, he paid no attention to such nonsense. Back he went to his real work, writing *Women in Love*. Otherwise he spent a good deal of time and energy arranging for William Henry to make a trip to London, something the farmer boy had long yearned to do. Lawrence's correspondence was full of requests to his London friends to look after William Henry in the big city, show him the sights, and see that he came to no harm. One or two of them were evidently somewhat annoyed by all this, finding it a nuisance.

However, William Henry or no, Lawrence finished *Women in Love*. About the middle of November he wrote Catherine

Carswell to say he was sending a copy of the manuscript to her
husband, Donald, and herself. Two weeks later, on the twenty-
seventh, he wrote again:

> I heard from Ottoline Morrell this morning, saying she
> hears she is the villainess of the new book. It is very strange,
> how rumours go round.—So I have offered to send her the
> MS.—So don't send it to Pinker [his agent] till I let you
> know. . . .
> Don't talk much about my novel, will you? And above all
> don't give it to anybody to read, but Don. I feel it won't be
> published yet, so I would rather nobody read it. I hope Otto-
> line Morrell won't want the MS.

How could he possibly have expected to get away with it?
Of course Ottoline did demand to see the manuscript, and after
reading it she objected strenuously to much of it, so effectively
that it was four years before the book appeared with several
offending passages deleted, and many more years before he and
Ottoline made it up. Nor was she the only person angered.
Many others of his friends were portrayed in similarly un-
pleasing guise, and one at least insisted on changes. Some never
forgave him. The pages of Nehls's record are full of denunciations that glow with righteous heat even today.

The year 1917 brought with it a landmark or two. In April
Lawrence scraped up the money to go to London, where he
stayed for a week and saw his friends—though not, one supposes, Lady Ottoline. And there was a young woman who
came to stay at Tregerthen, ostensibly to cure a broken heart
after an unhappy love affair, but she depended on Lawrence
to help her, and the dependence became so marked that Frieda
made her go away again. Lawrence made no attempt to stop
the departure.

Slowly, however, an unpleasant sentiment grew up among
their Cornish neighbors, a feeling that the Lawrences were
suspect. Even the Hockings were affected by the increasing

prejudice. No doubt Lawrence and Frieda had always been objects of suspicion in a mild way, ever since they first arrived, because they were both considered foreign, and Frieda's nationality especially could not possibly be mistaken, but things move slowly in the countryside and it took a long time for the hidden resentment to fester. A number of factors contributed to the Cornishmen's misgivings. When Lawrence went to Bodmin, they probably thought he had been caught at last and would have to go into the army like their own menfolk, but he got away and came home. That was annoying. It happened again, too; in June, 1917, he was called up for a repeat performance, but this time he was back within the same day, rejected for the second time. Then there were rumors. It was said that a British ship had been sunk off the coast near Zennor by a U-boat: were the Lawrences supplying German submarines with food by night? And it was generally known that Frieda's maiden name was Von Richthofen; the British had good reason to know that name because of Baron Manfred von Richthofen, Germany's top flying ace. To be sure he was only a second cousin, but Frieda was no doubt foolish enough to express pride in the connection. Sometimes, too, she and Lawrence sang German songs at the piano, and people passing by could hear them. It was all very touchy, and Lawrence at least was fully aware of the public's mistrust. One day when he and Frieda were basking on the beach, Frieda in an access of high spirits began dancing on the sand, her white scarf fluttering behind her.

"Stop it, stop it, you fool, you fool!" he shouted. "Can't you see they'll think that you're signalling to the enemy!"

No doubt they did think exactly that. Soon afterward when Frieda and Lawrence were walking home from a shopping visit to Penzance, a couple of coast guards halted them and accused Frieda of carrying a camera hidden in the old rucksack she used for such expeditions. Furiously and triumphantly Frieda brought out the suspicious object—a loaf of bread—but the men were not confounded: they kept on with their spying, and the villagers helped by watching whatever the Lawrences did. One night, when they were spending a weekend with Cecil Gray at Bosigran Castle, they had dined and were all three singing German songs when suddenly there came a loud pounding on the door. When Gray opened it, seven armed men walked in. They were muddy, Frieda noted, no doubt because they had been in the ditch outside the windows listening.

"You are showing a light," they said. And it proved to be true: his new housekeeper, just down from London, had not been careful in fastening her curtain, and its blowing in the wind had made the light flash on, off, on, off, in a highly questionable manner. The men insisted on searching the whole house before, with a final admonition, they departed. Frieda was of the opinion that Cecil Gray's uncle, an admiral, saved him from any more penalty than a stiff fine, but the consequences for her and Lawrence were graver. The visit to Bosigran came to an end; Lawrence went to Penzance for the day, while Frieda returned home. The minute she entered the cottage she knew someone had been there searching, and she hurried to the farm to find out if this was true. They said it was; two men had been asking for her. Next morning a small deputation came to see the Lawrences—a captain, two detectives, and the village policeman. They had with them an official order: the Lawrences must leave Cornwall within three days.

Frieda burst out with recriminations, but Lawrence hushed her. The iron of England had entered his soul again, said Frieda: "When we were turned out of Cornwall something changed in Lawrence for ever."

Where could they go? Garsington, of course, was now out of the question, and Lady Cynthia didn't have a house of her own. But Dollie Radford did, and Lawrence telegraphed to tell her what had happened and to ask if they could stay with her until they had located a permanent lodging in London. To her eternal credit, Mrs. Radford said that they could—to her credit, because she was afraid of what might happen to her for sheltering suspected spies. She need not have worried; the London authorities were not as sensitive as those in Cornwall. At any rate the Lawrences stayed only a night or so before finding another shelter in Richard Aldington's flat in Mecklenburgh Square.

Aldington wrote poetry and prose and was married to Hilda Doolittle, or H.D. as she signed herself, an American poet who was often called the first Imagist. They and Lawrence had met when Amy Lowell came to London in 1914 and organized the Imagist school. H.D.'s style was distinctive and had much effect on that of her contemporaries; Lawrence himself, as Aldington has justly said, was strongly influenced by it for a while.

Like so many dwelling places in London during the war, the Aldington flat was crowded. Another American woman, Dorothy Yorke, who for some reason was usually called Arabella, lived in the attic. Aldington was having an affair with her on the occasions that he came home on leave—he was in the army and spent most of the time in France at the front— and H.D., though not exactly complaisant about the arrangement, accepted it with reservations. Richard assured her that it wasn't serious, that she herself was his true love but that Arabella helped him to forget the strain and stress of war. H.D. was a tall, slender woman, carelessly beautiful. Years later she published a novel about the period, *Bid Me to Live*, really an accurate report of what happened, with only the names of the characters somewhat disguised. From it we learn of a typical Lawrence situation, beginning when Lawrence and Frieda arrived with their belongings and Aldington, his leave expired, departed at the same time.

Apparently the chief reason H.D. accepted her husband's behavior with composure was that she had been living an intense imaginary life with Lawrence. They had been corresponding; she sent him poems and cherished the long letters he sent in reply. Shortly after the novel opens, Aldington comes upon one of Lawrence's missives.

"What's this Orpheus that you've been writing for old Rico [Lorenzo]?" he asks in surprise.

"I wasn't exactly writing it for Rico," she replies.

"But she had . . ." the narrative continues; "it was Rico's pale face and the archaic Greek beard and the fire-blue eyes in the burnt-out face that she had seen, an Orpheus head. . . ."

Richard persisted: "What does Frederick [Lawrence] want, what does old Frederico want with you?"

And H.D. answered, "Well, he writes to everybody, his letters are around somewhere if I kept them, they're there in that stack of papers. . . ." But she knew they were not. "He's cerebral," she continued. "He has to write to someone."

She went on dreaming. It was no use talking to Richard, who was upstairs so often with Arabella. "Listen," he said, "it's perfectly clear; I love you, I desire *l'autre.*" It was perfectly clear.

H.D. went back to thinking of one of Lorenzo's letters in which he said, "We will go away together where the angels come down to earth." His flaming letters were no ordinary love letters, they were written to her in "pure being," he said. She reflected:

> It was not that she thought of Rico; but the fact that Rico wanted her, no matter how idealistically she might translate his letters, meant that there was something there, something that was wanted. Of course Rico did not really want her; he was harassed and distressed and he loved Elsa [Frieda], his great Prussian wife. He loved Elsa, yes, he said so; no, he did not say so. But it was now as if this cerebral contact had renewed her. She had not actually met Rico (he was in Cornwall) since the writing of the letter, *you are a living spirit in a living spirit city.* Yes, she was that.

> He had written other things she remembered, such as "Kick over your tiresome house of life."

Richard remained curious, asking questions.

"He came several times to the flat in Hampstead when you were out," H.D. told him in reply. "He watched me once peeling apples in one of those Spanish pottery bowls. . . ."

"What else?"

"Nothing else. He said he liked my Greek renderings better than Gilbert Murray; he said that there was a bite and sting in my writing—but he must have said that when we were all together. He sent me a cardboard box with some little lettuce-plants he had grown in his garden in Cornwall and some sea-pinks last summer. In a cardboard box."

"You didn't tell me about the sea-pinks and the lettuces."

"Didn't I? Well, he did."

After thinking it over a little, Richard asked her that if he didn't come back—well, did she love Lorenzo? No, said H.D., at least not at that minute. "He is part of the cerebral burning, part of the inspiration," she said.

It was at that point, or soon afterward, that the Lawrences themselves arrived. It was agreed that, with Aldington away, Arabella would come downstairs to sleep with H.D. while the Lawrences had her room. That evening there was a frenetically gay supper, and though Lorenzo shouted once at Frieda, "It's you, your fault, you damn Prussian," it was just Lorenzo's way; nobody took it amiss.

Next morning, with Richard gone, Frieda and Arabella went out shopping. (Frieda liked Arabella.) "I'll leave Frederico [Lorenzo] with you," said Frieda to H.D. as they left.

In the silence that followed their departure, Lawrence sat hunched up in H.D.'s armchair, looking discouraged. He had tried to find out from Dollie that morning if her Berkshire cottage was available, but she was out. H.D. waited expectantly for him to mention something about *them*, but he was silent. "The mud was still stuck to his rough ploughman boots, his corduroy trousers were tucked in at the tops. He had not even had time to shake, as it were, the dust off his feet. Cornwall was still with him. . . . They didn't seem to have anything to say to one another." H.D. thought of supper the night before when they had all been merry and she had sat between Lawrence and Frieda at the table. She wrote:

"Elsa [Frieda] is there," said Rico, "you are here. Elsa is there at my right hand," he said. "You are here," while Elsa went on placidly hemming the torn edge of an old jumper. Her work-bag spilled homely contents on the floor . . .

"You are there for all eternity, our love is written in blood for all eternity." . . . It was to be a perfect triangle, Elsa acquiesced.

"This will leave me free," she muttered in her German guttural, "for Vanio [Gray]."

Gray? H.D. had asked who he was and was told: a young composer who was coming from Cornwall to London for Christmas. Well, H.D. said to herself, Christmas was not so far off—but somehow the whole thing seemed too much, though Lorenzo really seemed to mean it: they could hardly live up to it, even though Lorenzo and Frieda had it all arranged between them. And now, alone with Lorenzo, she could think of nothing to say. As for him, he looked for a while at his knapsack, then rummaged in it and brought out a notebook. He dug in his pockets, found a pencil, and began scribbling. H.D. waited a moment and then, as he seemed absorbed, she walked over to the window and stood looking out.

When she turned and looked back at him, their eyes met, and

as if at a certain signal, she moved toward him; she edged the small chair toward his chair. She sat at his elbow, a child waiting for instruction. Now was the moment to answer his amazing proposal of last night, his "for all eternity." She put out her hand. Her hand touched his sleeve. He shivered, he seemed to move back, move away, like a hurt animal, there was something untamed, even the slight touch of her hand on his sleeve seemed to have annoyed him. Yet, last night, sitting there, with Elsa sitting opposite, he had blazed at her; those words had cut blood and lava-trail on this air. Last night, with the coffee-cups beside them on the little table, he had said "It is written in blood and fire for all eternity." Yet only a touch on his arm made him shiver away, hurt, like a hurt jaguar.

He was leopard, jaguar. It was not she who had started out to lure him. It was himself with his letters, and last night his open request for this relationship. Yet even this touch (not heavy on his sleeve) seemed to send some sort of repulsion through him. She drew back her hand. There were voices at the door.

Odd the way things turn out. Thus it was H.D. and not Frieda who was "left free" for Cecil Gray. Gray asked her to come back to Cornwall with him, to Bosigran.

"You [and Gray] are made for one another," Lawrence had said in one of his moments of irritability, and those words, like all his others, stayed in her mind. Arabella was trying to get Aldington to leave H.D. and marry her. Oh, well, thought H.D., and told Cecil she would go to Cornwall. Lawrence seemed shocked.

"You are really going to Cornwall?" Then he said, "Why don't you take our cottage? . . . It's not so very far from [Gray's]. He could come in every day to see you." He also said, "It would make a difference, don't you realise?"

No, she did not. She did not understand Lawrence. "Don't you realise," he said, "that this— This—I am not happy about this. You realise that."

H.D. went to Cornwall with Cecil Gray. She never did realize, as Lawrence put it, what had happened—that he and Frieda had only been playing their old game that evening, irritating each other at her expense. Martin Green has said that Lawrence was a flirt. We might go further and say that he was a tease.

"Friendship with Lawrence was essentially a one-way

traffic . . ." wrote Cecil Gray bitterly in his memoirs *Musical Chairs.*

Lawrence could not brook equals. One had to be a devoted disciple or he had no use for you. . . . I am naturally not so well qualified to speak of his relations with women; but from what I do know of them which is not inconsiderable, I am sure that they must have been equally unsatisfactory. Women admired him and cherished him for his genius and fame; they bathed and basked in the radiance of this reflected sunshine like beatific lizards—but for himself as a person they cared very little. He was definitely not attractive to women in himself, as apart from the seductive magic of his pen. His physical personality was puny and insignificant, his vitality low, and his sexual potentialities exclusively cerebral. There can be no possible doubt about that . . . It might not be true to say that Lawrence was literally and absolutely impotent— this, I am assured on medical authority, is a very rare physical condition—but I am certain that he was not very far removed from it."

And H.D. went on writing and writing to Lawrence, letters that she never sent.

# 10

## Cecily and Violet:
## "Attractive female disciples"

CECIL GRAY was not the only man who wondered vexedly what Lawrence had that made him so attractive to women, but Gray was probably the most honest in expressing his envy. In an angry outburst in his autobiography he wrote, "I am more than inclined to suspect that there was a certain element of sour grapes in my denunciation of his acceptance of adoration and homage from a worshipping circle of attractive female disciples, whom Frieda Lawrence had painted for me in glowing and slightly venomous colours."

Even Cecil Gray, however, would have admitted that there was nothing particularly enviable about Lawrence's life during the year that followed his expulsion from Cornwall; both he and Frieda suffered deeply from financial and emotional insecurity. In the autumn of 1917, it must have seemed that the war was going to last forever and there was nothing they could do with themselves as long as it went on—nothing, that is, but throw themselves on the mercy of friends. Dollie Radford had taken a risk and let them live in her London house; now she was called on to take a bigger one in giving them permission to occupy her daughter's country hideout in Berkshire. For some time she hesitated. There was the danger of official interference, and there was also the fact that Margaret

Radford had a prior claim to the place. While Dollie thought it over the Lawrences simply waited for her decision—after all, there was nothing else they could do.

Nothing, that is to say, except see their old friends, and Cynthia Asquith had a story about that. One day in London, lunching with Lawrence, she mentioned that she was going on afterward for a sitting in Augustus John's studio, where he was painting her portrait. Lawrence, who always had a good opinion of his own painting, pricked up his ears. He had never met John, but he also thought himself a good critic of art, and now he announced that he would accompany Lady Cynthia to the studio to see for himself the work of England's foremost portraitist. Perhaps unwisely, she agreed. The men were introduced to each other, Lady Cynthia assumed her pose, and John started to work, while Lawrence strolled about the studio examining the paintings that hung on the walls or stood stacked on the floor. In her memoirs Lady Cynthia told what happened.

"Then, like a clock rustily clearing its throat to strike, he [Lawrence] muttered, 'Mortuus est. Mortuus est,' several times. Gathering volume, his voice became a tolling bell. Suddenly, raising his head, he summed up the situation with the sepulchral utterance, 'Let the DEAD PAINT THE DEAD!' . . . John showed wonderful tolerance of this curious behavior." So, obviously, did Cynthia Asquith herself—but then she was used to being scolded, however lovingly, by Lawrence, in whose eyes she appeared rich as well as privileged. Though by the standards of her world she and her husband were poor, to Lawrence she seemed to lead a frivolous, glamorous life, and it gave him revengeful pleasure to scold her for it. As for his opinion of John's work, it was not the first time Lawrence had sorely embarrassed people by attacking artists. Before his break with Lady Ottoline she had urged him to look at the paintings of the brilliant young Duncan Grant, and to everyone's resultant dismay, Lawrence did so: that time, too, he disapproved.

At last, toward the end of the year, came Mrs. Radford's

decision. She said that Lawrence and Frieda could live in Chapel
Farm Cottage at Hermitage, in Berkshire, on condition that
whenever Margaret wanted to use the place the Lawrences
were to get out and stay out until the premises were free again.
It was an uneasy arrangement that was to cause much resentment. We might think that Lawrence and Frieda were unreasonable in objecting to this provision—after all, whose house
was it?—but those were the harsh facts, and they had nowhere else to go. They accepted. In ordinary times the so-called
cottage would not have been considered a prize piece of real
estate: it was really half of a double house, the other portion
of which was occupied by a family named Brown. After
Christmas at Ripley in Derbyshire, where Lawrence's sister Ada
Clarke was living, the Lawrences went to Hermitage.

Soon Lawrence was complaining that the cottage was
"cold, a little comfortless," but he and Frieda made friends
with the Browns next door and established cordial relations
with their next nearest neighbors, two girls who were struggling
to maintain Grimsbury Farm just down the road. From these
young women, Cecily Lambert and Violet Monk, Lawrence
got the idea for his story "The Fox," which Miss Lambert, or
Mrs. Minchin as she became, resented very much, since in it
she was represented as a peevish Lesbian. But that was all to
come: in the early days the Lawrences and the girls at the farm
got on splendidly. A snapshot taken then by Cecily shows
Frieda standing with her husband before the farmhouse door-
way, cheerful and fat in light blouse and very full, indeed
copious, checked skirt. The checked fabric impressed a number
of people; at least three of them have written about it. Next to
her Lawrence, who had been ill at Ripley, looks painfully thin
and fragile.

In addition to providing the photograph, Cecily also wrote
her impressions for biographer Nehls. When she first saw him,
she said, Lawrence was a most astounding spectacle, "a tall,
very slender creature clad in drainpipe khaki trousers, light

shirt, scarlet tie, and what appeared, in the distance, to be a blue dressing jacket, but on closer acquaintance turned out to be a butcher blue linen coat."

Above this garment was the reddest beard Cecily had ever seen, decorating a gaunt white face with penetrating, deep blue eyes. "A shock of mousey blonde hair [was] topped with a white floppy child's hat of cotton drill. Following a few yards behind was a very plump, heavily built woman, with strong features and blonde hair. The woman had yellowish eyes— "cat's eyes," the girls were to hear Lawrence call them—"and in her bold style was quite handsome," wrote Cecily. "She was dressed in a very full blue-and-white plaid skirt and a linen coat similar to Mr. Lawrence's which afterwards we were told was copied and tailored by him." (Catherine Carswell too saw those blue coats and mentioned that the Lawrences were "justly proud" of them.)

"With this she wore a very wide brimmed straw hat, devoid of trimming but which suited her," Cecily continued. "She was hurrying along, panting and rather disheveled, trying vainly to catch up with the man in front, who sped along on his toes almost as if he were being propelled by an invisible force and appearing as if he were trying to escape from the woman. This was not the case, however; the Lawrences were merely trying to catch the last post, which was explained soon afterward when the strange couple came to call on the girls.

Cecily did not envy them their cottage, which she called a tiny, bare sort of place; she was even less tempted by it when she and her friend learned of the inconvenient arrangement according to which the Lawrences had to evacuate the house whenever Margaret Radford arrived. In fact, the Lawrences ultimately took refuge in the farmhouse when this happened. Nor were Cecily and Violet pleased on the first afternoon when they had to be hospitable at such short notice and serve tea to the strangers. Even dishing up plain bread and butter, as they did, meant more than merely supplying food. Busy as they were, it was a nuisance to change their mucky clothes and neglect pressing duties for several hours. But the couple's charm, (especially, one suspects, Lawrence's), overcame their misgivings and they gladly accepted a return invitation to dinner at Chapel Farm Cottage.

Cecily remembered that things were rather topsy-turvy that evening; Frieda entertained the guests while Lawrence cooked, and this struck Violet and herself as unusual, though in time they were to get used to the arrangement. It was a delicious dinner—"rich stew with mushrooms and potatoes smothered with butter"—Lawrence dished it up right out of the pan, country fashion, talking animatedly the while. All went well until dessert was served—"toffee prunes," hard as stones and impossible to eat. They were Frieda's responsibility, and she had not known enough to soak the fruit first; she had simply sugared them and put them into the oven. Lawrence was very angry with his wife and there was a typical quarrel then and there.

"Frieda was a good raconteur," wrote Cecily, and was happiest telling amusing stories of the Lawrences' various adventures on their travels. She was quite happy to leave all the household chores to Lawrence, since she hated work of any kind. "I can see her now on that evening, sitting back on a low arm chair, purring away like a lazy cat and shewing a great deal of plump leg above the knee encased in calico bloomers probably made by D. H. himself. She was not permitted to wear silk or dainties."

Certainly not—if Lawrence had had his way none of the women he knew would have worn pretty underthings. Once when he came on Cecily making crêpe-de-chine undies for herself, he scolded her vigorously for using material that he denounced as "prostitutey." Cecily was startled and indignant even then, and her indignation increased vastly in later years when she read some of Lawrence's books. At that time she didn't know of Lawrence's reputation and had never heard of the fuss over *The Rainbow*, but her father, who sometimes visited his daughter, was better informed, and he objected to her friendship with such a man. He said that Cecily should put Lawrence out of the house—for the interview apparently took place while the Lawrences were staying at Grimsbury Farm. Cecily refused. She said it was not for her father to dictate to her. She liked the Lawrences because they brought a bit of gaiety into what was a hard life.

In May the Radfords announced that they would want the cottage for an extended stay in the country. This time Lawrence and Frieda were prepared and had acquired another cottage at Middleton-by-Wirksworth near Ripley, "a smallish bungalow," as Lawrence described it to Catherine Carswell, "—with rather pretty little grounds." It was Ada who arranged the lease and paid the rent, so it had the advantage of actually belonging to them, without interruption, until the following spring, but there were drawbacks. They didn't really like being so far away from London, where so many of their friends were and where Frieda could see the children from time to time without objection from Ernest. On the other hand, in Middleton Lawrence's old friends Willie and Sallie Hopkin were within easy reach, and people came to stay: Arabella, for one, spent a weekend at Mountain Cottage, as it was called. That summer Lawrence actually got paid work to do, when the Oxford University Press asked him to write a textbook on European history. When it was finished the embarrassed editor had to suggest that the writer sign the book with a pen name. Oddly enough, Lawrence did not resent this. He quite understood, he replied, that a book meant for young people could not appear under the name of a man whose work had been suppressed for immorality. In fact, he himself supplied the pen name: Lawrence H. Davison.

With what Lawrence often referred to as "the poverty" thus alleviated, he was happy to accept an invitation from the

Carswells that summer of 1918 to share a holiday in a house lent to Donald and Catherine in the Forest of Dean in Gloucestershire. Frieda and Lawrence were in fine spirits when their friends met them at the railway station, Frieda smiling broadly and exclaiming as always, said Catherine, and Lawrence like a boy let out of school. He was wearing a remarkable outfit: a badly shrunken green-and-red striped blazer which exposed inches of wrist, and an equally shrunken pair of trousers showing a considerable length of ankle. He cheerfully announced to Catherine that they were his only trousers: he washed them at night, he said, and let them dry as he slept. Espadrilles, worn without socks, and an old panama hat finished off the costume.

"With this strange attire and his beard he attracted some local notice," said Catherine, while Frieda "vied with her husband in the inexpensive gaiety of her dress. She wore the largest and brightest of cotton checks, and when out together we attracted, to Lawrence's displeased surprise, something of the attention that might have been accorded to a travelling circus." But was Lawrence's surprise really displeased? He once told Cecily Lambert that he *liked* people to look at him.

By the time the Lawrences got back to Mountain Cottage, it was early autumn, when, according to Murry, "the end of the war was in the air." If that was so, it had no effect on the authorities, who even in remote Derbyshire retained their grip on Lawrence and resented his lack of participation in the war effort. On September 24 he wrote angrily in a letter to a friend that he had to go up for yet another physical examination, and two days later, writing to Lady Cynthia, he said that he had duly reported to headquarters: "These accursed people have put me in Grade 3." This meant that he was still unfit for military duty but could do sedentary work. "It kills me with speechless fury to be pawed by them," he added. "They shall *not* touch me again—such filth."

Soon afterward Lawrence and Frieda came to London on a visit and took rooms not far from where the Murrys, now legally married at last, were living. Katherine Mansfield's health was steadily deteriorating and the doctors had told Jack that she had at most only five years more of life, but he kept this knowledge to himself. Lawrence often dropped in to see Katherine, possibly because both he and Frieda had had the flu and he was taking things easy while he recuperated. The old quarrels between households in Cornwall were completely forgotten; Lawrence enjoyed being with Katherine and she was again wholly charmed by him.

"Oh, there is something so lovable about him and his eagerness, his passionate eagerness for life—that is what one loves so," she wrote in her journal.

The London visit stretched out for some weeks. Because Frieda's usually robust health was slow in coming back after her illness, when she and Lawrence heard from the Radfords that the Hermitage cottage was again available they took it for a while and left Mountain Cottage empty, telling each other that Berkshire's climate was better for them. Thus it came about that they happened to be in London on November 11, Armistice Day, and Bunny Garnett met them there at a celebration party. It was the first time he had seen them in three years, and in the general happy excitement he naturally expected a warm reception. Lawrence, however, merely nodded to him, said "So you're here," and went on talking to someone else. Bunny would have felt really brushed off if Frieda had not given him a happy squeeze. A while later Lawrence was more ready to talk to young Garnett; in fact, he orated, and people began gathering around to listen. There in the middle of the jubilant crowd Lawrence took the gloomiest view. Did all these people really think, he asked, that the war was over and everything was going to be all right? If so, the more fools they. The war wasn't over.

"The hate and evil is greater now than ever," declared Lawrence the prophet. "Very soon war will break out again and overwhelm you. It makes me sick to see you rejoicing like a butterfly in the last rays of the sun before the winter. The crowd outside thinks that Germany is crushed forever. But the Germans will soon rise again." He probably had to lift his voice to be heard above the happy din out in the streets. "Europe is done for," insisted Lawrence; "England most of all the countries. This war isn't over."

He went on and on in a tone of "sombre joy" at being the only person in the room who was not celebrating. Bunny decided that he had had enough; after the party he made no attempt ever to meet either Lawrence or Frieda again.

But whatever her husband said, to Frieda the Armistice was a joyful occasion because she would be able to see her people again. She had never really lost touch with the Von Richthofens. In the comparatively permissive days of the First World War it had been possible for her to communicate with them by way of Switzerland; that was how she had received notification of the old Baron's death. She knew that her mother was now living in an old ladies' home for aristocratic females in Baden-Baden called the Ludwig-Wilhelm-Stift: she knew, too, that Else was in Munich. Now, of course, there was much more information. Soon after the Armistice came the news that there had been a revolution in Bavaria, and Frieda was amazed to hear that her brother-in-law Edgar Jaffe was Finance Minister of the new government there. Though he and Else had not lived together for years, Else being the mistress of Max Weber, they had never been divorced and were on good terms. It was hard to imagine quiet, self-effacing Edgar holding a prominent position like that, but before Frieda could really take it in everything was over for the Bavarian government, when assassins killed the President and a deputy, and wounded the Minister of the Interior. To be sure, Jaffe escaped injury, but the incident worried Frieda on account of Else and the others. She felt she must go and see for herself how things were going.

While she waited for her passport she fretted and sent one parcel after another of food and clothing. Lawrence too was feverishly eager to get out of England after feeling like a captive for so long. However sincerely he detested war, its end left him feeling empty. Now that he no longer felt threatened by having to enter some sort of national service he fell prey to earlier obsessions, especially the need to earn money. There was also the more immediate if comparatively trivial duty of making his peace with Ada. She had gone to all the trouble and expense of taking that cottage at Middleton for them, and then they had slipped away and taken up residence in Berkshire again, leaving the Midlands bungalow empty. Ada was angry. It was no use, Lawrence knew, telling her the truth—that the climate of Middleton, like Ripley's, was bad for him. No, he knew he and Frieda would have to go back and use up that lease, which would not run out until the following April, or have Ada for an enemy the rest of their lives. The affair was settled by compromise: Lawrence went back and Frieda stayed on in London until Christmas, using the children as an excuse.

It must have been resentment at his wife for thus neglecting him that started Lawrence brooding again over their endless struggle. Later in November, returning a book by Jung to Katherine Mansfield, he wrote in an accompanying letter, "I do think a woman must yield some sort of precedence to a man, and he must take this precedence. I do think men must go ahead absolutely in front of their women, without turning round to ask for permission or approval from their women. Consequently the women must follow as it were unquestioningly. I can't help it, I believe this. Frieda doesn't. Hence our fight." But domestic peace in one direction, at least, was preserved: Ada was no longer angry.

With Christmas and the family party out of the way, Lawrence felt refreshed and ready to think of the future. Gone were the gloomy reflections of Armistice Day when he wrote to Amy Lowell saying that they must prepare for the new year. He had seen Richard Aldington in London, he reported, looking very fit and looking forward to peace and freedom as soon as he was demobbed.

"Hilda also is in town," said Lawrence, "—not so very well. She is going to have another child, it appears." H.D. had lost one child before the war. "I hope she will be all right. Perhaps she can get more settled, for her nerves are very shaken: and perhaps the child will soothe her and steady her. I hope it will."

His chief aim in writing seems to have been to sound out Miss Lowell as to the advisability of going to America. He wanted to be in a new country, he said, but Frieda preferred going to see her people, so they would probably visit Germany first, as soon as the treaty was signed. For himself, he felt drawn to America. Amy Lowell did not rise to this fly, perhaps because it was merely a hint, but time soon showed that she didn't think it a good idea for Lawrence to cross the Atlantic.

January and February in the Midlands nearly settled the matter: Lawrence caught the flu again and almost died of it. Convalescent, he thought no more of the United States but played with the idea of going to Palestine with Dr. David Eder, who was working in the Zionist movement. No doubt the thought of the Near Eastern desert was tempting at the time. But the lease on the Derbyshire cottage expired at last, and the Lawrences joyfully rushed back to Chapel Farm Cottage, free at last of the onus. On May 26 Lawrence wrote again to Amy Lowell to tell her that the American publisher Ben Huebsch, who was going to put out a book of his poems, was of the opinion that Lawrence should do a lecture tour in the States. Lawrence was rather attracted by the idea. Admittedly, he said, he wasn't much of a lecturer, but no doubt he could do it if he had to, and he thought of going over in August or September, passports permitting. Frieda would follow after, once she had done her filial duty in Germany. Only one thing made him pause, said Lawrence. He heard from Huebsch that Amy Lowell had said something about Boston not being a good place for D. H. Lawrence to lecture in. Why had she said that?

"Are you shy of me?—a little doubtful of the impression I shall, or should make?" he asked.

Such a direct question demands a direct reply, and Miss Lowell gave it. Emphatically she said that Boston was not yet

ready for D. H. Lawrence; of all American cities Boston was
least likely to welcome a man who used such frank language,
even though he was a genius. Miss Lowell explained that she held
no brief for her own home town; she was ashamed of the fact,
but there it was. She told him that even *Sons and Lovers,* that
superb and comparatively discreet novel, was kept hidden away
by those in charge of the Athenaeum Library in what was called
the scruple room, and was handed out only to privileged readers
—which, said Miss Lowell, should serve to give Lawrence an
idea of what he was up against. No, Boston was not the place for
him. She felt so strongly on the subject that she wrote not only
to Lawrence but to Frieda, saying so, and they listened and took
heed—for the time being.

While they waited and waited for passports, things started
to move again in the literary world. Money actually began to
dribble in from this source and that. *The Rainbow,* somewhat
expurgated, had been published in America, and there were
several books of poems to be accounted for. All in all, Lawrence's agent in America, J. B. Pinker, was able to send him a
check for fifty-five pounds. Then Eddie Marsh, settling up the
late Rupert Brooke's affairs, told Lawrence that he had come in
for a legacy from the poet of twenty pounds more (though in
fact Marsh was using his own discretion to distribute the
money), and this was added to the budget.

Spring wore on. Jack Murry came once to see if he could
find a house in the neighborhood for Katherine—he couldn't—
and the Carswells brought the baby for Whitsun weekend. On
July 1, writing to Lady Cynthia, Lawrence said, "It was a great
mistake that we did not clear out in 1915, when we had those
other passports," especially as Thomas Cook, the travel agents,
now said that they didn't have a chance of getting documents
until the treaty was well and truly signed, and, as Lawrence
wrote Catherine, God knew when that would be. Still, little by
little England climbed to her feet again. In London, for instance,
the Asquiths were able to get back into their own house, which

had been let for four years, and Lawrence came to see them there.

Striding up and down our small drawing-room, Lawrence, in one of his moments of sudden tension, took a violent aversion to one piece of furniture [wrote Cynthia]. It was a not-very-good but fairly harmless little French table. Temporarily, however, it became to Lawrence the symbol of what he called the "Would be," the self-consciously pretentious. And, indeed, such was the persuasive force of his eloquence, that whilst he inveighed against the offending object, it did begin to look terribly trivial and strainedly elegant. We never liked that poor little table again. In fact before long we sold it. Inflamed by one table, Lawrence railed against all the "furniture of life" with which, he insisted, humanity was over-occupied—caring far too much for material objects, far too little for the essence of human relationships. "Come away!" he shrilled out, looking at me as though I stood in immediate deadly peril. "Come away. Free yourself at once, or before you know where you are, your furniture will be on top instead of under you." This admonition gave me a nightmare in which I was trampled to death by the legs of my own tables and chairs.

Lawrence's advice to Lady Cynthia to get away, considering the fact that he himself, for want of a passport, was unable to move out of the country in spite of many plans to go here, there, and everywhere, need not have been taken too seriously, but then he was always upbraiding her for something or other, usually for going out too much. She would be much better, he said, if only she would move to the country and do her own housework. It was with a natural feeling of triumph, therefore, that she was able at last to announce to him that she had a good job. She had never been able to do anything better, in the past, than work as a dress model, but now she was hired by J. M. Barrie as his secretary. So there!

"I wondered what sort of a rococo job you had found!"

was all Lawrence said as a retort, but he was impressed in spite of himself, for, unlike many contemporaries, he admired Sir James's writing. It will be remembered that he once told Jessie Chambers to read *Sentimental Tommy* and *Tommy and Grizel* if she wanted to understand his behavior. Moreover, Barrie had read *Sons and Lovers*, and liked it, and had written to tell Lawrence so. Everything considered, it was natural that Lady Cynthia should arrange a meeting between the two authors. Lawrence went to call on Sir James but, unfortunately, he took Frieda with him. I say "unfortunately" because of what Frieda immediately did.

"She never could understand any embarrassment about money or see any reason why it should not be transferred from a well-filled to an empty pocket," explained Lady Cynthia, adding, "—had the full purse been her own, her views would have been the same." This, as a matter of fact, is not necessarily true, but at any rate, Frieda said, "How do you do, Sir Barrie. I hear you make an income of fifty thousand a year. Why shouldn't you give Lorenzo enough money to pay for our passage to Australia?" Australia being one of the places Lorenzo said he would like to escape to.

It was the last time the Lawrences and Barrie ever met.

Otherwise, however, the summer was as busy a time socially as the Lawrences had ever experienced. Douglas Goldring, a writer and editor who had known of Lawrence since the days of the *English Review*, now met him personally through Koteliansky. Kot and Barbara Low, he commented, devoted themselves to Lawrence as if to a Messiah, so Goldring was taken aback the first time Lawrence said to him of these fervent friends, "These Russian Jews are so *heavy*."

Wrote Goldring, "He certainly dispensed with 'loyalty' in casual conversation, and no doubt he found them, as at times he found his wife and, indeed, all his close associates, irritating. Few people who knew him were lucky enough to escape occasionally getting on Lawrence's nerves. He constantly got on his own nerves. All the same, Lawrence was not *fundamentally* disloyal."

A week end the Goldrings spent at Hermitage was an unforgettable experience:

> The way he kept his Prussian wife, Frieda, "in her place" was slightly embarrassing at first. There was a painful moment just before the midday meal on Sunday. The potatoes were cooking in an open pot on the fire and Lawrence was watching them. Suddenly Frieda made some remark which he found particularly exasperating. His blue eyes crackled with rage, his red beard bristled, his hand shot out to the potatoes. Only our presence, I am certain, restrained him from "saying it with missiles." But in a few moments, the storm was over.

A high point of the day was to be the arrival of Lawrence's aunt and uncle-in-law, the Krenkows, for lunch. Lawrence, now in high spirits, confided to Goldring, when they went together to the pub to fetch beer for the meal, that he intended to borrow money from his uncle, to finance his and Frieda's newly projected passage to Italy. Lunch passed pleasantly and the Krenkows invited Lawrence to dinner that evening at their inn. Everyone in the cottage wished him luck as he set out, because everyone was in on the secret, and when he returned a few hours later, triumphantly waving a check for ten pounds, they all rejoiced.

"When I came downstairs the next morning," said Goldring, "I found Lawrence and Frieda singing South German folk songs at the tops of their voices while they laid the breakfast table. Life with Lawrence could never be *dull*, but I doubt if he would have found any Englishwoman with the nervous solidity to stay the course. Voluble, full-bosomed, Prussian Frieda was built to weather storms. Like a sound ship, broad in the beam, slow but seaworthy, she could stand any amount of buffeting."

Goldring added that Frieda doubtless found the Von Richthofen card a useful one to play. Unlike Cecil Gray and many others, the editor found Lawrence "less of a snob than most people," but it was obvious, even so, that the fact that Frieda came of a "baronial" family was not lost on her husband: "Indeed, he never seems to have discovered how little it really meant," said Goldring.

August arrived, but the passports did not, and the Radfords in their annoying way continued to borrow their own house from time to time. When this happened the Lawrences usually moved in on the Grimsbury Farm girls. Not that the girls really minded, though Violet might have complained a little. Like Goldring, Cecily felt that one could never be dull in Lawrence's company, or Frieda's either.

"They were so full of fun and life," she wrote, "and I regret that we were so busy and had so little time to spend with them. They occupied two bedrooms at Grimsbury Farm, and when I suggested to Frieda that it would ease things if they shared one, her reply was that she did not wish to be too much married. What that implied I have no idea."

Chattering confidentially with the girls, Frieda of course told them how she missed her children, and said that she longed to have a child by Lawrence. In Cecily's opinion, this sounded faintly unreasonable: after all, Frieda was several years older than Lawrence, who seemed old to her; Frieda was too old for children, one would think. In any case, she reflected, it seemed doubtful that an infant would really have been welcome to Lawrence considering the way he and Frieda lived; they were very poor and Lawrence hated staying in one place very long. At any moment he might have the urge to move on.

"He hated possessions and roots," commented Cecily, "and Frieda craved for a home and solidity."

At first there were difficulties with the guests. The minute they moved in Frieda went to bed for a few days and expected to be waited on, and most of the burden of taking care of her fell on her husband, since, said Cecily, "We were far too busy and overworked to do any nursing, except in an emergency, which certainly this was not. To this day I can see D. H. in a raging temper, carrying a brimming chamber [pot] down to the front garden and emptying it over our flower beds which rather horrified us, to say the least of it although there was little else he could do. The sanitation was of the most primitive."

But in spite of such drawbacks, Cecily was fascinated by the life-style of her guests: "The bohemian life of the Lawrences appealed to me, and D. H.'s desire to avoid being cluttered with possessions, free as air and untrammeled, excited my sympathies," she confessed. This is easy to understand in a girl whose existence was cabined and confined like hers, tied down to the unyielding routine of a working farm. It is to her credit that she seems never to have pondered the other side of the coin or reflected that if it had not been for "trammeled" people like herself, the Lawrences would have had no shelter, no beds or chairs in which to be comfortable. No, she envied them purely.

"Frieda I thought did not realize her luck in being able to go all over the world with all plans made for her," said Cecily. Once, it seems, Frieda begged Lawrence to let her buy red curtains, and he was furious. Less than fifty pounds in the bank, he said explosively to Miss Lambert, and his wife wanted red curtains! His attitude was natural enough, said Cecily, considering that he must have felt always to be racing against time: "So much must be accomplished before the dreaded bronchials gave up the fight." But it was hard on Frieda, she told herself; every woman really needs roots.

Besides, she said, Lawrence "had a diabolical temper in keeping with his red beard," and when it burst out the intensity of it was shattering. Once at the farm Frieda borrowed Violet's sewing machine and broke it in some way—nothing serious, said Cecily, but Violet was intensely careful of her things, and anything that happened to them, as in this case, appeared to her a major calamity. The mishap was mentioned in Lawrence's presence, with terrible results. He blew up at Frieda. He told her she was lazy and useless, sitting around while the other women did all the work, and then he ordered her to scrub the kitchen floor. As Cecily explained, the floor was large and made of well-worn bricks; it was very hard work to scour it, and the girls expected Frieda to rebel. Instead, much to their amazement she burst into tears and got down to work, though not meekly, "fetching a pail of water and sloshing around with a floor cloth in a bending position (although he had told her to kneel), bitterly resentful at having to do such a menial task quite beneath the daughter of a baron, at the same time hurling every insult she could conjure up at D. H., calling him an uncouth lout, etc."

It seemed to Cecily that Lawrence loved to humiliate Frieda, and the girl was surprised that Frieda should listen to his abuse or obey his orders at all. On this occasion the quarrel was not easily resolved. Frieda left Grimsbury Farm as soon as the floor was scrubbed, and went back to the Radfords' cottage. No doubt it had recently fallen vacant again and she saw her chance to make a protest. Lawrence, however, stayed on, finishing a book which Violet was typing for him. And it didn't really matter at that point who stayed where; now that the war was over the girls contemplated giving up their arduous life on the farm and were winding up their affairs. Also, at just the right moment the Lawrences' passports arrived, and smaller matters like the quarrel over the kitchen floor were swallowed in the excitement of preparation for going away.

In October Frieda left for Germany. Lawrence was still in the cottage when Cecily, passing by, stopped to say good-bye and found him dressed in city clothes, the first time she had ever seen him like that. She was surprised and impressed. "He looked the well-dressed and smart man-about-town and exceedingly handsome," she recorded, "striking in fact with his red beard (groomed) and his intense blue eyes." The girls never saw Frieda and Lawrence again, though they did not lose touch; several times Lawrence wrote to them from abroad, asking them to join in one of his plans. Once he suggested that they all meet in Mexico, but it didn't happen.

"How dull it was when he had gone," Cecily wrote. "Always there was some inspiration." Clearly she regretted the end of that chapter in her life, even though it had meant such hard work; she was still disconsolate over the loss of Lawrence as a neighbor in spite of the fact that she had made a happy marriage—and though Lawrence had betrayed her with that wicked story, "The Fox," in which Violet and a lover kill her with a falling tree, and which she never quite forgave.

Frieda had been moping after her family for nearly a year, and Lawrence did nothing to hinder her departure, though he himself refused to go; he saw her off at Harwich, and he was certainly writing of Freida at that moment when he said of Harriet Somers in *Kangaroo*, "She had a look of almost vindictive triumph, and almost malignant love, as the train drew out."

Afterward he went to meet Richard Aldington to discuss Chapel Farm Cottage, the complicated tenancy of which Aldington proposed to take over. He himself, he told his friend, intended to go straight to Italy. Deliberately or not, he seems to have failed to add that Frieda was going to meet him there after she had finished with her German visit, and Aldington naturally concluded that the Lawrences had split up at last, an ending which he considered regrettable. As he explained, he felt that a splendid love like theirs should never die, and in the light of later events, he admitted that he could have spared himself that sorrow, but certainly Lawrence had given him the idea that he didn't care if he never saw Frieda again. It is hard not to come to the conclusion that Lawrence meant to give that impression, out of anger with his wife for deserting him even for a short time. Just another case of Lawrence losing his temper.

In the meantime, poor Frieda was hardly leading the life of Riley. The journey to Germany was extremely uncomfortable. Her mother was living with the other old ladies in comfortless conditions: food was strictly rationed, and all shops and public buildings closed down at sunset, to save fuel and lighting. Shocked and grieved, Frieda stayed with the old

Baroness for a month and learned at last to be friends with her mother: no doubt the Baron's death helped to remove the barriers. It was to be a source of happiness in later years that Lawrence should have grown so fond of the old lady—but then he always did like elderly women, because they reminded him of his mother. Sometimes he ganged up with the Baroness in his constant warfare with Frieda. When he complained about her daughter, the Baroness von Richthofen would say, "I know her longer than you, I know her."

Frieda met Lawrence by prearrangement in Florence, a bit thinner, as Lawrence mentioned in a letter to Amy Lowell, but no doubt she rapidly regained her normal weight. "Katherine Farquhar was a handsome woman of forty, no longer slim, but attractive in her soft, full feminine way," he wrote later in the short story entitled "The Border Line" about a German woman living in England who revisits her native country after the war. "The French porters ran round her, getting a voluptuous pleasure from merely carrying her bags." In her memoirs Frieda tells of how she descended from the Florence train at the ungodly hour of 4 A.M., and Lawrence immediately took her on a drive because, he said, he had to show her the town.

"We went in an open carriage, I saw the pale crouching Duomo and in the thick moonmist the Giotto tower disappeared at the top into the sky. The Palazzo Vecchio with Michelangelo's David and all the statues of men, we passed. 'This is a men's town,' I said, 'Not like Paris, where all statues are women.'"

One of their first projects was to keep the promise made by Lawrence to an Englishwoman friend and explore the possibilities of a house she knew of in the Abruzzi Mountains near Monte Cassino. She had thought of living there, but she had no idea what it was like, so Frieda and Lawrence traveled down in the cold weather of December. They found the place, Picinisco, "a bit staggeringly primitive," as Lawrence wrote to the friend on December 16. To get to the house they had crossed "a great stony river bed, then an icy river on a plank," then climbed "unfootable paths," an ass carrying their baggage behind them. The walk was about two miles long, uphill. There was no furniture but beds, no floor covering, no crockery but one teaspoon, one saucer, two cups, a plate, and two glasses. Altogether it was so violently uncomfortable that Lawrence played with the idea of making it livable for Frieda and himself . . . but no, that sort of thing could wait; he was not yet ready to settle down, even so picturesquely. Frieda must have heaved a sigh of relief. It was his plan, instead, to travel to places in and near Italy and write travel books, thus earning his way to further countries still—even Australia. After four days of Abruzzi they surrendered and fled to Capri, where they could feel warm again.

Here they stayed two months, luxuriating in warmth and beauty, though they thought Capri very small and much too gossipy. Lawrence found an old acquaintance in the person of Norman Douglas, whom he had known in the *English Review* days, and, through Douglas, made the acquaintance of Maurice Magnus, a "European-American" (as Harry Moore described him) who hung around after Douglas and made the best of all opportunities. Magnus attached himself to Lawrence, borrowed money from him, and was generally a nuisance. He annoyed Frieda very much, but his character could not fail to fascinate Lawrence. Altogether, life in Capri was eccentric but pleasant. With other novelists Lawrence spent a lot of time talking about a projected trip to the South Seas; in the end, as one of the troupe remarked, he was the only one who actually got there.

Lawrence had not thawed out very long in the Mediterranean sun when—out of who knows what twinge of pain, what sinking of the stomach, what cataclysm of irritation—he flared out at, of all persons, Katherine Mansfield. The ailing Katherine had tried the climate on the Italian Riviera without satisfaction and was now in France, in Menton. It was early in February that Lawrence wrote to her an infamous letter, most of which has not survived. She wrote to Jack Murry:

Lawrence sent me a letter today. He spat in my face and threw filth at me and said: "I loathe you. You revolt me stewing in your consumption. . . . The Italians were quite right to have nothing to do with you" and a great deal more. Now I do beseech you, if you are my man, to stop defending him after that and never to crack him up in the paper. *Be proud!* In the same letter he said his final opinion of you was that you were "a dirty little worm."

Murry replied immediately in satisfactory terms, and Katherine, somewhat calmer, sent him another letter:

I wrote to Lawrence: "I detest you for having dragged this disgusting reptile across all that has been." When I got his letter I *saw* a reptile, *felt* a reptile—and the desire to hit him was so dreadful that I knew if ever I met him I must go away *at once*. I could not be in the same room or house, he is somehow filthy. I never had such a feeling about a human being. Oh, when I read your reply do you know I *kissed* it. . . . But you must hit him when you see him. There's nothing else to do.

"I am very sick of Capri," Lawrence was writing at about the same time to Catherine Carswell: "it is a stewpot of semi-literary cats." He could not bear it any more, and on February 25, 1920, he went to Sicily in search of somewhere else to live. He found the Villa Fontana Vecchia near Taormina, "a nice big house, with fine rooms and a handy kitchen . . ." he wrote to a friend in Florence. "It seems so peaceful and still and the earth is sappy, and I like the strong Saracen element in the people here."

The pattern was set, the transplantation complete. Thereafter Lawrence and Frieda were never to live in England again. When they did visit it they stopped for only a short time, like tourists. But then one might say that they were tourists wherever they were, as Lawrence's travel books can testify.

# *11*

# *Mary: "The elegant one of the company"*

FROM NOW ON it becomes possible to keep better track of Lawrence's woman friends, because there are fewer of them among the new faces. One does not know exactly why, unless it is because at this point he embarked on the series of restless journeys that were to keep him on the road most of the time and ended only with the last months of ill health. Perhaps there was simply no time to collect many new admirers, though of course there were some.

Life at the Villa Fontana Vecchia was fun for Frieda, who found herself at peace after many uprootings. They were living in a house they could call their own, with no danger of sudden summonses from the Radfords and no more forced sojourns in Derbyshire, suffering cold after cold after cold. Lawrence was in a better temper, working hard and earning money. If Frieda had still wanted red curtains he might even have bought her some, but curtains were hardly necessary in the Sicilian countryside.

"The sun rose straight on our beds in the morning, we had roses all winter and we lived the rhythm of a simple life. . . . Eating, washing up, cleaning the floor and getting water from the trough near the wall," she wrote. Housekeeping was not hard; they had old Grazia to do the shopping, though you had to watch her when it came to paying bills. ("She can rook me a little, but not too much," the thrifty Lawrence would say.) Frieda even learned to cook at last, probably because she didn't have to do it now. She actually enjoyed it.

This is not to say they stayed at home and met nobody. Lawrence was Lawrence, inveterate sightseer and incurably gregarious, and he and Frieda still wandered about the country, *"Vogelfrei"* as she described their style of travel. But now there was a welcome difference, a nest to which tired birds could return. And, though Lawrence declared when he first went to Sicily that he was doing so to get rid of the people around him, he was as inconsistent as ever once he was settled in at the Villa Fontana Vecchia; in no time he was writing to his friends, urging them to come on over and join him. One who was free to do so was their old friend Mary Cannan, who with her second husband, the novelist Gilbert Cannan, had lived near the Lawrences at Chesham.

"Cannan had first eloped with and later married J. M. Barrie's wife, Mary," wrote Bunny Garnett, describing how he had introduced the Lawrences to the couple. As Mary Ansell, the erstwhile Mrs. Barrie had been a successful actress. She was a pretty woman some years older than Cannan. Now she and the novelist were estranged—Cannan was soon to be certified insane—and Mary was at loose ends, with plenty of money and not much to do. She was living in Florence when she encountered the Lawrences again, and found it simple enough to move over to Sicily and take a studio in Taormina for five or six months.

In addition, Lawrence acquired a new group of friends, people who came from South Africa to live in Italy. Two of these were brother and sister, children of Sir Henry Juta of South Africa. Jan Juta, the man, was an artist who fell under Lawrence's spell and years later wrote a lengthy memoir about him for Edward Nehls, describing how he first heard about Lawrence and Frieda through other acquaintances in Sicily.

Frieda was rather summarily dismissed by his informants—
probably some of the other English in Taormina—as "a big,
gushing blonde," but the report on Lawrence was so enthusiastic
that Jan Juta, on first meeting him, was surprised and disappointed. Was this the wonderful man he had heard of, this
skinny creature with a red beard and a funny high voice? Soon,
however, Juta fell under Lawrence's spell and became aware
of what he called the man's "force, something powerful, yet
disciplined, nervous and alive as a flame," though the strange
voice belied it—"a little laugh, almost a cackle that left me
puzzled," he said. Frieda, on the other hand, was much more
impressive than he had been led to expect: "green-eyed and
handsome, a German mother-type full of conscious woman-
hood," was how he put it.

Juta had not been in Taormina long when he attended a
tea party and met there practically everyone in the British
colony except the Lawrences. They had stayed away, as he
gathered they usually did. Among those present, however, was
Mary Cannan, "a little lady . . . somewhat disillusioned, though
still attractive and conscious always of her feminine charms."
Consciousness seemed to be on Juta's mind. "She was the one
real friend of the Lawrences at the party, for she had known
them from the beginning, and despite flashes of violent jealousy
from Frieda, had encouraged and helped D. H." This sounds
very much as if Mary herself was Jan Juta's informant here.
At any rate, after the party he went on for dinner with the
Lawrences and gave them a "tactfully edited" account of it.
Predictably, Lawrence warned him against seeing too much of
foreign society in Sicily. He should emulate the Lawrences, he
said, and keep himself to himself.

While Lawrence talked, Juta watched admiringly as his
host deftly cooked and served the spaghetti. Frieda too, he observed, "watched him doing most of the work, smiling securely,
preparing her armour for her next attack on the defenses of
this elusive man, her husband." For, said Juta, he soon discov-

ered that Frieda loved Lawrence and was disturbed by his fight against the world, a "continual fight," he called it, "in order to stick to his principles," and "was not prepared to let him thus elude her." It sounds as if Jan Juta had read and digested much of Lawrence's writing.

> He admired the fighting spirit in her [he continued], but was confident he could always beat her down. And there were scenes of cold anger and floods of tears which gave rise to the rumour that they were not happy together. It was not true, for they were amazingly happy through every sort of difficulty, welded in a way most people could not understand. But Lawrence's unwillingness to compromise or break faith with the truth of himself roused even his wife to a sort of jealousy.

Or could her reaction, on the contrary, have been simple exasperation? Lawrence must have been very hard to cope with now, with the war over, their marriage six years old, and everything set fair for the future. Why, she may well have thought, shouldn't they live happy ever after? Yet here was Lawrence sinking again into his old awkward obsessions: he was beginning to sigh once more for Rananim, to tire of his surroundings, to hate the people among whom he lived, and to reach out longingly for something new. At the moment, the something new seemed to be Jan Juta, who sat there fascinated, listening to the master when Lawrence burst out:

"Why, oh why can't we find a little ship and sail away to an island, a Greek island, perhaps, or somewhere remote where we can start afresh and build a new way of life?"

Frieda is not quoted here as having said anything. She might not have been there at all; but if she were, there would have been nothing new to say: she had heard it all before.

The Murrys could have told this latest disciple of Lawrence something about the Rananim idea, but they weren't speaking to their lost leader. They were speaking about him, however. Katherine, still in Menton fighting her losing battle

for health, had received for review a copy of Lawrence's new
novel *The Lost Girl*, and her reaction was violent. In December, 1920, she wrote to Jack passionately, "It ought not to be
allowed to pass." By this she seems to have meant that the book,
or its author, should be burned at the stake; she was very angry.
Lawrence, she said,

> denies his humanity. He denies the powers of the Imagination.
> He denies Life—I mean *human* life. His hero and heroine are
> non-human. They are animals on the prowl. . . .
>
> He says his heroine is extraordinary, and rails against the
> ordinary. Isn't that significant? . . . Take the scene where the
> hero throws her in the kitchen, possesses her, and she returns
> singing to the washing-up. It's a *disgrace*. Take the rotten rub-
> bishy scene of the woman in labour asking the Italian into her
> bedroom. All false. All a pack of lies! . . .
>
> The whole is false—*ashes*. . . . Oh, don't forget where
> Alvina feels "*a trill in her bowels*" and discovers herself with
> child. A TRILL—what does that mean? And why is it so pe-
> culiarly offensive from a man?

Possibly because Katherine had herself been pregnant, she
knew that any talk of trills was nonsense. She asked Murry—
rhetorically, of course—if her violent reaction was due to her
own prejudice against Lawrence and concluded that she didn't
know: all she knew was that the book was "bad and ought
not to be allowed." Fortunately for Lawrence, this was not the
universal reaction to *The Lost Girl*, for which nearly a year
later he received a prize, from an English-literature professor
in Edinburgh, of a hundred pounds. As he rightly said, exulting,
that was no mean sum.

Meantime the Lawrences traveled about on short trips.
They went to Syracuse; they went to Sardinia. Frieda had
been to see her mother in Baden-Baden, and she and Lawrence
visited Jan Juta and his sister, Mrs. Réné Hansard, in Rome. But
of course for anyone intimately involved with D. H. Lawrence
such a peaceful, pleasant existence could not last indefinitely

and Frieda must have seen the writing on the wall when her husband began to complain of Sicily. It was always the same in a new place: first Lawrence was excitedly happy and enthusiastic, praising the scenery, the climate, and the people; then, little by little, the landscape became threatening, the weather was unhealthy, and the people proved perverse and malign. Sicily, it seemed, was too hot in summer and in the winter it was dull.

"The south is so lifeless," he complained. "There's ten times more 'go' in Tuscany." There is no telling what he might have done if Frieda's mother had not fallen ill early in 1921. When she heard of it from her sisters, Frieda rushed off, back to Baden-Baden, and though the patient's health quickly improved—in fact, the Baroness was to outlive Lawrence himself —Frieda, once there, decided to stay on until the summer, when Lawrence had agreed to join her for a holiday in Germany and Austria. Kicking his heels in the villa did not suit Lawrence; without Frieda he was disconsolate. "Don't like it at all," he wrote to his mother-in-law on March 16. People were very nice, he told friends; they invited him out to lunch and tea, but he didn't care for being alone in the house, and it was with considerable relief that he decided the time had come, shortly after he wrote the letter, to start out on his own travels. He planned to move at deliberate speed through Italy and end up in Germany. The first stop, somewhat off the direct line, was Capri, where he renewed old friendships and made new ones, in particular Earl and Achsah Brewster. The Brewsters were American painters. They were very much interested in Buddhist philosophy and planned to go with their little daughter to Ceylon, which they considered the fountainhead of Buddhism. They told Lawrence of their coming journey, and Lawrence rejoined with his vision of a happy group aboard a ship or, as he was now calling it, a "lugger." They would all go together in this lugger, he said, embroidering on the fancy: they could go anywhere they wished.

"Many happy hours we lingered, planning to lugger around the world . . ." said Achsah. "We seemed to need only the tiniest crew, in fact maybe we could manage it by ourselves, if we could do what was required by the captain. It looked as though Lawrence would be the captain!"

After this pleasant interlude Lawrence resumed the journey toward Frieda, but he paused again in Rome and then in Florence. In Florence he met Rebecca West, who was brought to call on him by Norman Douglas. She recalled later that Lawrence was staying in a small back room in a cheap hotel, where they found him busily "tapping away at a typewriter." At sight of this, Norman Douglas roared with malicious laughter, for he had just finished telling Miss West how eccentric Lawrence was, that on his travels he always went straight from the railway station to a hotel room and started writing about the temperament of the people without bothering to investigate them at first hand. Was Lawrence indeed writing about Florence? asked Norman Douglas, and Lawrence innocently replied that he was. However, the joke was soon forgotten when Lawrence put his work aside and became a host. Miss West was charmed with him.

"He made friends as a child might do," she said, "by shyly handing me funny little boxes he had brought from some strange place he had recently visited; and he made friends too as if he were a wise old philosopher at the end of his days, by taking notice of one's personality, showing that he recognized its quality and giving it his blessing."

He told the visitors, too, about his journey from Sicily to Florence by way of Capri and Rome. "There seemed no reason why he should have made these journeys, which were all as uncomfortable as cheap travelling is in Italy," she said, "nor did there seem any reason why he was presently going to Baden-Baden." We know there was every reason, but Miss West's imagination had the bit in its teeth and was galloping along, not to be deflected. It seemed to her that these were the journeys that mystics of a certain type have always found necessary—the Russian saint, the Indian fakir, and now D. H. Lawrence. "Lawrence travelled, it seemed, to get a certain Apocalyptic vision of mankind that he registered again and again and again, always rising to a pitch of ecstatic agony." This being so, she added wisely, why need he bother to meet people in a place and talk to them? He knew already what he wanted to see and hear. He carried it with him no matter where he went.

At last the saint, the mystic, arrived at journey's end in Baden-Baden, visited happily with his convalescent mother-in-law, and paid his respects to the other old ladies of the Stift. They adored him, but the Baroness was always in terror lest some one of them should happen to read his books. (As far as the record goes, this catastrophe never overtook her.) Afterward, he and Frieda went to stay with Nusch and her family in the Austrian Alps, where she and her husband had taken a house for the season. The Lawrences stayed there for some time, though Lawrence complained in a letter to Catherine Carswell that he couldn't breathe there.

"Perhaps it is one can't live with people any more—en ménage. Anyhow, there it is. Frieda loves it and is quite bitter that I say I want to go away. But there it is—I do." There it was, there it always was. Evidently he was persuaded to stay on for a bit, for they did not return to Italy until late in August. Then they borrowed a flat in Florence and moved in for a while. Lawrence had made an appointment to meet the Carswells in Florence, and after much arranging and rearranging the connection was made. It was important to see them, not only for the sake of the old friendship but for various other reasons. For one thing, Catherine Carswell had made a very generous gesture: on winning a prize of £250 for her novel, she sent Lawrence £50 of it on the grounds that he had helped her to make the book a success. Lawrence seems to have hesitated about accepting it, and in the end he destroyed Catherine's check and told her what he had done—he honestly didn't need it, he assured her with thanks. So that was that, but the Carswells were bringing, at Lawrence's request, several important papers to him, including new passport forms for Frieda and himself.

Donald and Catherine were on holiday. They had left their little boy at home and had been walking for miles, day after day, across what seemed like most of Europe. They now stayed for a week in Florence, having carefully chosen the cheapest pension they could find, and they saw the Lawrences every day of that week. One gathers that it was a strain. It often happened that way with Lawrence: after he had been completely charming to a friend, the wind seemed to veer and when one met him again in different surroundings the old warmth had somehow dissipated. We have seen a similar deteriorating process in the friendship between him and Ivy Low. Not that there was an outright break in this case, but everything was not as good as it had been in England, and the last meeting was canceled. Afterward, Lawrence wrote to Catherine with the old warmth and affection, saying that their week together had seemed only a moment, but she admitted to herself, and to those who read her memoirs, that it wasn't quite as simple as that. It had seemed "rather less than a moment" to her—

> a hazy moment, at that, and we seem to have said and done nothing in particular, nor to have been particularly happy. Though I never felt more drawn to Lawrence, there was about him something restless, remote and even impatient, which blurred the approach and made me doubt sadly once or twice if my sympathy found any response. I therefore did my best to conceal it. Sometimes I was relieved to get out of his presence.

Poor Catherine; Lawrence was bored with his old friends.

But he did talk with animation about his affairs. He told them that Taormina, and Italy altogether, were now finished for him. He was obviously in a hurry to get back to Fontana

Vecchia and pack up and be gone, said Catherine, and she made an interesting observation about the reason for his altered demeanor. Since the Carswells could not or would not accompany him on his next travels, she said, he identified them on the one hand with what he wanted to get away from. Yet on the other hand he needed them as friends, if only so that he might have friends to leave behind. It is an excellent explanation of Lawrence's complicated attitude.

At this stage his eyes were fixed speculatively on Ceylon, which was beckoning to the Brewsters; they in turn had urged him to follow and join them there, in a place where he could see how Buddhism actually *worked*. Lawrence wanted to hold on to Achsah and Earl Brewster. They were his newest adherents and he liked them for that: he had not yet written about them, and they offered a welcome change in a world that had grown stale to his fretful temperament. On the other hand, he still hankered after the imagined freshness of America. His speculations must have made him an absent companion indeed for the faithful, well-known, and probably boring Carswells.

There was an added complication, as far as Catherine Carswell was concerned: Mary Cannan, who had transferred herself from Taormina and now lived in the flat at the top of the house, just over the Lawrences' borrowed lodgings. Naturally the Carswells saw a great deal of her too. Once she entertained them with a meal that was much grander than the fare they ordinarily shared when they ate alone with Lawrence and Frieda. Mary, said Catherine, was "white-haired, and with exceptionally pretty features, [and she] was always the elegant one of the company"; she dressed beautifully. On a day when she was away from home, Frieda took Catherine upstairs to her quarters to show her a cupboard full of Mary's "enviable clothes," especially a number of hand-knitted silk *bouclé* dresses, fresh from Paris. Other women, said Catherine, had only ordinary knitted wool and silk; these clothes were all the more striking for that reason, and Frieda seemed to feel a kind of surrogate pride in the dresses, handling the stuff appreciatively as she boasted to Catherine that they were "enormously expensive." She offered a feel to Catherine, but Catherine frigidly refused it, and Frieda told Lawrence afterward that Catherine had no feeling for textures. It wasn't that, really. Catherine was reflecting that after all her wanderings, camping out, being rained on, and getting muddy, she had only one dress to wear on all occasions, a faded flowered cotton frock that had started life as a humble garden overall. In her book she admitted it frankly: she was jealous of Mary. Whenever they were all out together she seemed to have to walk behind the leaders of the troupe, Lawrence and Mary Cannan. They looked very nice, Lawrence dressed impressively in natural colored silk—because the Lawrences seemed to have more money nowadays to spend on such fripperies—and Mary "all that was urbane and charming." Catherine almost hated Mary, and it did not soothe her to be urged by Frieda to ask Mary about a special face-bleaching lotion the secret of which had allegedly been bequeathed to the ex-actress by Sarah Bernhardt.

"I saw that Lawrence liked to walk with a fashionably dressed woman," said Catherine, "and though he could and did make fun of Mary behind her back (as indeed he could and did of any of us) and was sometimes clearly bored before her face, he was fond of her and took a lot of trouble over her, largely because she looked always so nice."

The hardest part of the whole affair was that Mary had written a book about all the pet dogs she had owned, and Lawrence discussed it with her meticulously, making suggestions for improvements as if it were not the silly thing it obviously was; in just the same way he had once gone over Catherine's manuscript with her. Remembering those happier days, Catherine was distressed and took out her bad temper on the innocent Donald. She scolded him so hard over some trifle that at dinner that night he jokingly complained about it to Lawrence.

"You ought to hit her!" said Lawrence furiously. "Hit her hard. Don't let her scold and nag. You mustn't allow it, *whatever* it is you have done!" At which they all laughed and felt refreshed, said Catherine—but there seems no doubt that it was a relief when the week came to an end.

The next important incident in Frieda and Lawrence's life was the long-delayed publication in England of *Women in Love.* Immediately a storm broke over the author's head, precipitated in large part by an assistant editor of the periodical *John Bull,* who devoted some pages of the paper to his indignant views. The headlines seem amazingly unrestrained today:

"A BOOK THE POLICE SHOULD BAN. Loathsome Study of Sex Depravity—Misleading Youth to Unspeakable Disaster."

The reviewer reminded his public that Mr. Lawrence was an old offender. *The Rainbow,* he said, had been seized and suppressed by the police, and the same fate should overtake this book. The editor did not "claim to be a literary critic, but I know dirt when I smell it and here it is in heaps," he said. In terms that today would certainly advertise the book favorably and send up the sales to dizzy heights, he described the scenes he found most offensive of all—Hermione bashing Birkin with that lump of lapis lazuli, and Gerald and Birkin wrestling. "Sheer filth from beginning to end," he called that chapter, which is entitled "Gladiatorial." The article ended with a demand that the police act at once and remove from the bookstores "a shameless study of sex depravity which in direct proportion to the skill of its literary execution becomes unmentionably vile."

This was bad enough, though not unexpected. It made matters far worse that Philip Heseltine took umbrage at the picture he alleged Lawrence had drawn of him, under the name of Halliday, and threatened to bring a libel action if the text were not changed. It now appears that he would not really have gone so far, but the publisher, Secker, had no way of knowing that and was gravely worried as to his own liability. He told Lawrence something had to be done, and Lawrence mentioned the matter disingenuously to Catherine Carswell: "a fellow . . .

wants to bring a libel action because he says he's Halliday. . . .
Snotty little lot of people."

Of course Lawrence knew perfectly well that Heseltine
was justified; Halliday *was* Heseltine, and when Secker insisted
on action he changed the text very slightly and grudgingly.
Halliday's hair was now described as black where before it
had been yellow, and the girl Pussum, who had originally been
raven-locked, became a blonde. This did not satisfy Heseltine.
In the end Secker gave him five pounds and an additional ten
pounds for costs, the money of course to come out of Lawrence's earnings on the book. "Hell," wrote Lawrence in his
journal when he heard the news. Again one wonders why on
earth he was surprised by these incidents. Aggrieved, yes, even
righteously aggrieved, but why surprised? Lawrence never
learned.

Two other people, at least, did not resent being used in the
novel, partly because they didn't recognize themselves. They
were Katherine Mansfield, who served as the model for Gudrun
—much to her surprise when she was told about it—and Jack
Murry, the original of Gerald, who was equally startled. In
any case the Murrys were not the type to go to law with their
grievances, though one incident in the story might have given
them a clue. It is the scene where Gudrun in a tearoom over-
hears a group of men at a nearby table reading aloud from a
letter by Birkin and sniggering at it: she rises, goes over, and
takes the letter away from them. This incident, or something
very like it, really took place in the Café Royal, some time
before the estrangement between Lawrence and Katherine Mansfield. Katherine was sitting there with another woman when she
happened to overhear a group of men she knew slightly, Heseltine, Michael Arlen, and some others, at a nearby table. One of
them was reading aloud from a book of Lawrence's poetry, and
the others were laughing at the poem and making fun of it until
Katherine walked over to their table, possessed herself of the
book, and marched out of the restaurant.

In spite of increasing restlessness and an avowed intention not to spend another winter at Fontana Vecchia, Lawrence was still there with Frieda in the autumn of 1921. Having suffered another bout of influenza he was giving serious thought to moving on, but he could not quite make up his mind between two courses of action, and Frieda was equally at a loss, uncertain as to what to urge on him. On November 15 he mentioned in a letter to Donald Carswell that he had heard from an American woman named Mabel Dodge Sterne, who lived in a place called Taos, New Mexico: she wanted him to go out there and had said that she would give Lawrence and Frieda a furnished adobe house and everything they could want. It is unlikely that Lawrence knew what an adobe house was, but it all sounded very tempting, for Taos was on a mountain 7,000 feet high and twenty-three miles from a railroad—obviously exquisitely inconvenient, just the kind of thing that appealed to him. In addition, said Mrs. Sterne, close at hand were six hundred "free" sun-worshiping Indians, quite unspoiled, who were rainmakers. "It sounds rather fun," said Lawrence. He played with the idea of going to New Mexico by way of New Orleans or Galveston, bypassing "that awful New York." "Tell me if you know anything about such a place as Taos," he said to Donald.

Was he to go to America after all? On the other hand, however, were the Brewsters, who wrote enticing letters from Ceylon. Lawrence thought and thought and—one supposes—discussed the two choices with Frieda before he decided on his course of action and wrote to Earl Brewster, a fortnight later, that Kandy sounded lovely but he had decided to go to Taos. In Buddhism the goal was "that men should become serene," said Lawrence, but "I do not want peace nor beauty nor even freedom from pain. I want to fight and to feel new gods in the flesh." In America was that clamorous future that he sought.

There followed a brisk correspondence with Mabel Sterne, during which for some reason Lawrence's first keenness for the Western adventure faded. Perhaps Mabel was too enthusiastic.

Anyway, he felt misgivings. What was he doing, thus to trust himself and Frieda to the mercies of an unknown woman? Wasn't he taking a foolish, reckless decision? Such thoughts gave him pause, and he decided to put America off, though he was too canny to stamp on the idea entirely.

"I have once more gone back on my plan," he confessed to Catherine Carswell. "I shrink as yet from the States. . . . We had almost booked our passage to America, when suddenly it came over me I must go to Ceylon. I think one must for the moment withdraw from the world, away towards the inner realities that *are* real: and return, maybe, to the world later, when one is quiet and sure." However, he did suggest to Mabel Sterne that she too go to Ceylon and meet the Lawrences there; possibly they could all go on to Taos together afterward. Mabel did not accept the suggestion. She preferred to stay at home and wait.

The Brewsters had taken a "big old ramshackle bungalow" in Kandy where they invited the Lawrences to join them, and on February 20, 1922, the Lawrences set out for the East. It was a complicated trip which entailed taking a train to Messina, another to Palermo, and yet another to Naples, where they embarked on a ship. Ceylon was a fortnight's journey away. The Lawrences had a lot of luggage: four trunks, two valises, a hatbox, two very small bags, and Frieda's latest acquisition, a huge painted wooden side from a Sicilian cart.

"It had a joust painted on one panel, on the other St. Genevieve. It was very gay and hard in colour," said Frieda. "I loved it. Lawrence said: 'You don't mean to travel to Ceylon with this object?'

" 'Let me, let me,' I implored. So he let me. And off we set for Naples."

Lawrence was not really all that set against the object, for he wrote to his mother-in-law, "I am sorry you were not there to see us go on board at Naples, with trunks and bits and pieces —baskets of apples and oranges (gifts) and a long board that is a piece of a Sicilian wagon painted very gaily."

Even at this late stage, they were not absolutely sure they were doing the right thing in going to Ceylon. Characteristically, they kept their options open. One of their fellow travelers later recalled their saying that they were really on their way to Australia and were leaving the ship at Colombo "just to have a look at the tropics." Whatever his intentions, Lawrence felt well on the voyage out, better than he did ashore. One of the passengers, a Mrs. A. L. Jenkins, got on splendidly with the couple after she said she was reading *Sons and Lovers* and Frieda cried proudly, "That's my husband's book." Lawrence, she said, was "alert and active" and joined in many social activities (though he eschewed organized deck games), while Frieda sat placidly in her deck chair working on a highly colored rug and chattering about her husband, how he never read critical writing about himself and how hard he worked when he was in the mood.

Finally there they were, arrived at Ceylon. The Brewsters met them. "It is good to have gone through the Red Sea, and to be behind Moses," said Lawrence to Earl as soon as he was on dry land. He intended, he said, to get busy right away and study Singhalese, but there is no more mention of this resolve. The bungalow the Brewsters occupied was called "Ardnaree"; it stood on a hill overlooking the Lake of Kandy—a beautiful location, said Achsah Brewster, with views from all sides and wide verandas where each member of the group could have a separate place.

"I shall never leave it," declared Lawrence that first day, and, indeed, he was to remain there a full six weeks. They hung the Sicilian cart board on the wall and agreed that it looked perfect. Then Lawrence insisted on going out to walk around the lake, into which, in an access of good feeling, he threw his broken watch. Finished with time! They had come home at last!

The household rose very early every morning. Then Earl set out for a nearby monastery where he studied Buddhism and Pali, Frieda stretched out gratefully on a long rattan chair and

sewed or embroidered, and Lawrence worked. Presumably
Achsah played with her little girl, Harwood, or painted. In the
evening Frieda and Achsah took turns reading Harwood to
sleep, but they stayed together. Coming back in the dark along
the veranda to the drawing room, a person wanted company
because of boa constrictors that might tumble down off the
roof. Safely arrived in the drawing room, they closed all the
doors firmly. Even then Lawrence inspected the door cracks,
holding a lamp close and declaring that cobras could get in no
matter how fast the doors were shut. Sometimes in the night
the watchman shot a snake, which in the morning he invariably claimed was a deadly Russell's viper.

"There was always a consciousness of teeming life, by day
or night," wrote Mrs. Brewster. There were mongooses, chip-
munks, birds, and a "trotting-bull" that stayed close to the house
and sometimes mounted the veranda steps. In spite of his advancing deafness Lawrence was vastly irritated by one particular species of bird that sounded a bell-like note over and over.
He called it the "bell of hell," and sang at it a Salvation Army
hymn:

> "The bells of hell go ting-a ling-a ling
> For you, but not for me."

"This was done with a very personal emphasis and an air
of self-righteousness," wrote Achsah Brewster.

Not only birds and snakes annoyed Lawrence: one morning when he picked up his sun helmet to go out he found that
a family of rats had built a nest in it overnight. Altogether, said
Mrs. Brewster, "the teeming life of the place horrified him"—
even the people: he would sit quaking as the servants made
*puja,* a religious rite, to a Buddhist painting and chanted their
prayers.

"Who knows whether they are praying; they may be
planning to kill us in cold blood!" said Lawrence.

Nevertheless, life at Ardnaree was good for a while. Lawrence and Frieda were thrilled at witnessing Perahera, the great

festival that was held in honor of the Prince of Wales, with processions of elephants and gorgeous glitter. The jewel shops fascinated them, and Lawrence made Frieda happy by buying gems for her. There were walks in the jungle led by Achsah and Earl, when they looked at old rock temples that glowed white among fragrant flowers; often the party had to pause and step aside respectfully to let elephants pass. And the food at the bungalow seemed delicious at first, with great variety: every day the cook set out on the table six desserts: "camel's milk, preserved melon, jaggery-palm sugar, cocoanut sweets," and two more that he changed from day to day. "How wonderful!" said Frieda.

But after a while, as happens in the tropics, the sweet stuff began to pall. One after another, the Europeans shook their heads when the servant offered the dishes. Then Frieda produced a bottle labeled "liver mixture" and served it around to everyone in the party, and the day after that Lawrence announced in a melancholy voice that he wished they could have bread pudding sometimes instead of cocoanut cream with meringue. Achsah, who did not care for bread pudding—after all, she was American, not British—was scandalized, but according to his own lights Lawrence was quite right to wish aloud for anything he wanted. Had he not declared, the day he arrived, that in their communal life there should be no repressions? He intended to tell the party all their faults, he said, and he did his best to live up to the rule, as on the day Achsah suddenly decided to go to the village and asked if she looked all right for the expedition.

"If I were Frieda I should say you look perfectly *beautiful!*" said Lawrence, "but being myself I shall say, you look *decent.*"

Oddly enough, down there in Ceylon he seems to have had second thoughts at last about his mother. The question arose one day when he happened to be watching a good-looking workman fitting a screen on the veranda, and announced that the man reminded him of his father: "the same clean-cut and exuberant spirit." He said that he had wronged his father in *Sons and Lovers* and wished he could rewrite that portion of the book; he now realized that his mother had given the children a false picture of poor Arthur John. She should not have done what she did, making terrible scenes about his drinking and scaring the children needlessly. Their father, even in his cups, was perfectly harmless, and now Lawrence realized it. "The righteous woman martyred in her righteousness is a terrible thing," he said.

To us the existence they led in Ceylon sounds delightful, but there was one drawback: the climate. Admittedly it was trying. It was the warmest season Ceylon had known for many years, and as the rains continued none of the party felt really well. Frieda admitted that every day she dreaded the advancing heat, and Achsah said that all their rattan beds "sagged in the middle like hammocks." To anyone who knew Lawrence, who was seldom satisfied even at the best of times, the prognosis was not favorable. When he declared that the lush vegetation of Ceylon was "a little terrifying, a little repulsive," one knew he wouldn't stay much longer. Yet he seems to have indulged in fewer outbursts than usual against Frieda, though there was one occasion when he showed his old form, over a brooch that he had had made up for her of Ceylonese sapphires. Frieda lost it, and, not surprisingly, Lawrence upbraided her for her carelessness. Yet, said Achsah, hardly had he finished than he took it all back. Only big things matter, he said almost apologetically, and this was a little thing, not worth the passion he had shown. Obviously he was feeling really ill. Sitting glumly on the veranda of Ardnaree, he wrote to Mabel on April 10 that he didn't care for the East.

Its boneless suavity, and the thick, choky feel of tropical forest, and the metallic sense of palms and the horrid noises of the birds and creatures, who hammer and clang and rattle and cackle and explode all the livelong day, and run little machines all the livelong night; and the scents that make me feel sick, the perpetual nauseous overtone of cocoanut and cocoanut fibre and oil . . . all this I cannot bear. Je m'en vais. Me ne vo'. I am going away. Moving on.

Before quite giving up he made a suggestion that they all leave Ardnaree and move to a place, presumably cooler, that was higher in the hills, but Earl refused to consider it. What, he asked, would become of his Pali lessons then? Very well, said Lawrence: let Earl stay where he was and send Achsah and Harwood to America to cool off. But in the end they all left, the Brewsters for Europe and the Lawrences, on April 24, for Perth in Australia, where they planned to stay with that nice Mrs. Jenkins from the ship.

"By the way," wrote Lawrence to Kot, "I detest Buddha."

## 12

# *Mabel: "Wanted to seduce his spirit"*

FRIEDA AND LAWRENCE were in Australia a little more than three months altogether, first in the west and then near Sydney. As he always did, Lorenzo made a good impression on the local ladies. This time it was not only his charm that did it but the fact that he was an English writer of repute. This was a novelty, especially in Perth and Darlington where the Lawrences first stayed. Everyone was thrilled to meet him, even though the false rumor got around that he and Frieda were not yet married. (Fortunately he seems to have been unaware of this.)

Mrs. Jenkins took the visitors in hand when they landed at Perth on May 4, 1922; she introduced them to her friends and neighbors and was able to quote with authority from Frieda after they had gone on to Sydney that Mrs. Lawrence "would like nothing so much as a rest from vagabondage, and a home to keep neat and tidy." Probably Frieda would have said this sort of thing in any case because it was what women expected her to feel, but in Australia she really meant it. She was tired of traveling.

Mollie L. Skinner, a friend of Mrs. Jenkins, was helping to run a guesthouse at Darlington near Perth, and the Lawrences stayed there for a while. Miss Skinner was forty-four and had had a varied life. She studied nursing and midwifery in England and during the war worked in India and Burma. She had written newspaper articles on social subjects, and—as her friends were quick to tell Lawrence—had actually published two books, though she herself didn't want to mention them to such a celebrity because they were technical, not literary. She was more impressed by Frieda—the Countess, as people called her—than by Lawrence.

"She was beautiful, beaming and most fascinating," said Miss Skinner, "and it amazed us that she adored the little man and expected everyone else to do so." But as time went on, Mollie Skinner learned to appreciate "the little man's" quality, especially after she read *The White Peacock*. Here, she thought, was writing that approached her ideal, the work of Katherine Mansfield.

It is not on record whether she told Lawrence this, but since he never seems to have lost his temper with her it seems unlikely. He was very nice to her, reading one of her despised works and praising it. One day, following her out to the washtub where he intended to wash his socks, he said, "I wonder you don't write of the early days, tell us what drew these early Settlers. Tell us *what kept them here*."

Miss Skinner admitted that she longed to write such a book, but what was the use? Nobody in that "benighted land" would read it even if she did. Besides, she had a living to earn.

"His scorn, his sorrow, his contempt flung back in the words, 'You have been given the Divine Spark!, and would bury it in a napkin,'" Miss Skinner recollected.

This was exceedingly amiable. Lawrence during his stay at Darlington was always amiable, said Mollie, which she quite realized was a remarkable circumstance. She never saw that part of his personality so often described by other people with horror. Even Frieda commented on the phenomenon; Miss Skinner quotes her:

"I do not know this Law-rence. He is so gentle and kind, so—what do you call it?—angelic—since we arrived here. The mood will pass—you stupid people do not know him as he is, so cantankerous, so passionate and disconsolate. I wish he would remain like this, for I would like to settle down here and have a little farm in the amethyst atmosphere."

Miss Skinner shook with laughter at the picture conjured up by Frieda, "of the delicate little man with his frail body harnessing plough horses on a chill winter morning while the lovely Frieda lit the fire and cooked his bacon." An amusing picture, but the dream was never more than a dream and was soon dissipated.

On May 15, writing to his mother-in-law, Lawrence said, "So the new Jews must wander on. Frieda is very disappointed," and four days later they were aboard ship, sailing across the Bight to Sydney. From shipboard Frieda too stirred herself to write a letter, to the woman they were on their way, however slowly, to meet in Taos. Correspondence had been flourishing between Mabel Sterne and the Lawrences. Letters had just missed them in Sicily, Ceylon, and now Darlington, but others arrived in time, and both Lorenzo and Frieda replied. There was plenty to say. For one thing, they had discovered a friend they had in common with Mrs. Sterne: Leo Stein, one of Gertrude Stein's brothers. He lived in Italy, where he had met Frieda and Lawrence, and now it developed that he knew Mabel well and had actually visited her in Taos. When questioned, he wrote enthusiastically about Mrs. Sterne and the country she lived in, so now the prospect appeared to the Lawrences almost respectably reasonable. The letter Frieda wrote was characteristic of her: uninhibited, a bit malicious, a bit incoherent, occasionally echoing her husband in his more highflown moments:

I *love* the idea of spending some of the winter with you and Tony. I am so full of hope that it might be happy for all of us. . . . Ceylon was a wonderful experience and deeply satisfying but the past and the known. We will unite our efforts in a jolly life. . . . Achsah Brewster was quite simple and nice, but a kind of New England "culture" was very irritating; if she had only been content to be her simple self instead of all her flights! Pictures of huge St. Francis's and unbirdy birds

and white chiffon clouds of garments round her solid flesh.
. . . *Poor* Australia, we stayed in the bush but the pathetic pen-
scratchy attempts at civilising the poor country was oh so de-
pressing and the people are so *over*-civilised in one centre of
themselves!! I hope Sydney will be bearable for a few months,
it will be very hot, won't it, in the summer in New Mexico. If
we can only keep it dark for a little while that we are coming,
let's have our meeting without the spiteful comments of New
York on *all* of us.

Did they expect to be met with a brass band?

Sydney was too expensive, Lorenzo decreed within twenty-
four hours of disembarking, so they found a small house about
thirty-five miles from town on the South Coast, in a mining
township called Thirroul. Their life in "Wyewurk," the bungalow, was very quiet: nobody knew who they were, or cared,
and if this annoyed them it shows only in the many protes-
tations from Frieda in her letters that it was lovely not to be
bothered. Even the owners of Wyewurk were unaware that
they entertained an angel and did not find out until long after
the tenants had gone, when they learned that Lawrence was a
famous novelist who had actually published a book about Australia into which he wrote himself, his wife, and their very own
house, not to mention using their name for one of the minor
characters. No doubt Lawrence, who wrote *Kangaroo* at top
speed, grudged the time it would have taken to think up sub-
stitute details. It was really a lovely house, said Frieda, "right
on the sea . . . and a stretch of grass going right down to the
Pacific, melting away into a pale-blue and lucid, delicately tinted
sky," but it was in a mess and they had to clean it up. Wyewurk
was really a holiday place, a resort house which a large family
had occupied before them and had left in a bad state. There
were beds everywhere, torn papers blowing outside, old canvas
sails rotting on the veranda, and dirty floors and carpets. Fixing
it up was just the sort of domestic program Lawrence loved to
face: he and Frieda "set to and cleaned, cleaned and cleaned
as we had done so many times before in our many temporary

homes! . . ." she said. "But I was happy: only Lawrence and I in this world. He always made a great big world for me, he gave it me whenever it was possible; whenever there was wonder left, we took it, and revelled in it."

They would walk and walk along the coast, collecting shells. Living was easy, and people were amazingly generous at the farmhouses where the Lawrences bought food; when you asked for a pound of butter they gave you a piece that was closer to two pounds: "everything was lavish, like the sky and the sea and the land." They had no human contact apart from this, she exulted, "all these months" (though, to be exact, it was only about two months)—a strange experience, nobody bothering about them. Frieda wanted to stay forever and lose herself, but of course Lawrence had to move on to Taos. Early in July Frieda wrote to Mrs. Jenkins to say that they were leaving on August 10 for San Francisco. Why, she said, shouldn't Mrs. Jenkins accompany them? She went regularly to England, and from Sydney to England via America was no dearer than her usual way.

"*So come with us,* it would be fun, come before the 10th Aug[,] have a look at Sydney and stay with us here—I love it, the sea, the queerness of it all, there are all kinds of things to be done . . . though mostly I enjoyed the domestic part after all our wanderings—I seem to *cook* with a zest that is worthy of higher things." In a postscript she warned Mrs. Jenkins to be careful if she came in the boat as she herself had found "creatures" in her head.

A shipboard acquaintance who was emigrating to Australia looked up the Lawrences in Thirroul and thought they seemed lonely, Frieda especially, because they didn't know anybody in Sydney. He and his wife thought Lawrence looked delicate but Frieda, always sturdy, seemed to have put on weight. All that cooking, no doubt. There was no sign of tension, he added, and they seemed to love Wyewurk.

They departed according to schedule. Mrs. Jenkins decided

not to come along, so they sailed alone in the *Tahiti* for San Francisco by way of New Zealand, the South Sea Islands, and Honolulu. When the ship called in at Wellington, Lawrence thought of Katherine Mansfield, who had been born there, and on an impulse he sent her a postcard, on which he wrote the one word "Ricordi." Not knowing where she was (it was Gourdjieff's colony at Fontainebleau, where she was soon to die), he sent it to her care of Lady Ottoline Morrell. Katherine and Ottoline? He had quarreled with both women, and seriously, so what was this? It is likely he was saying that he was sorry and wanted to make up; he was clearing the decks, getting ready for a plunge into America's clean new world, leaving behind all the old anger and disagreeableness. Both women seem to have accepted the gesture, whatever it was, in the spirit in which it was offered. He didn't know that Katherine had already forgiven him.

Wellington, Raratonga, Honolulu. Frieda and Lawrence arrived with empty pockets in San Francisco, but this was not to be a permanent state; there was money in America as soon as Lawrence could lay hands on it, from the steady sale of *Women in Love*. Nevertheless he enjoyed writing to friends that he was broke, talk which often led to rumors of his insolvency. Like so many frugal people Lorenzo had a weakness for "poor-mouth" talk and often half believed it himself. So it was pleasant to find messages from Mabel at the hotel not only welcoming the couple but enclosing railway tickets to Taos. They were her guests in America, said Mabel.

"So American!" said Lawrence, gratified.

Actually, Mabel was not and never had been a typical American. Born in 1879, the same year as Frieda, she was the only child of rich parents in Buffalo and usually had her own way. Generally speaking, her life was a deliberate, successful struggle to get away and keep away from Buffalo. Her first marriage, to a man named Evans, ended when he was accidentally shot while duck hunting. Her second husband, Edwin Dodge, was an architect who willingly agreed with her desire to live in Europe. She bought a villa in Fiesole and he restored it, and for some years they lived in Italy. Mabel then set up house in New York and entertained lavishly, dabbling in radical politics and casually shedding Dodge on the way. The third husband, the painter Maurice Sterne, took her to the artists' colony in Santa Fe, and when she saw Taos she fell in love with it and decided to settle down. She got rid of Sterne when her roving eye lit on a Pueblo Indian named Tony Lujan, or Luhan. By the time the Lawrences arrived, Tony was a regular member of the household, and Mabel with her Indian lover was one of the sights of Taos and the villages around wherever there were ceremonial dances. The more conventional residents did not accept the situation uncomplainingly. They would have liked to snub Mabel, but how could one snub a woman who paid no attention and who was, anyway, very rich and did as she liked? On the whole the Anglo artists of Taos were rather proud of their eccentric millionairess.

Without realizing it, Mabel and Frieda were sister souls in that they shared the romantic philosophy which made of sex a panacea for most of civilization's ills. They both believed that sex must be free and untrammeled. Frieda, of course, had derived her faith from Freud by way of Otto Gross, whereas Mabel's had come around through other channels—not that the Viennese genius would have recognized either one—but in many respects they coincided. Both women found their beliefs admirably suited to their temperaments. Frieda had taken Lawrence because she desired him just as Mabel had reached out and grabbed Tony, and both redoubtable ladies felt completely justified in doing what they wished, but there was one important difference: Frieda was still minded to be satisfied with her bargain, but Mabel does not seem to have contemplated a lifetime of unbroken fidelity to Tony. Still unaware that Tony might have ideas of his own on that subject, she entertained hopes,

even before meeting Lawrence, of experimenting with an affair
with him. Genius, the abstract notion of it, appealed sexually
to Mabel because she conscientiously saw everything in terms
of sex, and she had plans for it.

The two couples met on September 10 at Lamy, the nearest
railway station to Taos, a long drive away. They met on the
platform, three well-rounded figures and one very thin one,
surveying each other warily. In her book *Lorenzo in Taos*
Mabel recorded her first impression of the Lawrences, hurrying
along toward them, "she tall and full-fleshed in a suit of pale
pongee, an eager look on her pink face, with green, unfocused
eyes, and her half-open mouth with the lower jaw pulled a little
sideways. Frieda always had a mouth rather like a gunman."
What Lawrence and Frieda saw was a stocky woman, not tall,
with hair cut in a Dutch bob around a calm, expressionless face,
wearing something arty and expensive and unclinging, standing
next to a stolid, handsome, tall, plump Indian with a black braid
over each shoulder, who was wrapped Taos fashion in a blanket
like a toga. Were the Lawrences startled by Tony? Mabel
thought they were, and was grimly pleased, but Frieda had
mentioned Tony in the letter to Mrs. Jenkins quoted earlier, so
he could not have come as a complete surprise. When the four
of them had supper in the railway café before starting home,
Lorenzo and Frieda may have seemed quiet and embarrassed, as
Mabel described them, but they were probably not so much
flustered as thrilled by the fact that they were actually sitting
with a real live redskin, the first they had ever known.

Furthermore, Tony's English was not very good, even
with people who talked American. No doubt the newcomers'
way of speech left him outside the conversation and unper-
turbed, majestically silent. This in its turn dampened Lawrence's
and Frieda's desire to chatter. But Mabel, the romantic, saw it
differently. Frieda was deciding what they should think of her
and Tony, she said. There they sat, Lawrence looking slim
and fragile next to his wife's bulk and being "agitated, fussy,

distraught, and giggling with nervous grimaces," while Frieda was "over-expansive, vociferous, with a kind of forced, false bonhomie."

It was clear to Mabel, said Mabel, that Frieda always did the sifting out of a situation for Lawrence and he lived through her, felt things through her. He didn't *want* to, but Frieda made him do it: "he must see through her and she had to see life from the sex center. . . . She was the mother of orgasm and of the vast, lively mystery of the flesh. But no more. Frieda was complete, but limited. Lawrence, tied to her, was incomplete and limited."

Thinking these things and looking impassive as always, Mabel was at the same time making up her mind to save Lawrence from his plight. As she put it, "the womb in me roused to reach out to take him." She knew he needed her; he needed another sort of force than Frieda's, now, and she made up her mind that he should have *her*. If Frieda had been able to read her hostess's mind, which seems not unlikely, she gave no hint of a reaction. Together they all moved on to Taos.

Mabel had prepared an adobe house—Tony's house, it was called, because it was built on Indian land next to the pueblo—for the newcomers. It was charming, "with Mexican blankets and Indian paintings of Indian dances and animals, clean and full of sun." But it was awfully close to Mabel at the Big House, center of what Lawrence dubbed Mabeltown, and they had to meet officially, as it were, every day for the evening meal, as well as during the day whenever Mabel felt like dropping in. Not immediately, however: Mabel, full of zeal to get Lawrence started learning about the Indians and the country, which she was determined he should interpret to the world, packed him off with a somewhat reluctant Tony to the Apache country, where there was to be a big dance. Left alone, Frieda welcomed company and listened approvingly when Mabel expounded her new theory about Lawrence getting all his experience filtered through his wife. Naturally Frieda was flattered and eagerly agreed with this interpretation. Mabel really understood, she said. It was pleasant, too, to have company, to chat with Mabel and her friend Alice Corbin Henderson, a poet from Chicago, about such feminine subjects as men and all that. Mabel was always willing to discuss her varied matrimonial ventures, and Frieda in return told well-polished anecdotes about her wanderings with Lorenzo. One thing led to another, until she was lured further into making confidences about her husband's lapses from strict marital fidelity. There was the infatuated American girl she sent packing—and also, of course, his crush, in Cornwall, on the young farmer, William Henry Hocking. . . . Mabel listened carefully and made mental notes.

"She was good company when Lawrence was not there, as is the case with nearly all wives," wrote Mabel. "She talked with heartiness and vigor—always with a real, deep, human warmth, albeit sometimes with such obtuseness, such lack of comprehension. So long as one talked of people and their possibilities from the point of view of sex, she was grand. She had a real understanding of that." (Look who's talking!) But, said Mabel, "any reference to the spirit . . . was antagonistic to her. The groping, suffering, tragic soul of man was so much filthiness to that healthy creature." She grew uneasy whenever her husband and Mabel—mostly Mabel, one feels—talked about what she called, with an indignant emphasis, "*soul*," just as she had resented his chats with Ottoline on such mushy subjects. However, Mabel added, she was "very alive to all the simple sights and sounds of the earth. To flowers and birds; to the horses and cows and sheep. She responded to things vigorously with boisterous explosiveness, and with passionate oh's and ah's!" Remember, Frieda was a gushing woman.

When Lawrence returned from the Apache country and found that his wife had made such good friends with Mabel, he was not pleased. Many a husband will understand that reaction, which is rooted in a fear that the creatures are ganging up on him, but Mabel saw in it something sinister. That, she said, was the end of the friendship between herself and Frieda: Lawrence stamped on it.

He now proposed that he write the story of Mabel's life. It was his idea, not hers, said Mabel, and this might well be true, because it was the kind of process in novel writing that attracted him, taking the life stories of his friends and acquaintances and interpreting them in his own way. But there can be no doubt she was delighted to agree; no doubt she had hoped for such a proposition. It is a fair guess that whatever he did with Mabel's life would not have delighted her, but the work was never completed, though it started out all right. The morning after they had agreed on it he hurried over to the Big House, notebook in hand, ready to get going, and found Mabel on the flat roof outside her bedroom, sunbathing. She had not thought to dress for him, she later admitted: she was clad simply and lightly in moccasins and "a voluminous, soft, white cashmere thing like a burnous." This deshabille startled and alarmed Lawrence, who was already distressed by the necessity of passing through Mabel's bedroom, in which her bed was as yet unmade, to reach the roof. It was a pretty bedroom, said Mabel defensively as she described that interview, white and blue colors, whitewashed walls, and everything "sunny, bright and fresh. . . . But Lawrence, just passing through it, turned it into a brothel. Yes, he did."

Obviously he was taking fright, and who is to say his instinct was mistaken? At her bidding he sat down on the roof and so did she. He said nothing for a minute but dropped his chin on his chest in a posture that would have been familiar to May Chambers and many others. Lawrence was shrinking away, drawing in on himself. After a gloomy silence he spoke. "I don't know how Frieda's going to feel about this."

But surely, said Mabel, she would understand? After all, it was his work. No, said Frieda's husband, she wouldn't. Frieda was German, he reminded Mabel, not Latin, which implied that she was down to earth, earthy. . . . According to Mabel's account, during the long talk that followed, Lorenzo repudiated Frieda forcefully, saying she was "the enemy of life—his life, the hateful, destroying female" incarnate. Why, he said, she wasn't even good at nursing.

"You cannot imagine what it is to feel the hand of that woman on you if you are sick," he confided—allegedly—in a fierce, lowered voice. "The heavy, German hand of the flesh."

The voice is not, strictly speaking, the voice of Lawrence, but the burden is recognizable. No doubt he did say something like this, though in better language, and there welled up in Mabel a great resolve to save him, no matter how, from that ham-handed woman. And it wouldn't be long either. She was jubilant as they walked together over to Tony's house. Frieda could be seen in the distance hanging washing on the line.

"She is mad!" Lawrence said gleefully as his wife caught sight of them and turned to wait for them balefully, hands on her hips. He had to lean over to conceal his laughter. Mabel, taking the hint, turned back to her house.

But alas, that long talk on the roof was the last tête-à-tête they were ever to have. That very evening Lawrence told Mabel that Frieda thought they'd better meet for work thereafter in Tony's house where she could keep an eye on them, and though Mabel protested, that is what they did as long as the book project survived.

Frieda told her version of the incident in *"Not I, But the Wind . . . ,"* with certain additions of developments ignored by Mabel.

Mabel and Lawrence wanted to write a book together: about Mabel, it was going to be. I did not want this. I had always regarded Lawrence's genius as given to me. I felt deeply responsible for what he wrote. And there was a fight between us, Mabel and myself: I think it was a fair fight. One day Mabel came over and told me she didn't think I was the right woman for Lawrence and other things equally upsetting and I was thoroughly roused and said: "Try it then yourself, living with a genius, see what it is like and how easy it is, take him if you can."

Might Lawrence really want to leave her? Frieda was miserable at the suspicion Mabel had instilled in her mind, until Lawrence came home and heard about the scene. Righteously indignant with Mabel—and possibly feeling just a bit guilty at the same time—he soothed Frieda and talked of leaving Taos, but he didn't leave, not yet. Instead he flew into a rage when malicious gossip reached him, as gossip had a way of doing in Taos, that Mabel's twenty-year-old son John Evans was going around saying that Mabel was tired of being sponged on by the Lawrences. It was probably untrue; it was not Mabel's style, but Lawrence believed it and declared that he would pay rent on the house before getting out with his wife as soon as possible. As for Mabel!

"All women are alike," he said to Frieda, "bossy, without any decency; it's your business to see that other women don't come too close to me." All very well, mused Frieda, but how was she to do it?

In time Lorenzo's rage cooled and for a while life went on with comparative calm. Mabel and Lawrence tried to collaborate on their book according to Frieda's rules, sitting and talking in a quiet corner of Tony's house while the mistress bustled to and fro through the rooms. In these unpropitious conditions Mabel still continued to struggle for the prize.

"You *need* something new and different," she urged Lawrence. "You have done her. She has mothered your books long enough. You need a new mother!"

But Lawrence merely answered hopelessly, "She won't let any other woman into my books."

The house was very nice, Lawrence wrote to Earl Brewster on September 22, but there were drawbacks to living under the wing of the "padrona"; she too was very nice, he added, but he hated living on somebody else's property and accepting their kindnesses. Nevertheless, Mabel was very kind. . . .

To the *padrona*, meantime, appeared a ray of hope. In spite of Frieda's watchfulness she felt that Lawrence was beginning to exchange with her, very subtly, glances of sympathy, more and more of them. It might be unconscious on his part, she felt, but it was there. To us, however, it seems that Lorenzo was playing his old game of delicate flirtation, leading Mabel on without intending ever to reach a conclusion. Once they washed dishes together on the porch outside the kitchen of Tony's house. They were alone for the moment, and in the soapsuds their fingers touched. Suddenly Lawrence exclaimed, "There is something more important than love!"

"What?" demanded Mabel challengingly.

"Fidelity!" he replied.

Now just what did he mean by that? Did he himself know? Mabel asked herself the question over and over and could not be sure of the answer, but of one thing she was not in doubt:

> I wanted to seduce his spirit so that I could make him carry out certain things. I did not want him for myself in the usual way of men with women. I did not want, particularly, to touch him. . . . He was, somehow, too dry, not sensuous enough, and really not attractive to me physically. But I actually awakened in myself, artificially, I suppose, a wish, a willful wish to feel him. . . .
>
> I did this because I knew instinctively that the strongest, surest way to the soul is through the flesh.

She never got her way, but days of watchful waiting gave her insight into her quarry's relations with his wife. She observed that Frieda never relaxed; the bond between Lawrence and herself was not allowed to slacken for an instant. If there should by accident be a quiet interval in their lives, she would drop a bomb to shake him up. She never let him become oblivious of her. Whenever she saw his attention wander she would prick him in a sensitive spot; she could always regain his notice and rouse his anger. After dinner, for example, if he had not paid her any attention for some time, she would start to mock him until he almost danced with rage. Then she sat "solid and composed, but with a glare in her green eyes," as she blew smoke in his face or let her cigarette droop from a corner of her mouth, a habit that infuriated him. Her head would be cocked, with one eye shut against the smoke—"a perfectly disgusting picture," said Mabel warmly, and though we may laugh we must admit that it is an excellent description of the febrile relations between Lawrence and Frieda. Once, it seems, he lost control and shouted at his wife in the presence of a whole party, "Take that dirty cigarette out of your mouth! And stop sticking out that fat belly of yours!"

Frieda retorted calmly, "You'd better stop that talk or I'll tell about *your* things."

In an appalled silence she gathered her needlework, put it into its bag, and said a pleasant good night to everybody. Lawrence went with her, head hanging in his characteristic "crushed" pose. Yet, when the others looked out of the window after them, they saw the couple walking close together, arm in arm in the moonlight. Jack Murry would have understood and sympathized with the puzzlement of Mabel's guests.

Perhaps rightly, Mabel took it as a compliment when the turbulent genius started to remold her. To begin with, he sharply criticized her style of dress. Those flowing robes so carefully designed to hide her square figure were all wrong, he said. He mocked them, calling them jibbahs, Mother Hubbards. Why did she wear them? Why should she hide her figure? Look at Frieda, said Lawrence; look at her clothes: full peasant skirt, laced-up bodice over her deep bosom; didn't she look nice?

"A woman is a woman. A waist-line is a waist-line," decreed Lorenzo. "I have always thought the kind of clothes my mother wore were the most lovely pattern any woman could have. . . . No, nice full skirts, with maybe a ribbon around the waist—and white stockings—that's the correct dress for a *woman!*"

In spite of inner doubts, the besotted Mabel immediately bought "yards and yards" of gingham, calico, dimity: very soon she was dressed in the style he approved of. She acquired a lot of aprons too, since he recommended aprons. Then came the next step, doing her own housework. Lawrence said he hated

servants and wouldn't have them because they got between one
and one's life; one should always do one's own cooking and
cleaning. To begin with, he told Mabel, she ought to get down
on her hands and knees and scrub her own floor. She wouldn't
*know* her floor until she had scrubbed it.

Obediently, Mabel, who had never in her life cleaned a
room, fetched a pail of hot water, a scrub brush, and a cake of
brown soap, and got to work. Fortunately for the smooth
running of the house, she did not go so far as to lay off her
domestics. She got only halfway across the floor before giving
up, and one of her Indian maids took over from there. Nor was
she any more successful with breadmaking. Her bread was calamitous; Lawrence after one bite threw his piece into the fire.
However, Mabel added, he was awfully nice about her failure.
The failure of others always put him into a good temper.

Frieda's anger at Mabel's attempts to lure her husband away
did not put an end to the women's friendship. Though they
never achieved quite the rapport of those first few days, they
still had good old heart-to-heart talks now and then. Mabel
heard all about the Weekley children and Frieda's maternal
anguish. Mabel, a mother herself though not a notably protective one, sympathized when it seemed required of her, and at
least once she was able to render a service concerning them
when Frieda wrote her an agitated letter from Tony's house:

Dear Mabel,
        I want you please to send a cable about the children. I feel
    worried about Elsa. She is frail and overgrown and was *not*
    well when I last heard. Two of her father's brothers died of
    consumption. If she isn't well, we must find somebody who
    would bring her to America. We could find somebody surely.
    . . . I feel so happy, otherwise, but this worries me.
                                                                F.

This was the kind of thing Mabel was good at, because
she was kindhearted and loved to act as go-between. It is not
clear why Frieda found it necessary to request her help, as the

most acrimonious days between Ernest and herself were over, but perhaps she thought Ernest would resent any attempt on her part to take Elsa away. No doubt, too, she was tempted by the fact that New Mexico was a popular haven for consumptives. In any case Mabel cabled, giving her own name and address for reply, and the answer was that Elsa was better. Frieda relaxed.

Tony taught Lorenzo and Frieda to ride on some of the horses he and Mabel kept. The Lawrences loved the exercise and went out every day—a good thing, as it turned out, because later on when they lived in the country they had to depend on horses for transport. For a time life was tranquil; and Lawrence began thinking again about setting up Rananim—a group of young people gathered "somewhere away from the city. . . . They could be *themselves* there, and they would form a nucleus"—until certain affairs in Mabel's family distracted his attention. John Evans, still an undergraduate at Yale, had left the university without his mother's permission and come home, full of determination to marry. The object of his affections, "Little Alice," lived in Santa Fe. Though John was not yet twenty-one and his Alice a mere fifteen, none of the three parents involved opposed the marriage, because they were good friends: Mabel, Alice Corbin, and her husband, William Henderson, a painter. Preparations were soon under way for the wedding, which was to take place before the year was over.

At this happy time Mabel began thinking about John's preparation for man's estate. After all, the boy's father was dead and, as far as his mother knew, nobody had given him that little man-to-man talk considered essential before a wedding. She asked Lorenzo if he would take a father's place and give John the advice of a man of the world, and he readily agreed. That evening he visited John in the boy's log cabin, where the two stayed for more than an hour behind closed doors. When at last they emerged and joined the others in the Big House, Mabel's anxious eye saw that her son looked elated, and she felt re-

assured. At last the others had said good night and left mother
and son alone together; she asked him what words of wisdom
Lawrence had spoken.

"He said a lot," John replied. "He said for me to be always
alone. Always separate. Never to let Alice know my thoughts.
To be gentle with her when she was gentle, but if she opposed
my will, to beat her. And he said, above all, to be alone. Always."

It was not quite what Mabel had meant when she suggested a little talk.

As for beating, she told one story about the Lawrences that
has raised many eyebrows. Now and then she took them to the
Hot Springs, a sort of mineral-water spa in the canyon near
Taos where people can immerse themselves in the shelter of a
stone room, built directly over the water. When she and Frieda
bathed, she said, she sometimes saw "the big voluptuous woman
standing naked" in the dim light, and often there were "great
black and blue bruises" on her body. "And sometimes I found
her with eyes red and swollen from weeping," added Mabel.
It is hard to believe the implications of this unless we accept
the likelihood that Lorenzo too was bruised—but then, Mabel
never saw *him* stripped; Frieda took care of that. Mabel and
Lawrence were seldom alone. Mabel was convinced Frieda had
stipulated that her husband should never, never be caught in
such a perilous position.

On one of their local expeditions the Lawrences were taken
to see a small ranch in the mountains that Mabel had bought
some time earlier and presented to John Evans for use as a hunting lodge or week-end place. It was seventeen miles from Taos, a
good deal higher in wild country. It had a tremendous view
and was altogether beautiful. How lovely it would be to live
somewhere like that. Lorenzo and Frieda talked of it wistfully
more than once, especially when life at Mabeltown became
strained and complicated and a new friendship put fresh ideas
into their heads. From the time he arrived, Lawrence had been

"protected" by Mabel from everyone in Taos but members of her immediate circle. She had not gone to such lengths to capture a genius, she felt, just to turn him over to hoi polloi, who in her estimation included most other residents of the town, and her indignation was great when Lawrence got away from her, as he did, and made friends with outsiders. Two of these were young Danish artists, Knud Merrild and Kai Gótzsche, who had driven to New Mexico all the way from the East Coast in a dilapidated tin Lizzie and paused for a while in Taos to paint. They met the Lawrences through another painter named Walter Ufer and became friendly, and the friendship grew in spite of Mabel's obvious disapproval. (Later Knud Merrild wrote of the friendship in a book, *A Poet and Two Painters*.) Lorenzo invited himself with Frieda to see the Danes' work; naturally his reaction was hostile.

"I really can't bear to look at pictures!" he said, but Frieda —as always—scolded him and said the paintings were very nice. As she moved around commenting on them, Lawrence hammered away, saying, "The art of painting is dead." The Danes' feelings were not hurt; they liked the Lawrences and got to know them better. Soon Lorenzo was telling them just how to ride horses, taking it for granted that they were beginners— which they were not—and behaving, himself, as if he were a veteran cowboy. Even then they liked him, though it was always a relief when he shut up about horses.

They were not acquainted very long before Lawrence was inveighing against Mabel. He said he was tired of it,

tired of her, the bully, with that bullying, evil, destructive, dominating will of hers.—Oh, these awful cultured Americans, how they lack natural aristocracy.—She doesn't let one alone, we have no privacy, and wherever we go, she has to drag that fat Indian along, that Indian chauffeur of hers, Tony Luhan. I hate it. I hate her and the whole atmosphere. . . . Why don't people know their places? I hate having servants around me, they poison the air. Not that I hate Tony, he is all right in his own way, but I want to choose my own company.

The Danes, knowing nothing of Mabel themselves, were willing to grant Lawrence might be right. They had met Mabel once and she had snubbed them; that was all they knew of her. Lawrence said contemptuously that she wanted to bully him into writing a book on her, but he would never, never in his life do it.

"To think of it!" chorused Frieda indignantly.

Lorenzo and Frieda gave the two young men a rush. They showed them how to use the Hot Springs. Lawrence insisted on giving them a multicolored scarf Mabel had knitted for him. They went out all together in the Danes' car, and Mabel watched balefully from her balcony as they drove past. One evening she gave a party at which Pueblo Indians danced, and Lawrence made her invite the Danes. At these parties everyone was supposed to join in and dance with the Indians; Lawrence, said Merrild, was no good at it because he seemed to have no sense of rhythm. At length the guests began dancing in the Anglo way, though Lorenzo would not, but stayed on the sidelines making acid remarks about tail-wagging. Both young artists asked Mabel, most politely, to dance, but she turned them down, saying she was tired, only to appear a moment later partnered by another guest. War had been declared, as the Danes fully realized.

Soon afterward the Lawrences threw a bombshell at Mabel, saying that they wanted to get out of Taos, where Lorenzo couldn't work properly. They wanted to go and live on John's ranch and asked Mabel's permission to do so. She was shocked and grieved and urged them to change their minds, painting dreadful pictures of the rigors of winter up there, but they would not be moved. Unwillingly she consented then to their occupying the ranch. It was infuriating to learn soon after, as she did, that the Danes were going to take them there in the tin Lizzie, thus rendering them independent even of her car. But for the moment she held her fire.

On December 1 the party set out in the battered car, which stopped several times on the way. Lorenzo, sitting in the back

seat, kept making rude remarks about motor cars, which he
didn't approve of, but he didn't get out, and when they were
nearly there and Lizzie paused for the last time he actually
spoke as an authority on the matter: "I think she needs more
water. Shall I give her some?"

Merrild understood. Lawrence couldn't bear not to be master of the situation, even this one. Politely they refused the offer,
however; they didn't need water.

The ranch's cabins, not having been used for a long time,
were filthy and evil-smelling, so everyone got to work cleaning
and scrubbing until they were habitable. Everyone was happy
and excited. Lawrence named the place "Lobo Ranch." They
had just finished supper by candlelight when he was telling the
young men that he and Frieda wanted them to stay for the winter as guests, to help out. Gótzsche was all for it immediately,
but Merrild was dubious and need persuading. He pointed out
that they might not continue to be friendly. Lawrence, he said,
was apt to get irritated by people and rapidly tired of everyone.
Look how fast he had used up Mabel, said the Dane—he had had
enough of her in one month! But Lawrence persisted, Gótszche
was eager, and in the end they agreed to stay. Everyone was
happy—until the next day, when a messenger arrived from
Mabel to Lawrence to say that he was to use one cabin only;
the other was to stay vacant in case John wanted to use it for
hunting. Of course Lawrence immediately went up in smoke
and flame. Very well, he raged; they would all four stay in one
cabin.

"Why Mabel ought to go down on her knees before the
honour!" he ranted. "Instead of which, she puffs herself up,
and spits venom into my face like a cobra."

The Danes were uncomfortable and offered to leave, to go
on with their journey to the West, but Lawrence would not
hear of it. Instead they went out looking for somewhere else
than John Evans's property, and they found it quite easily—
Del Monte, a working ranch at Questa not far off, that belonged

to and was worked by a young couple named Hawk. The Hawks had two cabins they weren't using and were willing to rent them. Fortunately Lawrence could afford to pay, and the move was quickly effected.

Lorenzo wrote to Bessie Freeman, announcing it. Bessie was a Buffalo woman, a friend of Mabel's who was visiting her when he and Frieda first arrived. He had struck up an immediate friendship with her, possibly, as Mabel maliciously suggested, because she had white hair and seemed safe. She seems to have reminded him of the many elderly ladies he liked. Now he wrote with characteristic lack of loyalty, "Mabel was too near a neighbour." And he sent a long letter to his mother-in-law elaborating on the theme:

You have asked about Mabel Dodge: American, rich, only child, from Buffalo on Lake Erie, bankers, forty-two years old, has had three husbands. . . . Now she has an Indian, Tony, a stout chap. She has lived much in Europe—Paris, Nice, Florence—is a little famous in New York and little loved, very intelligent as a woman, another "culture-carrier," likes to play the patroness, hates the white world and loves the Indians out of hate, is very "generous," wants to be "good" and is very wicked, has a terrible will-to-power, you know—she wants to be a witch and at the same time a Mary of Bethany at Jesus's feet—a big, white crow, a cooing raven of ill-omen, a little buffalo.

The people in America all want power, but a small, personal base power: bullying. They are all bullies. . . .

Basta, we are still "friends" with Mabel. But do not take this snake to our bosom. You know, these people have only money, nothing else but money, and because all the world wants money, all the money, America has become strong, proud and over-powerful.

If one would only say: "America, your money is sh. . .', go and sh. . . more"—then America would be a nothing.

Mabel missed all the brouhaha of the move because she went to Santa Fe as soon as the Lawrences left, to avoid, she said, the desolation of not having them close by. She was back before Christmas, however, when there was a slight *contre-temps*. Lawrence wanted to go to Taos for the holiday. He expected his publisher, Thomas Seltzer, and his wife to arrive about that time from New York, and he doubted if he himself and Frieda could make the pair comfortable up at Del Monte. He therefore attempted to bury the hatchet with Mabel, proposing that they all stay at her place. But Mabel was still angry at being deserted, and she certainly didn't want to put up the Danes, so she said she regretted that this was impossible; she was unable to take in anybody, as she planned a family Christmas with the young newlyweds and the Hendersons as her only guests. She did, however, take rooms for them in another house, Danes and all. Lawrence promptly took offense and said they had decided not to come at all.

They did come just the same, having made their own arrangements; Mabel ran into them at the dance at the pueblo. "I saw, from our car, Frieda's foolish grin flashing in the flickering light as she talked to a Dane," she wrote. Lorenzo even came over to the car and exchanged a few courteous words, but the rift was far from healed. When, some weeks later, Mabel invited the Lawrences to accompany her and Tony to another Indian dance, to be followed by a motor trip to Old Mexico, Lorenzo haughtily refused, saying that he wanted to be alone for a while. (The Seltzers had come and gone, having had a lovely time at Del Monte Ranch.) It was too much for flesh and blood to bear, thought Mabel, and she wrote a long letter about her grievances to an old friend in the East, Walter Lippmann.

"It's your own fault," replied Lippmann. "Don't you know that you can't make a pet out of a snake?"

The thing was getting out of hand. When Mabel heard from a Taos gossip that Lawrence had been talking maliciously about her—"He said you tried to make him fall in love with you. He said you tried to take him up on your roof and make him make

love to you. He said you have an evil, destructive, dominating
will and that it will be the end of you"—she fainted away and
knew no more for twenty-four hours. At least that is what
she said, adding indignantly, "And when Lawrence heard about
this, he said it was just defeat! That my will had been defeated
for the first time and that it couldn't stand it."

One would think that this was the end of Mabel, at least
for that season. But there was one trace of her at Del Monte
Ranch—Bibbles. Bibbles, or Pips as she was sometimes called,
was a French bull-terrier puppy Mabel had given the Lawrences when her prize bitch Lorraine had a litter. The pup was
a little black creature, a wriggly bouncy little dog, friendly to
everyone. At first Lorenzo reported cheerfully from the ranch
about her, telling Mabel that she was growing at a great rate,
but soon she developed a will of her own, and when Lawrence
went in too strongly for discipline she signified her displeasure
in a marked manner by going over to the Danes' cabin and
staying there for several days. The fact that they were looking after an Airedale for a friend probably had something to do
with it, too. Lawrence did not like this desertion; he had in his
mind some ideal of canine fidelity which Bibbles had failed to
live up to, and he took such things personally. He carried her
home once, giving her another chance as it were, but the next
day she went back to the Danes. Then Lawrence gave the dog
to the boys. They didn't really want her—she made trouble
with their cat—but there was nothing for it until one day she
returned to the Lawrences' cabin of her own free will, and they
heaved a sigh of relief.

Then, alas, Bibbles came in heat and showed signs of interest in a dog from the main house which belonged to Bill
Hawk. The Danes urged Lawrence to keep her indoors or on
a leash for the time being, but he refused. He was sure he
had her trained; she would obey him no matter what the urge.
When she ran away for a preliminary run with her suitor he
brooded fiercely, his head sunk on his chest, and beat the dog up

on her return that evening. Next morning there was no Bibbles; she had run into the mountains with her friend, and nobody saw her for the following day and night.

Sensibly, she went to the Danes' cabin when she did come back. That afternoon everybody there was sitting around peacefully, Bibbles in Gótzsche's lap, when the sound of rapid footsteps was heard, the door burst open, and Lawrence stalked in, his dirty boots marking the floor unheeded. He looked around, spotted Bibbles, rushed over, stopped short, and began screaming curses at her. He knocked her off Gótzsche's knees and she scuttled for cover, while Lawrence and Gótzsche stood there bristling at each other.

"Lawrence was completely out of his mind," reported Merrild. He threw himself on the ground and tried to reach Bibbles, then scrambled up and tried to catch her, chasing her all over the room, shoving chairs and tables out of the way, until the little dog saw the open door and rushed out of it like a bullet, Lawrence after her. Then she made the mistake of plunging into the fresh snow, where with her short legs she couldn't make headway, and Lawrence caught up with her, kicked her several times, lifted her in the air, and threw her as far as he could. Then he caught up with her and started all over again.

In the meantime the Danes, temporarily paralyzed from shock, recovered their senses and ran over to interpose themselves between the genius and his victim. There followed a gláring match during which nothing was said, and finally Lawrence backed down and went home. When he next came to see the Danes he didn't mention Bibbles, who was still living with them, except to say, "Best she stay with you." He had brought with him a lot of fresh bread and cake, something he always did when he felt apologetic. After this experience the little dog was much quieter generally, and a few weeks later went back to the Lawrences of her own accord.

There has been much comment on this incident. Lawrence's admirers flatly refused to believe it because they couldn't bear to. Others, who never liked him anyway, pounced on the story and flourished it as one more example of his depravity, saying flatly that the man was stark staring mad, at least in fits and starts. Long after Bibbles was reconciled with her master the battle raged over her little black head, but amid all the sound and fury nobody seems to have offered the obvious explanation, which is that Lawrence simply didn't know anything about dogs. According to his own account, the family never had a pet dog except for a few weeks once during his childhood, when a sporty uncle left a pup with them to look after, then came and took it away. Lawrence wrote an article about that occasion; clearly it was something remarkable in his childish life.

The Chambers family at The Haggs owned a bull terrier, and once when Bert wanted to talk seriously with Jessie he said to the animal, "Go away, Trip. We don't want you, you're not nice."

Catherine Carswell on this subject has already been quoted; let us remember her words: "He hated the domestic dog on account of its too public habits."

Many readers have been delighted by Lawrence's writing of animals. They say that he really saw animals, understood their feelings, and helped his readers to share this understanding. But the truth is that everything Lawrence said of animals—everything interpretive, at least—is anthropomorphic. To him they reflected human traits, human attitudes, and Bibbles was no exception. Her sex obscured the issue, too. She was a dog, but she was a female dog, and Lawrence blamed her behavior on this irremediable fact. To him she had all the faults of womankind. When she left him and went to stay with the Danes he saw it as betrayal, just as a woman might have betrayed him, and when she committed the ultimate infidelity, running away and mating with a dog, she was the woman taken in adultery. Disgusting! Of course he beat her, poor little Bibbles.

# 13

## *Frieda Again: "A household Brunhilde"*

WINTER OVER, Lawrence and Frieda prepared to go south, to Old Mexico. The Danes took Bibbles to Taos and found her a home before they set out for California, but long before they got started Frieda and Lorenzo had departed. One is always surprised by the short time limits of Lawrentian adventures: this first visit to Mexico lasted only three and a half months, but Lawrence managed, nevertheless, to write a long novel about the country before leaving it.

They arrived on March 23, 1923, and waited in Mexico City for friends who had arranged to make the trip with them: Witter (Hal) Bynner, the poet, who lived in Santa Fe, and Willard (Spud) Johnson, his secretary and lover. The Lawrences' acquaintance with this pair dated back to their first night in New Mexico, when Mabel and Tony met them at Lamy and started back to Taos. Because the drive upcanyon was dangerous in the dark, Mabel arranged for the Lawrences to spend that night at Bynner's house, she and Tony having rooms elsewhere. As Lawrence got out of the car, clutching the famous Sicilian cart board, Tony inadvertently backed up and bumped Lawrence, cracking the board. Lawrence flared up at his wife: "It's your fault, Frieda! You've made me carry that vile thing round the world, but I'm done with it. Take it, Mr. Bynner, keep it, it's yours! Put it out of my sight! Tony, you're a fool!"

Bynner's first impression of Lawrence, therefore, was hardly favorable, especially as he liked Frieda: "Her smile from the first had meant, 'I'll like you till I find a reason not to and I'll be all of myself whether you like it or not.' Her body had German breadth and stature; she was a household Brunhilde; her fine profile was helmeted with spirit; her smile beamed and her voice boomed. . . . She never had to insist that she was there."

Now they were together, the Lawrences and Hal and Spud, in Mexico City. Naturally, one of the first sights they went to see was a bullfight. Lawrence and Frieda were appalled by the goring of the horses and did not wait to see the whole thing, but they found other aspects of Mexican life more pleasing. They visited Xochimilco, "where Frieda, like an expanded Cleopatra, lolled on a flower-decked barge," to quote Bynner, and Lawrence caught a bad cold. In Orizaba, where they arrived early on a chilly morning, he made a scene. (Hal called it a nervous seizure.)

"We are not staying here, Frieda," he declared on the railway platform the minute they got out of the train. "We are leaving."

He asked the railway people when the next train left for Mexico City; Frieda sighed with relief to learn it was quite a bit later. She asked her husband what was wrong.

"Don't you feel it?" he railed. "Don't you feel it through your feet? It exudes from the platform. The place is evil. I won't go to the town, I won't go to a hotel, I won't go anywhere. I can stay here at the station till train time. You can do as you like. The place is evil, the whole air is evil! The air creeps with it!" And he screamed at the finally intimidated porters to go away.

At this point Bynner lost patience and announced flatly that he, for one, intended to visit the town and, if he liked it, spend the night there; Frieda could come with him if she wanted. Hal noted:

"He looked extremely and childishly surprised . . . as if it was an unwarranted attack on him out of the blue. He was instantly docile and dumb [and] followed us into the vehicle. He sank his beard into his breastbone."

After the journey, returned to Mexico City, Lorenzo gave further signs of what can only be called aberrant behavior, and Bynner was not the only man to be outraged by his treatment of Frieda. The Lawrences were staying at what the American writer Carleton Beals described as "a smelly Italian hostelry," and there they received the various admirers of Lawrence's work who came to pay him homage. One day Frieda, described by Beals as "a fine handsome woman, one of those Teutonic types that remind me of delicious home-made bread, a woman of great poise, calm and breeding," was sitting in the reception room blamelessly chatting with a female friend. In came Lawrence and began shouting at her about something. Frieda paid no attention to him but went on talking. "Finally, his face purple, he screamed at her: 'Why do you sit with your legs apart that way? You're just like all the other dirty sluts.' "

Still she ignored Lawrence and his outburst and went on talking quietly, without any acknowledgment. "Her passivity merely incensed him the more," said Beals; "he literally frothed at the mouth and flounced out."

Those better acquainted with the Lawrences could have told Beals that Frieda was deliberately goading her difficult husband; what seemed well-bred passivity in the face of extreme provocation was, in fact, her own form of provocation. But Lawrence was undoubtedly, observed Beals, "a very sick man . . . greatly frustrated physically and physiologically by her full, healthy body and poise." An outing Beals made, accompanying Frieda on a sightseeing expedition, gave him no reason to change his warmly complimentary opinion of her: he thought her "a grand human being," a phrase he was unable to apply to her husband, and he somehow got the idea that Frieda in her quiet way "found means of compensating herself for Lawrence's numerous spleens and infidelities, putting on the horns, as Mexicans say."

Frederic Leighton, an American importer who spent much time in Mexico, was another man who called on the Lawrences and got an unfavorable impression of the genius's treatment of Frieda. It is only fair to point out that Americans were predisposed at the best of times to disapprove of the way Englishmen cope with their wives. But certainly Lawrence, more than most of his compatriots, gave them reason.

"His bad manners shocked me," said Leighton in a letter to Bynner, "made me wish to apologize for him to somebody, to anybody. Never before or since have I heard a human being, in educated society, repeatedly release such flow of obscene vile abuse on his wife (or on anyone) in the presence of comparative strangers as Lawrence did on Frieda; nor, I must admit, have I heard such apparently uninhibited response." (This, at least, gives us a slightly different view from Beals's of Frieda's long-suffering tolerance.) "Lawrence was far more eloquent," added Leighton, "more varied in his vituperation, but Frieda hardly less emphatic."

Frieda wasn't the only one to suffer. Lorenzo's terrible temper was apt to spill over on everybody within distance of his shrill voice, as when Fred Leighton arranged that the writer should meet José Vasconcelos, the Minister of Education, at a luncheon party to which were invited the Lawrences, Witter Bynner, Willard Johnson, Carleton Beals, and Leighton himself. The guests were kept waiting a long time in an anteroom and were then told that the Minister, much to his regret, could not attend the party because of urgent matters of state. Would they, therefore, postpone the luncheon and return the next day?

Lawrence, leaping to his feet, shouted, "No, I shan't!" and walked out, to march furiously up and down an inner balcony for ten minutes before he could be calmed down. All the others, Frieda included, accepted the invitation and had a charming lunch next day with the Minister, but Lawrence refused to go. He had been insulted, he maintained; "Art, Literature, History, the British Empire, Civilization itself had been insulted! How anyone's body, to say nothing of a sick, fragile one, could withstand such berserk bursts of passion I did not know," said Leighton.

Lawrence talked often of returning to England, but letters home show that he was irresolute about it, and finally he decided, in his own words, to give Mexico one last chance. Attracted by the description of the place in a guidebook, he went to Chapala, a resort thirty-five miles from Guadalajara, situated on a large lake forty miles long and twenty miles wide, to examine its possibilities as a dwelling-place. He wanted to go alone, and Frieda did not demur, saying wisely to Bynner, "When he finds a place by himself, he always likes it."

Sure enough, he liked Chapala, so he took a house there and telegraphed the others to come along.

While he was away Frieda had a most enjoyable time with Hal and Spud, shopping, eating at different restaurants, and seeing the sights without hindrance. On May Day there were celebrations in Mexico City, and her friends threw themselves enthusiastically into a ceremony at the cathedral, climbing the tower with hundreds of others and reappearing on the roof at last to wave a red flag. They had been busy inside helping to toll the bell in commemoration of working-class martyrs. Standing in the milling crowd beneath, Frieda was alternately thrilled and frightened when mounted soldiers arrived to put a stop to incipient revolt, but nothing serious happened, and the men got away in time to take her to lunch. All three went to Guadalajara on the following day in answer to Lorenzo's summons, but there Hal and Spud "swerved off" by themselves for a day or so of liberty to explore the town, away from Lawrence's tantrums, before rejoining the couple at Chapala.

"Mind you, I like Frieda better than ever," wrote Bynner in his journal after separating from her. "A solid, hearty, wise, and delightful woman. The few days we had alone with her in

Mexico City were a solace. Her love for Lawrence, probably her worst fault, is genuine and forgivable."

It was owing to their liking for Frieda that the two men eventually came and put up at a hotel near the house Lawrence had taken. Fortunately, everything worked out pleasantly. The Lawrences stayed at Chapala from May 2 to the second week in July—of course, Lawrence started a novel on Mexico, which was to be *The Plumed Serpent*—and Bynner and Johnson were with them nearly as long. Life was quiet and peaceful. Undisturbed days of writing, with daily dips in the lake's milky waters, had a soothing effect on the genius's fretful temper. In a memoir he wrote after Lawrence's death, Spud recollected that they would all sit for hours on the *portal*, or veranda, of the house, "either on warm afternoons over tea, or in the evening when the moonlight made the garden beyond into mysterious shapes which Lawrence, I think, always fancied were bandits."

Lawrence did fancy they were bandits, and he was afraid. Frieda too was nervous, especially at night, so they made the cook's son, armed with a revolver, sleep outside their bedroom door to guard them. During the afternoons while Lorenzo and Hal wrote, Frieda sat in a New England rocking chair knitting, while Spud, in a twin chair, just sat, smoking. Frieda stopped swimming with the men because one morning when she was in the lake a huge snake rose from the water "yards high," as it seemed to her, only a few feet away.

"All that time in Mexico seems to me, now, as if I had dreamt it, dreamt it intensely," she wrote.

Lorenzo resented her warm friendship with Bynner. Perhaps he had reason even though he knew the poet was homosexual; there are other infidelities than the simply sexual. One day when Hal was mixing the afternoon cocktail, his regular chore, and Lawrence was not present, he said to Frieda, "If you and Lawrence quarrel, why don't you hit first?"

It seemed good advice and she took it to heart. The next

time Lorenzo lost his temper and began steaming up for the attack, she surprised him by flying at him. Of course he resented Bynner!

The halcyon existence worried the Puritan in Lawrence; he wrote to Earl Brewster that he loathed the "playboy" attitude to life (could he be thinking of Hal?) and detested "having a good time," but he still couldn't face England. A man wanted him to run a banana hacienda with him there in Mexico, he said, but . . . no, he knew he should first go to England. Anyway, he probably shouldn't try to bury himself in inaccessible places. Frieda, he added, wanted to go to England much more than he did.

The high point of the Chapala sojourn was when the party hired a boat. They had long admired the great flat-bottomed sailboats, heavy as barges, that moved back and forth over the lake carrying on the trade of the region, and when one day they saw a brand-new one, clean and not yet loaded with cargo, they promptly chartered it complete with crew and set out on a leisurely tour.

"Our craft moved when the wind moved, and lay becalmed under myriad stars whole nights," wrote Spud. "She was poled into quaint old ports where we bought fruit and chickens, eggs and tortillas. She glided magnificently over gentle, choppy waves to islands where mangos and goats' milk replenished our larder—where sometimes a shepherd would kill a kid for our pirate appetites."

With them on the voyage were two Americans living in Guadalajara; Dr. George E. Purnell, a dentist, and his daughter Idella, who had been one of Bynner's students in his writing class at the University of California. Idella, later Mrs. Stone, was editing a new poetry magazine, *Palms*, for which she asked Lawrence for contributions and was roundly snubbed, but later he relented and gave her some poems. She was seasick on the trip and Hal got dysentery, so that both had to be taken ashore, but all the others had an enjoyable time. One evening after the voyage some of the party were sitting in the local hotel lobby when Lorenzo entered, "looking pale and pursued," probably after an encounter with the local prostitutes. He sat down by Frieda, and Idella heard him say, "Oh, Frieda, protect me from these wretched women!"

"He almost put his head down in her lap, like a little boy," continued Mrs. Stone. "My feeling about him, after all these years and in the light of the things I know now, is that he was sexually immature, upset by misinterpretations of wisdoms, and preoccupied by a desire to understand, with his head, something he could never really understand with his body." A case, perhaps, of sex in the head? ". . . I remember how he enjoyed baking, lovely crisp loaves of white bread; and he liked to mend things, and sew."

When the Lawrences left Chapala she saw them off at the station. Frieda blew her nose emotionally and said, "I *like* Chapala! I *like* Chapala!" but Lawrence, Idella could see, was happy to be leaving. Yet three days later he was regretting Mexico. All the way to New York he regretted it, in New Orleans which he hated and in New York which he hated more. He had no use for the United States at all. On the other hand, he shrank from going back to England; he and Frieda quarreled about it steadily. She was determined to go, arguing that she had not seen the children for four years, but Lawrence grew more and more stubborn. The day after getting to New York they moved out to the Seltzers' cottage in New Jersey where he was to correct proofs of his Mexican book undisturbed. On August 7 he wrote to Jack Murry, the Baroness, and Merrild, telling each of them that he wasn't going to England.

"I find my soul doesn't want to come to Europe, it is like Balaam's ass and can't come any further," he wrote to Frieda's mother. "I am not coming, but Frieda is." Instead, he said, he would go out to California and join the Danes, and if it was nice there Frieda could rejoin him in October. "I don't know why I can't go to England," he continued. "Such a deadness comes over me, if I only think of it, that I think it is better if I stay here, till my feeling has changed. I don't like New York—a big, stupid town, without background, without a voice. But here in the country it is green and still. But I like Mexico better."

In *"Not I, But the Wind . . ."* Frieda was to say that Lawrence was right and she was wrong, that he should not have had to come to Europe as he did later to catch up with her. What gave her this feeling of compunction is not clear, apart from the remorse one always feels about one's dealings in the past with someone now dead. She said that she realized when she got to England that the children were grown up and didn't need her any more (not that they ever had, if one comes down to it) because they were leading their own lives. Also, it was winter in England and dreary, and she missed Lawrence. But there is probably another reason for her qualms of conscience.

Jack Murry had found her in a rebellious mood, righteously indignant with Lawrence. She must have begun to boil over in Mexico when he behaved so badly again and again, and those last weeks of indecision on his part—to go with her, or not to go?—put the finishing touch on her anger. For what was probably the first time in her good-natured life, Frieda found herself capable of prolonged fury, able to be angry with Lawrence whenever she thought about him. Still, she was not accustomed to living alone, and she welcomed Murry's company. He, lonely without Katherine, who had died in the past year, came often to see her in the flat that was part of a Hampstead house owned by Catherine Carswell's brother; the brother lived there in other rooms, and so did the Carswells. Murry had started a new literary magazine, the *Adelphi,* and he told Frieda he hoped Lawrence would use it as a platform from which to spread his ideas. This pleased her, but the frequency of Jack's visits caused Mrs. Carswell to raise her eyebrows. She didn't like Jack Murry, had never liked him, and now she asked herself—and probably Donald, as well—what was going on between Lawrence and Frieda that she was alone in London. Frieda was somewhat cryptic as to when she expected to see her husband again. Could it be . . . ?

Catherine's watchful presence must have made Frieda uncomfortable. At any rate, things did not come to a head until she and Murry embarked on a journey to Germany together, she to see her mother at Baden and he on another errand from which he meant to move on to Switzerland. It was on this trip that the question of a love affair was broached. Letters exchanged between Frieda and Jack in after years are specific: Frieda, it seems, suggested that they go to bed together, but Jack consulted his conscience and decided against it, saying it wouldn't be fair to Lawrence. In 1955 he asked her, writing from Norfolk, "Tell me, Frieda, for my own private satisfaction—it shall be buried afterwards—did you love me as much as I loved you in those queer days? It drove me crazy—really crazy, I think—wanting you so badly: the comfort and delight of you, and then feeling Oh God, but Lorenzo will never get over it." Lorenzo, he went on, was always lecturing him, telling him to untwist himself. But if he *had* untwisted himself . . .

Frieda replied that after their journey she felt happy about things: "something ultimate and deeply satisfactory and new had happened to me . . . an inner lovely fact, that I accepted without question. . . . No, you did the right thing," she said. "Lawrence was already very ill. I think you averted an ugly tragedy." She also owed Lorenzo loyalty, she said; she had to see him through, and Jack helped her. "It was tough going at times as you know. . . . Do you remember the sweet names he called me? . . .'——' was the one I hated most. When you say I was a comfort and delight that pleases me no end."

In a letter to Merrild, Lawrence said definitely that he was going out to California, taking it for granted that the Danes would willingly join him in whatever program he felt like following. "We might like to spend the winter in Palm Springs or among the hills. Or we might go again to Mexico." In any case, he said, he wanted to see them and talk about the future. Failing anything else they might make a pack trip into the mountains or find some boat that would take them to the South Sea Islands, "you as sailors, myself as cook." Frieda would probably want to join him again in October, he told them, by which time no doubt they would have chosen what to do. Perhaps they might build an adobe house in the foothills? They had told him that friends of theirs had done this, and it gave him the idea.

The Danes were staggered by the news that Frieda and Lawrence had separated, even for a short time; it seemed to them inconceivable. They were worried by the prospect of taking care of Lorenzo on his own, because they had a full-time job decorating a room for a friend, who was going to let them use it as an advertisement of what they could do, and they knew that Lawrence was very demanding. Still, there was nothing for it but to try. He was already on the way, writing now and then from various stopping points. He stayed for a few days at Bessie Freeman's house at Palm Springs and sent word that he was arriving in Los Angeles on August 30. They met him at the station and went through the usual fuss about the room they had found for him—he didn't like it, of course, but he put up with it for that night.

And after all things went well enough. Their friends who had given them the work, the Johnsons, were thrilled to make the acquaintance of the great man. There was an eclipse of the sun coming up, and all of them went together to see it. Lorenzo *was* a problem when it came to the work, just as the Danes had expected, because he wanted to do it himself. "He wanted desperately to help us paint," said Merrild. "But we didn't let him. As we were using the technique of fresco, it was too risky to let an amateur try his hand."

The work was finished in due course and the Danes were at liberty. Lorenzo still had in mind his romantic notion of the three of them hiring out as part of the crew of a sailing ship, and he insisted that they try to find such a vessel. They knew it was no use, but they humored him and joined in the fruitless search. One evening during this period Lawrence invited the young men to dine with him and asked where they would like to go: they elected to eat their dinner in a dance hall, and their host had to go along, though he did not like it at all. He sat there gloomily as they disported, telling them between numbers that he loathed the music and detested the dancing, which he called tail-wagging. Did the Danes, could they, really like that sort of thing? They assured him that they liked it very much and urged him to try for himself. Why not dance with a pretty girl? It was a silly question that didn't deserve an answer. Everyone went home early.

Lorenzo decided to go back to Mexico and urged the Danes to come with him. He might buy a banana ranch, he said, and they could all three work it, or perhaps they might find some other project. How about it? Gótzsche listened to the siren song, but Merrild would have none of it because, he explained in his book, he was heartily tired of living as Lawrence dictated. He had his own ideas of what he wanted in life, and they didn't include trotting at the heels of a genius. If he went anywhere it would be the South Seas, not Mexico. But Gótzsche felt great reverence for Lawrence, and though Merrild, he admitted, was probably right when he said you couldn't depend on Lorenzo, who always changed his plans in the middle of things, he wanted to follow him, come what may.

That wasn't hard to prophesy, Merrild retorted. Lawrence without Frieda was even less stable than he was with her. No matter what he said, he would soon throw up whatever he was doing and rejoin her in England, leaving Gótzsche out on a limb.

Probably, said Gótzsche, but it didn't matter; he was willing to spend his last penny to be with the great man as long as possible. Against such fervor Merrild fought no more, feeling it was no use and none of his business anyway. So the Danes separated, and Lawrence and Gótzsche set out for Mexico toward the end of September. Very soon a letter came to Merrild from Lorenzo:

"When I look at the ranches," he wrote, "I doubt very much whether I shall ever try to live on one for ever and a day. But very nice to stay the winter." Hmmmm, said Merrild.

The travelers reached Guadalajara on October 15, and Lawrence found there a letter from Frieda urging him to come to England. No, said Lawrence, discussing it with his companion; no, he wouldn't—at least not during the winter. Gótzsche wrote to Merrild that he couldn't help being amused by Lorenzo, who always scorned sentimentality but was very sentimental himself. On the way to Chapala he admitted that he didn't like to go there without Frieda—"He is longing for her," said Gótzsche—and when they arrived he was deeply moved because it seemed so changed. "Somehow it becomes unreal to me now. I don't know why," Lawrence said.

"He is always so concerned about the 'spirit' of the place that he isn't aware, I believe, that it is he, himself, his own mood or frame of mind, that determines his impressions of the moment, or the landscape," said Gótzsche wisely. "It is, of course, possible that the place has changed, it is fall now and he was there with Frieda in the spring. But of course that isn't it. It is the 'spirit.' "

Lawrence was greatly put out, said the Dane, that Frieda was happy to be in England and kept telling him to come and join her in what she called the best country in the world. Naturally, all this uncertainty worried Lawrence's companion. What of the future? Within a month the plan was already beginning to disintegrate. Three days afterward he was telling Merrild that he believed Lawrence was going crazy. Frieda had not written again, probably because she was annoyed with Lawrence for going back to Guadalajara, and he was very irritable.

"You know his ways," wrote Gótzsche, "and how he bends his head far down, till his beard is resting on his chest and he says (not laughing) 'Hee, hee, hee' every time one talks to him. A cold stream always runs down my spine when he does that. I feel it is something insane about him." Doubtless, said the Dane, who was now an experienced Lawrence-watcher, the genius was arguing himself into going back to England as Frieda wished, and Gótzsche was glad, in spite of everything, that they hadn't found a ranch to live on in Mexico. He realized how difficult it would be to live with Lawrence for very long. "Frieda is at least an absolute necessity as a quencher," he commented.

Clearly, Gótzsche added, Lawrence was in dread that Frieda would run away from him—if, indeed, she had not done so already—and the Dane was not at all startled when Lawrence announced that he had decided to go to England soon, probably the middle of December. That settled, he cheered up amazingly. On the third of November Lawrence himself wrote to Merrild to tell of his decision: "Gótzsche will have told you that Frieda won't come back: not West any more. I had a cable yesterday asking me to go to England. So there's nothing for it but to go."

After all, Gótzsche told his old friend, he himself would be all right; Lawrence was paying his way for an inexpensive trip back to Denmark. Much to his relief, he said, Lorenzo was himself again, now that he had made up his mind, but all was not quite easy, evidently, in his conscience: "He is afraid Frieda will avoid him; he says that she can have a house in London and have her children with her, then he can travel alone. 'She will hate it before long,' he says, biting his lower lip and nodding small, quick nods. Do you know him? The fact is that he is afraid she will like that arrangement only too well."

It is clear that in the struggle Lawrence always saw between man and woman, *his* woman had come out triumphant, and the knowledge was galling. But he could do nothing about it—nothing, that is, but write about it bitterly to his mother-in-law on November 10. It is a letter Frieda describes in her book as cross and unjust, one of the very few occasions in which she permits herself to speak ill of her dead husband, and one can hardly blame her for it. Lawrence at the time was in Wagnerian mood, possibly because, as always when corresponding with the Baroness, he was writing in German. The word *courage* recurred over and over in the letter. One must be seventy before one is full of courage, he told the seventy-year-old woman. The young are always halfhearted, and women have more courage than men. Continuing in *macho* strain, he said that he liked it in Mexico:

> I don't know how, but it gives me strength, this black country. It is full of man's strength, perhaps not woman's strength, but it is good, like the old German beer-for-the-heroes, for me. Oh, mother-in-law, you are nice and old, and understand, as the first maiden understood, that a man must be more than nice and good, and that heroes are worth more than saints. Frieda doesn't understand that a man must be a hero these days and not only a husband: husband also but more. I must go up and down through the world, I must balance Germany against Mexico and Mexico against Germany. I do not come for peace. The devil, the holy devil, has peace round his neck. I know it well, the courageous old one understands me better than the young one, or at least something in me she understands better. Frieda must always think and write and say and ponder *how* she loves me. It is stupid. I am no Jesus that lies on his mother's lap. I go my way through the world, and if Frieda finds it such hard work to love me, then, dear God, let her love rest, give it holidays.

One wonders if the Baroness showed this letter to Frieda before she died, or if Frieda found it in her mother's belongings after her death. The hero continued:

> Oh, mother-in-law, you understand, as my mother finally understood, that a man doesn't want, doesn't ask for love from his wife, but for strength, strength, strength. . . . And the stupid woman keeps on saying love, love, love, and writes of

love. To the devil with love! Give me strength, battle-strength, weapon-strength, fighting-strength, give me this, you woman! England is so quiet: writes Frieda. Shame on you that you ask for peace today. I don't want peace. I go around the world fighting. Pfui! Pfui! In the grave I find my peace. First let me fight and win through. Yes, yes, mother-in-law, make me an oak-wreath and bring the town music under the window, when the half-hero returns.

After which purging outburst, he probably went out and paid for the ticket that was to take him back to Frieda.

But she was not really talking all that much in her letters about love, not at that time; her amorous propensities were aimed elsewhere. Frieda was never good at concealment in these matters, and Lawrence was very clever at guessing what women were thinking. For all his posturing as a deliverer in shining armor, going round and round the world to do battle (and for what?), he must have been aware of something in England that threatened him, and he shrank from confronting it. Much to Gótzsche's exasperation, even after making his decision he kept faltering. The sailing date was near when Lawrence declared that he couldn't go after all: "I am sure I will *die* if I have to see England again," said the doughty warrior. He really looked ill, said Gótzsche, with his chin resting characteristically on his chest. Then, once more, a quick change followed in his mood; the next day he wondered why one must make such a fuss over a little thing like going to England, and, in the end, he actually got aboard and sailed away.

In spite of all the travel and the incertitude, the time spent in knocking about California and Mexico, trying to recapture the past at Chapala and the rest of it, Lawrence didn't stop working. He had on his mind the novel written by Mollie Skinner of Darlington about the early settlers of Australia. After his words of encouragement she had set about writing it: she completed it after he went away and sent it to him for his opinion, catching up with him in California; Lawrence wrote to Miss Skinner in September from there to say that he had read it carefully.

"He slated it [attacked it], then praised it," wrote Mollie in her account of how their collaboration came about. He told her that he hated to think of the book being wasted because he liked much of it. But, he added, she had no "constructive power," so, if she liked the idea, he himself would write it over again "and make a book of it."

Now nobody, even a comparative beginner like Mollie Skinner, is quite happy to think of her work taken over and changed, not even by a famous genius like D. H. Lawrence. On the other hand, what else was she to do with the book? Without him, she couldn't even be sure of finding a publisher. She decided that she would be a fool to decline the offer; with a pang, she consented; and Lawrence, on the way to England, went ahead rewriting. There was no nonsense about consulting her as he went along. He had a completely free hand, and she didn't see the work until he had done it all. Resentfully, she noted that he had, after all, used her construction all the way through until he reached the last two chapters—which, she grieved to see, were drastically altered in a manner she would never have dreamed of. Love affairs, dramatically described, had been added. Mollie wept, but again submitted. The book finally appeared under the title *The Boy in the Bush*, signed by both authors. Everyone Mollie knew condemned it, and her with it, which was only to be expected in Australia. But when she came to England soon after the publication date, saw the "magnificent reviews," and found that she was to share equally in the royalties, she was comforted. *The Boy* had considerable success.

Lawrence arrived in London early in December. A little deputation met the boat train—Frieda, Kot, and Jack Murry. Murry thought Lawrence looked ill, with "a greenish pallor," but the pallor may have been in the eye of the beholder, who was feeling a twinge of conscience. Catherine Carswell saw Lawrence as soon as he got to the flat, and she denied the pallor, though she had no doubt he had summed up the Frieda-Jack situation at a glance and could hardly be expected to look pleased. Admittedly, Catherine was prejudiced. She didn't like Murry.

Lawrence, whose first words as he emerged from the train were, "I can't bear it," was within a few minutes suggesting to Jack that the *Adelphi* attack everything in sight and "explode in one blaze of denunciation," a program Murry found untempting. No doubt Lawrence saw the magazine as an obstacle to the dream that had been born afresh during the long voyage: Rananim, with Murry as a founding member. With such a glorious future, why should Jack want to edit a magazine? Lawrence talked a good deal about it. They would make up a party and leave for New Mexico as soon as possible, he said, there to live happily ever after. There would be Jack, and Catherine Carswell, and Brett, that shy deaf girl from the Slade, whose father was a peer and who had once joined with Lawrence in being catty about Ottoline. Within a few days, however, Lawrence's plan was running into trouble. Jack was markedly noncommittal about it, and in the 1974 edition of Brett's book *Lawrence and Brett: A Friendship,* we learn why. Brett has announced at last that she is not a virgin, though it has long been the fashion of her world to describe her as such. It seems that one afternoon or evening in 1920 she went to bed with Jack Murry. She regretted this lapse because Katherine Mansfield was furious with her about it, and it made trouble, too, between Katherine and Jack, though they later became reconciled. Naturally, however, Jack as a sorrowing widower did not want to be thrown into Brett's company too markedly: he suspected Lawrence of matchmaking, and he was probably right. As for Catherine Carswell, she replied to Lawrence's proposal with genuine sorrow that it was quite impossible to count on her for a long time to come, for Donald couldn't go, and she could hardly leave him and the child. A "terrible sadness" fell on her as she said this, and Lawrence replied gently, "No, a woman can't choose if she's really married," and went on to speak approvingly of Brett because she was free and untrammeled.

For the first time since they had grown up, Frieda's daughters met Lawrence at a little party in Frieda's flat. Barbara thought him "a queer, unearthly creature" with his fragility and high-pitched voice. She preferred John Middleton Murry, who sat near, "dark, smiling and inscrutable, but more like the other men we had known." Though Lawrence was very friendly, he puzzled the girls. He talked to Barby about her art school, but as always when art was mentioned he became critical, of the school and even of her, saying later to Elsa, "Barby is not the stuff of which artists are made." She might reasonably have wondered how he knew on such short acquaintance. Two years later when he encountered their brother, Monty too noticed the Midlands accent and quoted a very typical remark of his stepfather's to illustrate it—"Sargent, sooch a bad peynter." But then, the British are always very conscious of accents. During that 1923–24 visit, at any rate, Lawrence met only the girls, and he was not flattering about them when he and Frieda went to visit her mother. He told the Baroness that her granddaughters were "just little suburban nobodies." Poor Barby. Poor Elsa.

Rananim continued to be very important to Lawrence, and as soon as he got over the regulation bad cold that always attacked him after a journey he made up his mind to give a supper party for all the group and settle the thing. He took a private room at the Café Royal and ordered a supper for nine. It was not at all his usual style of entertainment, which as we know was an informal meal of stew or spaghetti cooked by himself in whatever place he and Frieda had borrowed to live in. No, this was to be a slap-up affair for his best friends; Kot, Murry, Mark Gertler (an artist whose work he did not quite condemn), Donald and Catherine, Brett, and Mary Cannan. Of course he went into a rage because, when he ordered the meal, the manager insisted on a cash deposit, but he got over it, and the party went ahead.

Catherine Carswell thought there was something "piquant and touching" in the way he received his guests at the café, all dressed up as they were and on their good behavior. "It emphasized the lack of sophistication in him which, combined with his subtlety, was so moving a charm," she said. It would be wrong, she added, to apply the word schoolboyish to "this mature and refined, disciplined and impassioned artist," but there *was* something schoolboyish about him just the same: "You'll see I'm quite up to this," he seemed to be saying. "Mind you play up to me, so that nobody will have the slightest idea that we don't dine in marble halls all the year round."

The story of that party has been told many times. Everyone drank a lot of claret, and Kot stood up and made a speech in praise of Lawrence, punctuated by smashing wineglasses whenever he made a particularly telling point. (Kot, after all, was Russian.) "Lawrence is a great man," he said, and broke a glass. "Nobody here realizes how great he is." Smash. "Especially no woman here or anywhere can possibly realize the greatness of Lawrence." Smash. "Frieda does not count. Frieda is different." No smash. Kot and Frieda were not really friends.

Then Lawrence, looking pale and ill, stood up and talked in less formal manner, breaking no glasses, about the future and his plans for them all. He said that he couldn't stay in England; he must return to New Mexico, and he wanted them all, his good friends, to come with him. He talked glowingly, but vaguely as ever, about what they would all do together. They would struggle with the world in a new way, he said, withdrawing their essential being from the common struggle and turning their strength into a new channel. Catherine thought it beautiful, though she didn't understand it. Then Lawrence asked each one of the party in turn if he would come to America.

He asked Mary Cannan first, and she replied unequivocally that she would not; she liked Lawrence, she said, but not that much. Gertler, when he was asked, turned off the question sardonically. Of course he'd come, he said, in a way that meant of course he wouldn't. Kot? Indeed yes, said Kot, patently lying. Donald? Yes, said Donald, with a similar lack of conviction. His wife at least knew he didn't mean it. Brett? Yes—and Brett did mean it. Murry? Yes, he said. Catherine? She too said yes, knowing in her heart that it would never happen.

By this time dinner was over, they were drinking port, and nobody was responsible for his actions. The exact account of what happened next is confused, and the version given by Catherine Carswell does not jibe with Murry's, which is more convincing. According to him, he kissed Lawrence and said, "I love you, Lorenzo, but I won't promise not to betray you."

Probably he did say it. It was a message to Frieda, sent to her over the heads of the others as she sat there, silent in her pretty dress.

Port was not good for Lawrence, and at this moment he vomited. There was a great shuffle and a lot of excitement among people who wanted to do something about it, chiefly Catherine and Brett; it was Brett who held his hand and stroked his damp hair, waiting for the men to fetch a taxi. Frieda did nothing of the sort but continued to sit calmly. Lawrence was carried out of the Café Royal, put into the taxi, and borne up to his bed, where he remained for a day or two in thoughtful mood.

Afterward, said Brett, he dropped in often on her Hampstead house. In the book she wrote about Lawrence she addressed him all the way through, telling her story as if speaking to him. "You hate that house, you hate my furniture, you hate the whole thing," she said, "but you come, nevertheless. We sit opposite each other, making flowers in clay and painting them; and you talk to me in that soft, midland voice, probing delicately into my life and ideas and feelings, sensitive to my sensitiveness; and I evade shyly, you laughing at my adroitness. And thus we sit, happily, sometimes quite silently, intensely aware of each other, modelling and painting pots of flowers."

But Brett didn't get off any more easily, when it came to her work, than Augustus John had. Looking at her paintings, Lawrence cried, "They are dead. Like all the paintings now; there is no life in them. They are dead, dead! All these still-lives —no life in the painting." He seems to have talked himself into a passionate anger, too, that any woman should bother about art. Also, he declared, painters of the day never faced life itself. Brett didn't take this meekly and wanted to argue with him, but Murry took him away. Still, he came back, often.

Others can bear witness that "the Brett" from that time on was one of the circle of Lawrence intimates. The South African writer Sarah Gertrude Millin and her husband, a judge, were visiting England and met the Lawrences about the turn of the year. She described Frieda as a German woman who was stout, untidy, but pleasant, and mentioned that Lawrence talked so much about the snobbery and class distinctions of the English that he seemed rather a snob himself. The Millins invited the Lawrences to dinner with Murry and Koteliansky; Lawrence asked if they might bring, as well, the most charming girl in the world—who was, of course, Brett. Naturally Mrs. Millin said yes, and she went to a lot of trouble to find a young man for her.

"The Lawrence party arrived very late, and without Mr. Koteliansky," said Mrs. Millin. "There had been, it appeared, a row with Mr. Koteliansky about Tolstoi, and this row had made them late, and it had prevented Mr. Koteliansky from coming at all." Though the men were in evening dress, Frieda wore "a brown fur cap, a white Russian blouse, a black velveteen skirt, white cotton stockings and black velveteen shoes." Brett was of course carrying her hearing-aid case (she called the trumpet Toby) and explained to her hostess that she couldn't hear a thing without it; Murry, in further explanation, told Mrs. Millin *sotto voce* that Brett had gone deaf in early youth trying not to hear what her upper-class relatives had to say. The young man Mrs. Millin had brought in was tongue-tied when it came to talking into Brett's hearing aid. Altogether it was not the most successful dinner party Mrs. Millin ever gave.

Informal parties among the group were more fun. After supper in the Lawrences' flat, said Brett, they would sit around the fire and model flowers in plasticine, then paint them. One night, with much merriment, they modeled Adam and Eve, along with the tree, the apples, and the snake. Lorenzo wouldn't trust Brett to do the human figures; he was insolent about it, but the others laughed and yielded to him. Murry made the snake. But when they looked at Adam they were shocked.

"Lawrence, you just can't leave Adam like that."

Lawrence was amused by their scandalized faces. He said, tartly, "Do you good, Brett." But when they continued to protest, he snipped off the "indecency" and then mourned for Adam's loss, "poor, thin, indecent Adam." One wonders what Lorenzo's reaction would have been if anyone else had done this.

On another evening things were not so gay and funny. They were all there in the same places, around the fire, and talking about something Brett found hard to follow with her trumpet. Frieda was knitting as usual. All at once, said Brett, Frieda launched a verbal attack on her husband, contradicting him, denouncing him, and declaring that he wanted to make a God of himself. "You expostulate wearily," said Brett, making it clear whose side she was on—indeed, was always on. . . . "Your temper rises to meet the sledge-hammer blows. You break into the midland vernacular. The rich Yorkshire dialect pours softly from your lips with an ever-increasing force, a steadily rising anger. In that language, strange to our ears"—strange indeed, as it was Nottinghamshire rather than Yorkshire—"you fiercely denounce her." Small wonder that everyone stared, spellbound.

Suddenly Lawrence seized the poker and, as he talked, emphasized his words by striking the cups and saucers. It was "terrible to watch and hear," said Brett, "—the slow, deadly words and the steady smash of the poker," until he said, slowly and menacingly, "Beware, Frieda! If ever you talk to me like that again, it will not be the tea things I smash, but your head. Oh, yes, I'll kill you. So beware!" Down went the poker on the teapot.

Still nobody spoke. At last, sighing heavily, Lawrence held out his hand to Brett. She took it and held it. Running his other hand through his hair he laughed a little, nervously, and said, "Frieda should not make me so angry." Things returned to normal, and Frieda later brought a dustpan and brush and swept up the broken crockery.

Many years later, Frieda in a letter to Murry (December 19, 1951) spoke of such outbreaks; she was terribly sorry for Lawrence, she said, or she could never have stood it. "Sometimes he went over the edge of sanity," she admitted. "I was many times frightened but never the last bit of me. Once, I remember he had worked himself up and his hands were on my throat and he was pressing me against the wall and ground out: 'I am the master. I am the master.' I said: 'Is that all? You can be master as much as you like, I don't care.' His hands dropped away, he looked at me in astonishment and was all right."

Time drew on toward the sailing date. After a visit to Baden-Baden there was a flurry to get ready. Murry had intended to go along, even though it meant relinquishing the *Adelphi*, which was no small sacrifice. But when he discovered that Brett was going too he made up his mind privately to bow out. He would *not* be one of a party of four, he resolved. Lawrence had no right to make such arrangements without consulting him first. It was bad enough, going along with Frieda in the party and being unable to explain his feelings about her; to be paired with Brett—no! He pretended until the last minute that he would follow after, but even Lorenzo was not fooled.

It comes as a surprise, perhaps a welcome one, to discover that there was in England one woman at least who actually *did not like* Lawrence, much less have a crush on him. This was Carrington, the former Slade School student who had once shared a flat with Brett. In a letter to a friend dated March 4, 1924, she said:

> I saw on Saturday afternoon D. H. Lawrence and his fat German spouse Frieda and the great decaying mushroom Middleton Murry and an attendant toadstool called Dr Young at Brett's house in Hampstead. I went up there to say goodbye to Brett [the Lawrences, with Brett, were taking off next day for New Mexico] but found to my dismay this dreadful assembly of Adelphites. Lawrence was very rude to me of course, and held forth to the assembly as if he was a lecturer to minor university students. Apparently he came back this winter expecting to be greeted as the new messiah. Unfortunately very few saw his divination. . . . A few critics called him a genius but that wasn't enough. "England is rotten, its inhabitants corrupt." Mexico is the only country where prophets, and great writers are appreciated. So tomorrow Lawrence, and Frieda and Brett set off in an ocean liner for Mexico.

More discussion brought out the fact that it wasn't really Mexico they were going to, but New Mexico, "which is a state of U.S.A.," Carrington explained kindly, but they continued to refer to it as Mexico. She quoted Lawrence scornfully: "We lead a very primitive life, we cut our own wood, and cook our own food." To this, Frieda came in like a Greek chorus, as always the minute Lawrence stopped speaking:

"And Lawrence makes the mo-ost beau-ti-ful bread."

Then Lawrence turned his unwelcome attention to Carrington: "And here is Carrington, not very much changed, lost a little of her 'ingenue' perhaps, still going to parties, still exactly the same, except I hear you are very rich now, and live in a grand country house."

Furiously, Carrington wrote, "I took the shine off his Northampton noise and his whining 'ingenue' accent. I told him I had 130 £ a year which I had always had. 'Ah but yer married a rich husband!' "

She retorted "He has £80 a year."

"And yer don't mind the change, that's very fortunate."

Scathingly, Carrington told how Lawrence then turned back to the subject of Mexico and held forth "with some fine literary passages." Everyone listened respectfully, taking notes, as it were, in imaginary notebooks: "The decayed Murry sat on a sofa and said nothing; he swayed backwards and forwards like a mandarin, with hollow eyes, toothless gums, a vacant smile and watery eyes." She continued:

"Only once he spoke. 'Say, Brett your butter's bad. It's not good.' (D.H.L. 'They've scalded it Brett, butter should'na be scalded. They've boiled the milk.') Otherwise the great Murry never spoke. It is reported he has given up the *Adelphi* and is, in a few months, going to follow the Messiah, Frau Messiah, and Brett to Mexico."

# 14

## Brett: "A kind of buffer"

"21 MARCH 1924: SANTA FE," Hal Bynner dated a
letter to his mother. He told her that the Lawrences had just
arrived that evening "with an English viscountess or something,
deaf but likable. . . . They go along to Taos tomorrow, to see
whether this time he can refrain from quarreling with Mabel.
He's a man with a mind, anyway. I was glad to see him and
really joyous in seeing the great-hearted Frieda."

The hatchet had been buried. Mabel was ready to admit
that she'd been a naughty girl, while for his part Lorenzo was
willing to accept her "submission," as he liked, rather oddly, to
phrase it. He had been lecturing her for weeks by letter, also
keeping her up to date on his plans for Rananim. The colony
as he saw it would live at Mabeltown, under her various hospitable roofs. For the moment, of course, there were only
three of them.

"I rather hope Murry won't come to Taos," he confessed
from Baden-Baden. "Don't trust him very well."

Later Lawrence wrote a short story, "The Border Line,"
which gives a clear idea of how his mind was preoccupied by
Murry. In it we meet—not for the first time—the daughter of
a German baron, who has been married twice. Her first and

late husband was tall and splendid-looking and red-haired, a hero of a fellow, a giant Lawrence, but the second, living husband is a mean little creature with Murry's features. This miserable specimen falls mysteriously and fatally ill. During his dying moments the dead man comes back, picks up the woman in his arms, and takes her to bed *right there in the room.* Writing the story must have made Lawrence feel a lot better about Murry.

Mabel and Tony had spent the winter in California and came home a day after the Lawrence party arrived to be joyfully greeted. The impact of Frieda's personality, larger than life as it was, took Mabel by surprise even though she should have remembered it.

"I don't know how to describe . . . the hearty sounds she gives out," wrote Mabel. "Shouts and shrieks, but muffled ones, blasts of energy with her big, wholesome mouth open and her white teeth shining." In the excited confusion and much to her own surprise Mabel actually kissed Frieda "on her hard, pink cheek," at which Frieda started back, her smile gone. Obviously she didn't want Mabel's kiss.

Brett Mabel saw as "a tall, oldish girl" with "pretty, pink, round cheeks and a childish expression," harmless in herself, but the same could not be said for Toby, her ear trumpet. Brett was always turning Toby around, pointing it at people to pick up scraps of conversation; the bad part of this was that almost always it was pointed at Lawrence, and Mabel didn't like that. She found it inhibiting to know that Toby scooped up everything she herself said to Lorenzo. Toby was an eavesdropper, Mabel decided—a spy; curious and relentless. Mabel was still determined to be a good girl, but before long she was complaining about Brett to Lawrence. He brushed it off, saying (according to Mabel) "that he had brought Brett along to be a kind of buffer" between himself and Frieda, as life alone with his wife was too hard. Perhaps he really did say this, but it sounds suspiciously like a similar yet very different argument he had already used on Frieda when she, like Mabel, wondered why the young woman should be included in their circle:

"You know it will be good for us to have the Brett with us, she will stand between us and people and the world."

Frieda confessed that she was not convinced; she had a suspicion that Brett intended, rather, to stand between Lorenzo and herself. "But no, I thought, I won't be so narrow-gutted, one of Lawrence's words, I will try."

Naturally Frieda saw at once that Mabel too did not wish Brett to be quite so present. She attempted to comfort Mabel— a galling thought, that it should come to this!—saying that she was not to mind "the Brett."

"She doesn't count," said Frieda. "She helps Lorenzo. She plays piquet with him and types for him."

The Lawrences and Brett, housed on the estate, took their main meals in the Big House and stayed on reasonably good terms one with another. Inevitably, however, Lorenzo grew restless, complained of all the social goings-on around Mabel, and pined for a change. During a nostalgic visit to the ranches, the Lawrences said so many nice things about the peace and beauty of John's property that Mabel impulsively and generously, not to say recklessly (since it wasn't hers), gave it to them, all 166 acres and the three cabins on it. Lawrence refused to accept, on the grounds that he didn't like presents, so Mabel gave it to Frieda instead. She made it up to John by giving him in exchange four hundred dollars and a buffalo-skin robe. (John and Alice were glad to have the robe because he drove a very cold touring car; it came in handy when they went shopping. Unfortunately someone smashed a dozen eggs over it and they had to bury it.) Naturally, Frieda was delighted, but after some reflection she had misgivings about accepting such a magnificent gift, and suddenly remembered a way to get around it by handing to Mabel the manuscript of *Sons and Lovers,* which had been in Elsa's possession in Germany. Lawrence did not ordinarily save his manuscripts, but

Elsa happened to have this one intact because she had translated it into German. Lawrence consented to the transaction, and so it was arranged.

Five weeks after Mabel handed over the ranch, the Lawrence party moved up and took possession. They renamed the property, hitherto called The Flying Heart; from then on it was known as Kiowa Ranch. Certain politenesses were observed: for example, Tony and Mabel had been in the habit of leaving horses at the ranch, and the Lawrences assured them that the animals could stay. After all, they themselves habitually rode Luhan horses—even Brett had learned to ride and loved it. Also, it was agreed that one of the houses, of which there were three on the ranch, was to be reserved for Mabel when she felt like coming to stay. A lot of work had to be done on the buildings, and a number of Indians were hired from the Pueblo to do it. They came up with Tony and Mabel and set up camp higher on the hill, back of Kiowa Ranch, with a large tepee. Before the cabins were habitable Mabel and the other Anglos slept out of doors in the warm summer nights.

Brett described the life in the early days. "The cabin is built up slowly. I chop wood for Frieda's little kitchen stove. You are working all day with the Indians. Frieda cooks, lies on her bed smoking, cooks again."

When it stormed and the tepee was flooded Mabel came and slept in the guest house, though she often got bored and went down to Taos for a day or two. She was away at the time of the first Frieda–Brett crisis at the ranch. It began in the evening, after a day's hard work, when Lorenzo, Frieda, and Brett met for supper in the newly built kitchen in the big house. Brett, cut off by her deafness from ordinary conversation, was sensitive to moods, and she realized that something was wrong: there was a queer feeling in the air. Were they all tired, perhaps? She wondered. No, no more than usual. But after the meal, when the dishes had been washed and she went out into the yard, Lawrence quickly came after her and attacked her verbally, out of the blue as it seemed. "You . . . say suddenly that I have no respect for Frieda. I stare at you in astonishment. Your voice begins to rise. You shout at me that I have no respect for either you or Frieda, that Frieda says I never talk to her but only to you. Your voice is rising higher and higher."

Brett took hold of his wrist and said calmly, "No, Lawrence, that isn't so."

It stopped him for a moment; he hesitated. Then Frieda popped out of the house and egged him on, shrieking at them both until she set off Lawrence again. He continued to rant, but Brett held on to his wrist and repeated quietly that it just wasn't so. Lawrence's anger subsided and he went back indoors. Brett could not dismiss the matter, however; she was upset. She went off into the woods and stayed there until dark, when she came back to her little house and went to bed without lighting her lamp. Someone came in with a lantern, but Brett kept her head under the blanket and stayed quiet until the intruder went away.

"Next morning Frieda comes over, very upset, and weeps," reported Brett. "We are both upset. When I go over to your house, you come in and, looking at me with a gleam and a twinkle in your eyes, you say:

" 'Storms, Brett, storms.' "

It would be strange if Frieda had not resented Brett at times, if only because the young woman was witness to various of her humiliations, as when Frieda acquired a new horse, a big gray named Azul, with which she was delighted. She rode along with Lawrence and Brett to fetch the milk at Del Monte, and called out happily, "Oh, it's wonderful; wonderful to feel his great thighs moving, to feel his powerful legs!"

"Rubbish, Frieda!" replied Lawrence. "Don't talk like that. You have been reading my books: you don't feel anything of the sort!"

Not long afterward he and Brett managed to fell a tree and drag the trunk from the woods to the house, where Frieda loudly admired them for their strength and cleverness. Law-

rence said, "We will have to saw it. You can sit on it as you
are the heaviest." Frieda didn't care for this remark, but she
did sit on the log, "solidly and firmly," while the others
worked on it with the two-man saw. One can hardly wonder
if her temper suffered from treatment like this, but what really
infuriated her was Brett's open adoration of Lorenzo, her
complete acceptance of everything he said and did. No doubt
Frieda could have done with a bit of this admiration herself,
but it was never forthcoming. In any dispute, Brett immediately
lined up on Lorenzo's side. Once at tea Lawrence asked Brett
how she liked *The Boy in the Bush*, which she had read in
England. Brett replied that she liked it very much except for
the ending, which was artistically wrong; Lawrence should
have let the man die.

"I know, I know," said Lorenzo. "That is how I wrote
it first; I made him die—only Freida made me change it."

Sitting there with her embroidery, Frieda boomed, "Yes,
I made him change it. I couldn't stand the superiority of the
man, always the same self-importance. 'Let him become ordinary,' I said. Always this superiority and death."

"Well," said Brett. "It's spoiled the book."

And Lawrence sighed and added, "Yes, he should have
died."

Surely this was playing with fire; we cannot wonder that
Frieda said angrily, "The Brett always agrees with you; always
sticks up for you." Nobody answered this remark. Really,
one should not condemn Frieda out of hand, especially as she
seems sometimes to have dealt with the situation with humor.

"Brett, I'll give you half a crown if you contradict Lawrence," she once said, but Brett never did. Another time she
said, "Brett, I detest your adoration for Lawrence, only one
thing I would detest more, and that is if you adored me."

Compared with this constant irritation, even Mabel was
far less of a menace than she had been before. The Lawrences
were now more social than they had been in the old days and
usually came down to Taos with Brett for week ends. Living

in Mabeltown was a new man, Clarence, who had been passed
on to Mabel by a friend in the East. Clarence was a pretty boy
who loved to dress up, and Mabel liked him. He adopted her as
a mother figure and would have taken on Tony as a father
except that the Indian remained carefully withdrawn from such
goings-on. Excited at the idea of meeting a great man like
Lawrence, he persuaded Mabel to take him up to the ranch
when she went up there with Tony. The visit began unfortunately.

Like many people, Lorenzo's feelings about killing things
were mixed, as the Danes had discovered in the old days when
they made a practice of shooting rabbits for food. Lawrence
and Frieda approved at first, and were glad to have the extra
meat, until one awful day when Gótzsche shot a particular
rabbit that had been nibbling the greenery close to the Lawrences' cabin. There was hell to pay over that bunny. Now
Tony too came under a cloud by shooting a porcupine. The
Indians always shot porcupines when they got the chance, because the beasts killed pine trees by ringing their bark close
to the ground, but Lorenzo was furious.

"I don't want any shooting here," he told Tony angrily.
"I *like* the porcupines."

Tony, his feelings hurt, took the porcupine and his rifle
straight up to the Indian tepee, off the ranch's land, and that
night he and Clarence stayed there. Mabel had to sleep alone
in the guest house and she was unhappy. It sounded as if
Clarence and Tony and the Indians were having a much jollier
time than she was. In vain did she tell herself that Lawrence
was justified; the ranch was his, and he had a right to forbid
shooting if he wanted; Tony was her husband, and she felt
indignant on his behalf. In the morning, therefore, she went up
to the encampment, flouncing her skirts as she passed the Lawrence house, and when she reached the camp she sent Clarence
down to tell Lawrence, peremptorily, that she wanted to see
him. As might be expected, Lawrence retorted that if she
wanted to see him she could come down the hill. Mabel did.

She took him to the guesthouse, slammed the door, turned around to give him a dignified rebuke, and—

"How *can* you treat me like that?" she demanded, and burst into tears, flopping down on the bed. Lorenzo, head bent to chest, sat there on the edge of the bed and waited for the storm to pass. Mabel howled and sobbed for quite a long time, but at last she regained control, and they had a talk. It went on for hours, she reported, and in a strange way was very enjoyable for both parties, but she may have been mistaken about Lorenzo's reaction; the incident may well have sparked off an irritable statement he later made to Frieda that he would like to *kill* the woman. It was not the first time he had spoken so extravagantly of killing Mabel, but it seems to have come as news to her when Frieda mentioned it to Clarence and Clarence rushed back to tell Mabel. The fat was in the fire. Tony, when he heard of the threat, waxed wroth and sent up for two of his best horses from Kiowa Ranch. In other words, back to Square One, but everyone made up ultimately. The Lawrences even went along with the Luhans to see the Snake Dance in the Hopi country.

Soon after this jaunt, however, disaster struck at Kiowa Ranch. Lawrence had had a cold and sore throat for some days when one afternoon he spat blood. This was a dreadful omen for a man who never, never admitted to himself, let alone anyone else, that he might be tuberculous. Both Brett and Frieda, who were present, experienced the kind of embarrassment that accompanies an inadvertent sign of weakness on the part of a loved person; Lawrence, observed Brett, cast a look of consternation at his wife, who appeared flabbergasted. Brett herself pretended to have seen nothing. Lawrence went to bed and stayed there. When on the next afternoon he spat blood again, Frieda sent down to Taos, without telling him she was doing so, and asked the doctor to come up and see her husband.

Brett and Spud Johnson, who was visiting Kiowa at that time, carried the message by way of the Hawk ranch, and Lorenzo found out about it only when they came back and

Frieda, in his hearing, asked if Dr. Martin was coming. Lawrence was sitting up in bed at the time, his supper on a tray on his knees.

"Why have you sent for the Doctor?" he screamed. "How *dare* you!" and he seized the iron egg ring he used as an egg cup and flung it at Frieda's head, missing her by a hair's breadth. "You *know* I dislike Doctors . . ." he ranted. "I *won't* see him— I *won't!* I'll go out and hide in the sage brush until he goes. I'll teach you!"

He didn't carry out his threat, possibly because he was too weak to get out of bed. Dr. Martin arrived with a car full of blankets, just in case the turbulent patient had to be carried down to the hospital, but such stringent measures were unnecessary, as a beaming Frieda reported afterward to Brett and Spud, "It is all right. Nothing wrong; the lungs are strong. It is just a touch of bronchial trouble—the tubes are sore."

A large mustard plaster was procured and put on Lawrence's chest, and that was that. But Brett, remembering how Katherine Mansfield spat blood at the onset of her fatal illness, continued to worry.

Autumn comes early in the Taos mountains, but the Lawrences did not hurry. It was October 11 when they left the ranch neatly locked up and set out with Brett for Mexico. They stopped for a while in Mexico City: "everybody in this damned city coughing and sneezing: it's been very chilly: snow low down on Popocatepetl," wrote Lorenzo peevishly to Mabel. "And the town uneasy and depressed: as if the bottom had fallen out of the barrel. Don't like it.

"We think to leave for Oaxaca on Monday. . . . If we don't like Oaxaca, we shall probably toddle back. If I'm going to waste my sweetness on the desert air, I'll damned well choose my desert."

They got to Oaxaca on November 9, 1924, and found good rooms in the hotel, but when they began unpacking Brett discovered to her horror that she had lost Toby. They put up notices everywhere, offering a reward, but nobody brought back the ear trumpet; the thief would be afraid to bring it back, the hotel proprietress told them. So they found a tinsmith, Brett drew diagrams, and he made a new Toby that worked to some extent, though not perfectly or always.

Other complications soon arose. There were rooms to let, the foreigners discovered, in the English padre's house, and when they went to see them they were charmed with the patio and the large, cool rooms. But Frieda stalled: there was not enough space, she said, for all of them. Brett knew what was expected of her and quickly did the right thing: she could easily stay on in the hotel, she said. Frieda immediately cheered up. Having moved, Lorenzo acquired an Indian servant and found that the young man was trying to learn to read and write. Morning lessons were set up, and Rosalino studied hard.

"He is observant," wrote Brett, adding the—to us—rather surprising comment, "and discovers that you take a bath regularly every Saturday evening." After that, Rosalino also had a good wash every Saturday, though he got his in the public baths. But . . . only every Saturday for Lawrence? Never mind. The three visitors got to work happily on the usual routine, scrubbing the new rooms and painting furniture, and Lawrence, as soon as he felt settled, got to work again on *The Plumed Serpent*. It was easier to write in Oaxaca, he said, than it had been in Chapala, and on the ninth of December he wrote happily to Earl Brewster that the climate was lovely, "hot and sunny, roses and hibiscus and bananas, but not tropical heat. . . . One needs a *rest* after America: the hardness, the *resistance* of all things to all things, inwardly, tires one." Soon, however, the inevitable discontent crept in. There were soldiers everywhere, a hint of trouble between Indians and Mexicans and, possibly, North Americans too. At least, Lawrence scented trouble.

"In spite of the beautiful climate I don't believe I will ever be able to stand the lack of freedom," he said to Brett. "I wish we could buy huge revolvers and knives and kill somebody. It's all so silly and tiresome."

Walking past the barracks one day they were badly frightened by what seems to us, in our less peaceful era, a trivial incident, but then Lawrence was always timorous in Mexico and his feelings infected the others. The soldier on guard, "a huge Indian," said Brett, with a rifle, gestured to the two women to get off the pavement and walk farther off, in the road. "His motion is silent and savage," said Brett. Lawrence, as usual, turned white with fury but did nothing. "The soldiers, the terrible dreaded soldiers!" commented Brett. Yet the story ends there.

Drinking cocktails one evening with a friend in the town, Lorenzo asked their host if he had a book to lend him, and Dr. Miller picked one out and handed it over, saying laughingly, "This is just the book for you." Oh, dear, what could be more unfortunate?

"On the cover," said Brett, "is the picture of a woman pulling off her chemise, a man in evening suit watching her. You take it in your hands, a look of astonishment on your face. You hold it for a few minutes in silence, then hand it quietly back to Miller without even saying a word. He looks baffled." And well he might, at this reaction from a man who wrote what the world called pornography.

That the Lawences lived in one place and Brett in another did not bring to an end their close relationship, as Frieda had hoped. Brett was always coming over on the street car to see them, and Lawrence took this as natural and right. One day he and Brett decided to go out into the country, he to write, she to paint. To Lawrence it seemed a very daring thing to do, but—"Let us try. Two of us must be safe," he said. Frieda and Rosalino could come out to join them with lunch, he said. Frieda said nothing.

They spent the moring in complete safety, each under his own bush, Lawrence writing and Brett painting. Looking at her picture, Lorenzo was not at all pleased with it, declaring that there was something very wrong with her portrayal of the mountain. "Here, let me have a try." And so much did Brett love him that she handed it over. "You are dumb, Brett," he said happily as he worked; "you don't look at things; you have no eyes."

That, too, she accepted. Unlike the Danes, she never objected when he took over. Years later this writer asked her, "How could you, Brett? You're a painter, a good one, and he was a rank amateur. How could you have let him meddle?"

She laughed a little sheepishly. "He was such a dear," she said.

That day they waited a long time for lunch, until Lawrence looked at his watch, sighed, and said, "Frieda can't be coming, after all; so we must start home." They did.

On January 10, 1925, Frieda's long period of watchful waiting came to an end. Brett woke up that morning feeling "a sort of apprehension," which was amply justified when Rosalino arrived with a letter from Lawrence. Brett could hardly believe it when she read it—a "fierce, cruel" letter telling her that the three of them were not "a happy combination" and must separate. Frieda in her memoirs was to state her side of it, how she had come to put her foot down. Brett had always bothered her, she said; Brett seemed to be always there, and Frieda had no privacy.

"Like the eye of the Lord, she was; when I washed, when I lay under a bush with a book, her eyes seemed to be there, only I hope the eye of the Lord looks on me more kindly. Then I detested her, poor Brett. . . . When I finally told Lawrence in Oaxaca: 'I don't want Brett such a part of our life, I just don't want her,' he was cross at first, but then greatly relieved."

Characteristically, Brett did not give in to her wounds. She needed time, she said, to think things over, and in the meantime she tried to carry on as usual, even going over to the Lawrences' house that afternoon for tea. There she was quiet,

as always, and did not speak of the letter. Lawrence was gentle
to her, but Frieda seemed hostile, and who can wonder. Brett
felt it wise not to stay after tea. She went back to her hotel
room and had set to work typing one of Lawrence's manuscripts, when in came Lawrence himself.

"Frieda broke out again the minute you left. She made
such a scene that I can no longer stand it. . . . The only thing
I could think of was to come down and ask you not to come
up again to the house."

They should keep things calm and sensible, rejoined Brett.
All this strain couldn't be good for Lorenzo; suppose she went
back to New Mexico and stayed at Del Monte for a while?

Lawrence immediately cheered up. He protested a little—
was she sure she could make the journey by herself?—but he
did calm down, and now a new element entered. He was watching her with puzzlement, as if asking himself how she could
keep so tight a rein on her emotions. It was as if this lack of a
scene *annoyed* him. (Probably because of her deafness, Brett
was unusually good at reading people's reactions. She seems to
have seen Lawrence whole, without for a minute faltering in
her adoration.) In the end everything was settled. They agreed
that she was to start for Taos at the beginning of the week.

Next morning Frieda, too, came to the hotel, bringing with
her a letter defending her position because, she said, she could
not bear it that Brett should blame the trouble on her. Brett
took it and read it in amazement as Frieda waited balefully.
"In it she accuses us, Lawrence and myself, of being like a
curate and a spinster," said Brett; "she resents the fact that we
do not make love to each other. She says that friendship between man and woman makes only half the curve." This was
spoken as befitted a true and faithful adherent of Otto Gross's
theories; it also recalls the argument Frieda had used against
Ottoline and the "soul-mush" between her and Lawrence, which
Frieda so hated.

But Frieda, expostulated Brett (who knew nothing of Otto
Gross), how on earth could she be expected to make love with

Lawrence when she was the Lawrences' guest? That would be indecent.

Such an admirably British sentiment had an oddly maddening effect on Lawrence's wife. Make love? She, Brett? How dared she think it possible? Why, Brett couldn't, not in a month of Sundays, seduce Lawrence! He could never love a woman like her, "an asparagus stick!"

Well, Lorenzo wasn't all that fat himself, retorted Brett. But this was the lowest ebb to which she sank, and afterward things took a more civilized turn. The women talked themselves into a good humor at last, and laughed together at some pleasantry. When Monday came, Frieda and Lawrence saw Brett off at the railway station: Brett and Lorenzo shook hands warmly in farewell, and Brett actually kissed Frieda good-bye. "She is astonished; so am I," said Brett. And so ended the experiment in communal life which was the nearest Lawrence ever came to achieving Rananim.

They themselves were going to Europe by way of Mexico City, Lawrence said in a letter to A. D. Hawk at Del Monte Ranch on January 30, probably leaving on February 20. There was a hint of uneasy conscience in the next words: "I am wondering very much how deep the snow is, and how Miss Brett will stand the cold. But if she goes into the Danes' cottage, it is so sunny, and warm with a fire."

But almost immediately he fell ill again. It was malaria, he wrote to Bill Hawk, son of the rancher, on February 7, mixed with "the remains of the old flu," but he had seen the local doctor and was better. Not really, however; soon he was seriously ill. The English and Americans in Oaxaca rallied round and did what they could. Lawrence himself was sure he was dying and told Frieda that he would be buried there in the Oaxaca cemetery.

She laughed, though she too was frightened. "It's such an ugly cemetery, don't you think of it," she said.

She was even more frightened when he continued, "But

if I die, nothing has mattered but you, nothing at all." In a way, of course, she was gratified, but this was so uncharacteristic that she thought he really might be dying. As if this were not bad enough, they had a severe earthquake. The terrified Frieda saw the room's beams moving in their slots, and she warned Lorenzo that they might have to hide under the bed. Things didn't come to that however, and as soon as he could manage it they moved back to the hotel, where Lawrence seemed to improve steadily if slowly, until they were able to set out for Mexico City on the first leg of their trip to Europe. Because he suffered, they had to stop halfway so that he could rest in a hotel overnight. Frieda had never, in all her time with Lawrence, shouldered any of the responsibility of travel, but now she had to cope with buying train tickets, finding hotels, and watching out for the luggage, carrying all the time a gnawing, terrified grief in her heart. For once her natural optimism failed her, and she told herself that he would never be completely well again. He was ill, he was doomed. She cried all that night in the halfway hotel, which made Lawrence angry.

In Mexico City she found friends to help her bear the weight of Lawrence's care. One of them called in a doctor, who made tests, took another opinion, and finally said to her openly, in Lawrence's presence, "Mr. Lawrence has tuberculosis."

There it was, that dread word, out in the open at last. Nothing could cancel it, and Lawrence looked at her with "unforgettable eyes," wondering what her reaction would be. She spoke as cheerfully as she possibly could: "Now we know, we can tackle it. That's nothing. Lots of people have that." But when the doctor spoke to her alone there was no reason for cheerfulness. Lawrence was very sick, he said, too sick to attempt the Atlantic crossing. His only chance lay in getting back to the ranch, and even then it was the doctor's opinion that he would live a year or two longer at most. This was to prove a considerable underestimation, but of course Frieda had no way of knowing it.

In spite of her private despair she was careful to maintain a smiling demeanor always before Lorenzo, and he responded; he rallied and was soon deep in plans and preparations for the journey back to Taos. He wrote to the Hawk family and asked them to alert Brett, when late in March he and Frieda set out toward the north. At El Paso, on the border, there was a frightening hitch when the American immigration authorities refused to allow Lawrence to enter the country on grounds of health. The couple waited in painful suspense while influential friends in Mexico City tried to rescue them. It was the American Embassy, in the end, that carried enough weight to get Lawrence back into the United States.

Perhaps his return to the mountains of New Mexico added to what was left of Lawrence's life. The air of that desert state was considered exceptionally good for sufferers from tuberculosis, so much so that Taos and Santa Fe were well provided with sanatoriums—not that Lorenzo would have considered living in one. The couple hastened through Santa Fe, in a rush to get to Kiowa Ranch. Of course Mabeltown was open to them, but Mabel, who was undergoing a difficult menopause, was in New York consulting a psychiatrist. She and Lawrence were never to meet again, but they exchanged letters and books and maintained friendly relations at long distance.

As for Brett, "She wanted to come up here but Frieda said no," Lawrence told the old Baroness. She stayed on, therefore, at Del Monte. Frieda did not object too strenuously when she rode up to Kiowa almost every day, ostensibly to pick up manuscripts and take them home for typing. Lawrence now completed a play, *David*, which he said was to be a vehicle for Ida Rauh, the actress married to the Taos painter Andrew Dasburg. Lorenzo liked Ida and saw a lot of her; it was the Dasburgs, in fact, who brought the Lawrences up from Taos when they came back from Mexico. One day she and Brett rode from Del Monte to see Lawrence, and he read the play aloud to all three women, Frieda and Brett and Ida. There were to be songs in the production, for which he had supplied the words but not the music. Brett urged him to write out the music as well, and after a little modest protest he began to do it, humming and tapping out the melodies as he made notes on lined paper.

Suddenly Frieda gave way to a fit of exasperation, brought on, no doubt, by the rapt attention the other women were paying to her Lorenzo. She said abruptly, "Oh, you get on my nerves! Go out—get away—I don't want to hear you!"

Lawrence's reply was superb in its way. "You are impudent," he said. "Don't be so impertinent."

Ida and Brett escaped to the kitchen, from where they heard Lawrence resume his humming as if nothing happened. Frieda, however, remained silent.

No doubt every day that brought increased health to Lawrence relieved Frieda's mind of morbid fears but left that much more room for the old jealous resentments. Brett must still be warned off, she felt: Frieda still had a man to fight for, not a corpse. She wrote to Brett, attacking her and telling her to stay away from Kiowa Ranch. She didn't want her life mixed up with Brett's, she said. As usual, Brett serenely ignored the attack and remained living at Del Monte, from which neutral territory no Brunhilde however furious could evict her. She came to Kiowa Ranch whenever she felt like it, which was often, and sometimes Lawrence even went to see her at Del Monte. After one of Frieda's letters, when they were riding together, he attempted to apologize to Brett for his wife's behavior, and Brett replied, "If Frieda starts her spinster and curate and asparagus nonsense again, I will rope her to a tree and hit her on the nose until she has really something to yell about." This outburst, she noted with glee, flabbergasted Lawrence and left him wordless for once.

As the days passed and the sun shone through the crystalline air, Lawrence felt better and better. It was wonderful, said Frieda fondly, to see the life flow back into his body. Before half the summer was over, he was making plans again to go to Europe. They would do it in the autumn, he decided, and so avoid spending the winter in the cold mountains of New Mexico. Only one difficulty stood in the way: Brett. What was he to do about this woman who had followed him all the way and was loyal to the nth degree? He could not, like Frieda, ignore his obligation to her; he was really responsible for her presence in America. No, he could not sail off and leave Brett sitting on a mountaintop all alone. He broached the subject, asking what her plans were for the winter.

None, said Brett glumly, except to stay in New Mexico. She couldn't, she said, travel much alone because of her deafness.

Lawrence told her emphatically that this was nonsense; of course she could travel. He pointed out that she had what he called "plenty of money"—an exaggeration, but it was true, Brett reflected; she had a certain amount of income. It would be far better for her to travel, he said bracingly. Had she ever been to Italy?

No, said Brett.

"Well, you ought," Lawrence declared, "everyone who can ought to see Italy." He might even be there himself, he said; he hadn't made plans as yet. "Why don't you go to Capri?" He brushed aside her protest that she didn't know anybody there. Earl and Achsah Brewster were there, he said; they had gone to live on Capri, and he would give Brett a letter to them, so that was settled. He might even go to Capri himself.

Brett was willing to take the chance, and for a while she was happy in her hopes, but a cloud appeared on the horizon. Something was the matter, something unspoken. Lorenzo sent his latest manuscript away for someone else to type, and there were other things; certainly something was in the air. She asked Frieda what the trouble was; Frieda was noncommittal. Then Brett happened to mention an old folk rhyme she had promised

to Frieda. She had written it down, she said, but lost it somewhere. Now she quoted:

> "Matthew, Mark, Luke and John
> Went to bed with their trousers on."

Lawrence looked up angrily at the words and said, "That
is a very vulgar joke. Indecent and nasty."

Brett was amazed. "But, Lawrence, my nurse used to sing
it to me when I was tiny," she said. "What is the matter with
it? I wrote it out for Frieda, but I lost it."

He snapped "Do you mean to say that you do not know
that is a vulgar, dirty joke?"

No, Brett insisted, she didn't. Lawrence dropped the subject, but that night he gave her something else to type, and
she suddenly realized that he must have found the rhyme in his
manuscript book, where she had left it, and felt insulted. What
*was* dirty about it? She never knew.

Toward the end of September the Lawrences left for
Europe by way of England and arrived in London the night
before October 1. The invaluable Catherine Carswell arranged
to borrow a flat for them from her younger brother. Family
ties were looked to: Barbara came to see them, and soon afterward Lawrence and Frieda went up to visit Ada Clarke in
Ripley. Barbara saw them there, too, coming over from
Nottingham where she was staying with friends of the Weekleys, a professor and his wife. Lawrence had decided to like
Barbara better. In London she had brought her fiancé to meet
her mother and stepfather, and they didn't like him; now Lorenzo, who was in bed with a cold, set to work to persuade her
to give him up. (She soon did.) In Ripley there was a slight
awkwardness after dinner when someone suggested that Barby
spend the night. More than willing, she telephoned to her
hostess, whose husband was horrified. What, stay overnight
under the same roof as That Man and That Woman? Whatever
would her father say? No, they could not allow it. Poor Bar-

bara returned to Ada's living room with the news, and Lawrence leaped to his feet, white with rage as usual.

"These mean, dirty little insults your mother has had to put up with all these years!" he yelled, fighting for breath.

The Lawrences did not stay long in England, but they were there long enough to make the acquaintance of the writer William Gerhardi at a party and to ask him over for tea. In the end the afternoon stretched out to include dinner. Gerhardi was fascinated by Frieda—"A real German *Hausfrau*," he thought at first, just the right type for Lawrence; she could look after him and minister to his creature comforts. But no, he was wrong, as he soon learned; Mrs. Lawrence scorned housework and it was Lawrence who did it. During the evening Lorenzo rebuked Frieda for showing too much violent feeling during a discussion of—of all people—Lord Beaverbrook, whom neither she nor her husband had ever met.

"Not so much intensity, Frieda," said Lawrence quietly.

To which Frieda retorted, "If I want to be intense I'll be intense, and you go to hell!"

"I'm ashamed of you, Frieda," said Lawrence. Whereupon, commented Gerhardi, "Frieda's hatred for Lord Beaverbrook transformed itself into hatred for her husband, and was soon a spent cartridge."

Lawrence continued to see the young writer. On one occasion, in the street, Lawrence pointed to a crowd and said, "These London girls. I would as soon sleep with them as with a water closet."

"And I pictured a number of attractive young girls," said Gerhardi, "for no crowd is without them, mortified at the refusal of a sickly, red-bearded, untidy individual of middle-age to meet their advances, which in fact had not been forthcoming." But he liked Lawrence, in spite of his "curiously adolescent habit of derisive generalities."

Once Murry came up from Dorset, where he was living with another consumptive wife, and spent the night in the flat, but Frieda was not there.

Then the Lawrences were off again, to Italy via Baden-Baden and Switzerland. Lawrence didn't like Switzerland: "Horrid." Spotorno had been recommended, so they went there to meet Lawrence's publisher, Martin Secker, and possibly also to find a house for the winter. Almost immediately Frieda saw a place she liked the appearance of, "a pink villa that had a friendly look." They asked the caretaker about it and found that it belonged to a "Tenente dei Bersaglieri" or army lieutenant who lived in Savona. Actually it was the property of Lieutenant Angelo Ravagli's wife, but the result was the same: Ravagli came to the Lawrences' hotel to arrange to let the house. He was an imposing figure, though rather short; it was the Queen's birthday, so he was in full uniform, with a plumed hat and a bright blue sash. Lorenzo went down to talk to him and came back to fetch Frieda just so she could look at the lieutenant's splendor. The Villa Bernarda was rented to the foreigners for four months, and Ravagli became their friend, coming over from Savona on Sundays to study English with Lawrence. He found it interesting, though puzzling, that Lawrence was always doing housework: never, he said, did he see the genius writing. One day Ravagli arrived to find the house full of smoke from the kitchen stove, which always gave trouble. Lorenzo was swearing, saying that the smoke was choking him, so Angelo, like a good landlord, took off his uniform, put on overalls, and set to work with Lawrence to clean out the pipe. He disconnected it, and the men found the elbow to be choked with soot. Having emptied it out, Angelo climbed to the roof and cleaned out the chimney, lowering a swab to dislodge the soot while Lawrence, beneath, caught it in a bucket. Lawrence was much impressed. He later told Frieda that Angelo would be a useful man to have on the ranch.

Barbara, her engagement ended, came out to Spotorno for the Christmas of 1925, though Ernest was reluctant to permit it and insisted that she stay at a *pensione* in a nearby village instead of at the villa. It would have surprised him to learn that Lawrence was even more fussy than himself about preserving the nineteen-year-old girl's virtue. When Barby, painting out of doors, made the acquaintance of an English admiral and actually went to tea with this stranger, Lawrence was heavily disapproving. She ought to be very careful of "that kind of man" he said, and he also reprimanded her for having traveled out to Italy third class. "An English girl doing that here gives the impression that she is looking for an *'adventure'*," he said darkly.

Tired of going back and forth, Barby soon gave up the *pensione* and moved outright into the Villa Bernarda. She was there only one night before experiencing a typical Lawrentian outburst: she woke up suddenly in the morning, disturbed by loud thumps over her head, and ran upstairs to find Frieda in tears, her neck scratched, and Lawrence sitting glumly on the edge of the bed.

"He has been horrid," said Barbara's mother. Later Barby learned that the fight had been over herself, Frieda having told Lawrence that he was not to interfere between mother and daughter. The warning had set him off.

Barby was exhilarated rather than horrified by all this, but a few days later, at the dinner table, she lost her equilibrium when Lawrence said to her, "Don't you imagine your mother loves you; she doesn't love anybody, look at her false face," and flung into that face the contents of his glass of red wine.

It was too much. Barby shouted, "My mother is too good for you . . . it's like pearls thrown to the swine."

However, a few minutes later when Frieda had left the room to change her clothes, Lawrence and Barby talked things over in a calmer spirit. Did he love Frieda? Barbara asked, and he retorted that it was an indecent question to ask. "Look what I've done for your mother!" he said, and later, "Why does your mother want to be so *important?* Why can't she be simple and talk to me naturally, as you do, like a woman?"

This was better, thought Barby. All the man needed was a little sympathy, a woman who understood him. Sympathetically, therefore, she listened to the complaints he poured out. It seemed to soothe him.

"Afterwards when someone told me that he had said, 'Frieda's daughter tried to flirt with me,' I thought it mean of him," she confessed. But she bore no grudge. She was thoroughly happy in Spotorno, painting and lying in the sun.

In February her elder sister Elsa joined them, which of course delighted Frieda. Lawrence was not so cheerful, perhaps because Frieda again forbade him to interfere between her and the girls, or perhaps merely because his old jealousy had come back rampant. Ravagli, admittedly not a detached observer, reported to Nehls years later that he realized something was wrong when he came to see the family: "I sensed that Lawrence did not share Frieda's happiness in having her daughters with her for the first time since she had married him."

Lorenzo sent for his sister Ada to come out—evidently to counterbalance her show, said Frieda—and Ada came, bringing with her a friend named Mrs. Booth, so there were what Frieda called two camps. At night she heard brother and sister talking and talking, "complaining to her about me," said Frieda. "I did not hear the words but by the tone of their voices I knew."

Elsa and Barby had been sent away from the villa, where there wasn't enough room for everybody, and were lodged in a little hotel nearby. The morning after they moved, Frieda came to their room in a temper because, she said, Ada and Mrs. Booth had tried to put her out of her own kitchen. The truth is that Frieda and Ada had never been too fond of each other, though Frieda would not admit her part in the dislike. Ada fiercely resented the married woman with whom her darling brother had eloped, setting the whole town talking, and Frieda, always sensitive to any threat to her ascendancy, resented Ada's resentment. Lawrence had pulled the plug from the bottle and let the genie escape; the women's rage blazed forth. If what he wanted was women fighting over him—and it was, all his life—he got his wish, and richly.

He was ill, with what he diagnosed again as flu, but Frieda felt that the real cause was all the hostility in the house. One night she went to his room and made it up.

"In the morning Ada and I had bitter words," said Frieda. " 'I hate you from the bottom of my heart,' she told me. So another night I went up to Lawrence's room and found it locked and Ada had the key. It was the only time he had really hurt me; so I was quite still. 'Now I don't care,' I said to myself." For the second time in her life (the first was when he refused to go to England with her) she was really angry with Lawrence, so angry that it was touch and go if she ever forgave him.

Lawrence was too perceptive not to realize that he had gone too far at last, though he would never have admitted it. In a letter to Bill Hawk, announcing that he was going away with Ada, he only touched on the subject: "Somehow everything feels in a great muddle, with daughters that are by no means mine, and a sister who doesn't see eye to eye with F. What a trial families are!" In such a coil, the best thing he could think of was to repair to other women who could give him solace and incidentally enrage Frieda still further. Ada and her companion wanted to see Monte Carlo, and Lawrence went with them on February 22. Monte Carlo was an incongruous place for him and he knew it, but Ada, no doubt, wanted a taste of high life on her trip abroad, and it didn't really matter to him where he went as long as Frieda was angry with him. He did his brotherly duty; then, having put Ada and Mrs. Booth on the train at Nice, from where they went back to England, he telegraphed Brett in Capri, where she had been obediently living for the past five months, to say that he was coming. The Brewsters were her constant companions on the island, but they were on the verge of going East again, this time to India. Like Brett they were excited and happy at the idea of seeing Lorenzo, and when he proposed to stay at their house they were delighted to say that he could. Brett, of course, was in heaven.

"I only want to be quiet, quiet and peaceful," he told her, leaving her to imagine what kind of rackety, disturbed home he had fled. Accordingly they went out for a gentle, peaceful walk, not too long a one because he was still weak, and sat down to look at the sea. Lorenzo sighed.

"I am so tired of it all, Brett. Oh, so tired!" he said.

Pityingly, she made the appropriate soothing speeches. Why didn't he go away on a long trip, she asked.

"Sometimes I think I must," said Lawrence. "My life is unbearable. I feel I cannot stand it any longer." He continued, "Chopping and changing is not my way, as you know"— chopping and changing women?—"but I get so tired of it all. It makes me ill, too. I don't know what to do. I just don't know what will happen."

Though Brett was sure she knew what he *ought* to do, she shrank from telling him. Of course, she told herself, he should keep away. (Away from what? She couldn't say the name.) She looked at Lorenzo, wondering if he had enough strength and courage to break away—again, from what or whom? Ah, that was the rub: one mustn't say it. He didn't quite say it either. He just went on as if he were thinking aloud:

"If only I had enough money. But I never do have enough. Then I could go away for a time. But it would mean letters and telegrams all the time. I would like to buy a sailing ship, and sail among the Greek Islands and be free . . . free! Just to be free for a little while of it all! . . .

"You have no idea, Brett," he said later, "how humiliating it is to beat a woman; afterwards one feels simply humiliated."

The days passed quietly, with little walks and picnics and charades and painting. Once Brett saw a letter arrive for Lawrence; he glanced at it with "a weary look of annoyance," frowned, and shoved it into his pocket. After dinner one evening with the Brewsters and Brett present, he talked of the great poverty of his childhood, painting what Brett described as "a vivid and very terrible picture." The time came for the Brewsters to leave, and Lawrence and Brett saw them off, promising to go to India the following year to stay with them. Now, because Lawrence had nowhere to stay, they left Capri and went to Ravello, because Lawrence had friends there, two elderly ladies of the kind he always liked.

In Ravello Brett and Lawrence spent most of their time with the two ladies, despite Brett's feeling that they did not like her, "for the reason, I suppose, that they felt that they did not have Lawrence to themselves." One evening, after they had finally left the ladies for the night, Lawrence suddenly walked into Brett's room in his dressing gown.

"I do not believe in a relationship unless there is a physical relationship as well," he said, and got into Brett's bed and kissed her.

"I was frightened as well as excited," Brett recalled many years later.

I can still feel the softness of his beard, still feel the tension, still feel the overwhelming desire to be adequate. I was passionately eager to be successful, but I had no idea what to do. Nothing happened. Suddenly Lawrence got up. "It's no good," he said, and stalked out of the room. I was devastated, helpless, bewildered.

All the next day Lawrence was a bit glum. Nothing was said. And I was too tense and nervous to say anything, even if I had known what to say. That night, he walked into my room and said, "let's try it again." So again he got into my bed, and there we lay. I felt desperate. All the love I had for him, all the closeness to him spiritually, the passionate desire to give what I felt I should be giving, was frustrated by fear and not knowing what to do. I tried to be loving and warm and female. He was, I think, struggling to be successfully male. It was hopeless, a hopeless horrible failure. He got up, finally, stalked out of the room, and turned on me saying, "Your boobs are all wrong." This left me ashamed, bewildered, miserable. . . .

Next morning, early, I heard a movement in the next room. I got up and opened the door, to find Lawrence busily packing. "I have to go," he said, "I can't stay." He was in a towering rage.

She managed to dissuade him for the moment. However, it now appeared that she was the one who would have to go. Some time earlier she had applied for American citizenship. In Ravello she got a letter forwarded from Capri, telling her that her quota papers had arrived at the British Consulate in Naples; she would have to go there and fill them in, the consul wrote. Brett was rebellious and said that she would let the matter slide, since it meant leaving Lawrence alone. Without her, she was sure he would really go away. But he said no, no, she would have to attend to it; she must not lose her place in the quota. As she still argued, he told her that he would probably move on to Florence, where she could join him again. Almost reassured, she was prepared for the trip, but by the time she was packed and ready to go, Lawrence was once more irresolute.

"I don't know, Brett, I don't know what I will do. I may go back to Frieda soon; she is quieter, now, more friendly."

Frieda was also, though he did not say so, talking of leaving Spotorno soon and taking the girls to Germany. He would have to follow her. He needed Brett—or someone—to look after Kiowa Ranch. So Brett went to Naples to fix up her quota and then on to Taos.

Back in the Villa Bernarda, Frieda was not as quiet and friendly as Lawrence seemed to think. She was happy to be with the girls, but when she got a card from Lawrence that might well have been an olive branch—a picture of Jonah threatened by the whale, with the message, "Who is going to swallow whom?"—she may have smiled, but she did not relax. She was still angry.

When the news came that he was arriving soon and wanted to be back, as she put it, she hesitated. She was not at all sure that *she* wanted to make it up. But the girls scolded her and talked her round.

"Now Mrs. L.," they said, "be reasonable, you have married him, now you must stick to him." They made her get all dressed up and go with them to meet him at the station, and she submitted.

"Then we all four had peace," wrote Frieda. "He was charming with Else and Barby, trying to help them live their difficult young lives. . . . But for his sister Ada he never felt the same again."

"They are nice girls really," wrote the indefatigable Lawrence, surreptitiously, to his sister-in-law Else about her nieces, "it is Frieda, who, in a sense, has made a bad use of them, as far as I am concerned."

# 15

## *Frieda at the End: "Come when the sun rises"*

LAWRENCE'S ATTITUDE toward the struggle between men and women was changing somewhat, probably for excellent reasons. A new note is apparent, for example, in *The Plumed Serpent*, the novel with a Mexican background which was published in January, 1926. Its heroine, Kate Leslie, one of Lawrence's many Frieda-figures, allies herself with a Mexican leader, Don Ramon, who is heroic in every way save stature: he is rather small. When making love with Kate, the hero, for some reason known only to himself and his creator, does not permit his partner to reach orgasm—*ever*. It was in 1926, too, that Lawrence became totally impotent. Frieda complained about it to all her best friends, but there it was: in his next novel, *Lady Chatterley's Lover*, he was not Mellors the gamekeeper but Clifford Chatterley the cripple.

Until the end the couple kept moving about, in search of a place where Lorenzo might feel better. It was unusual when they stayed more than two months in any one house. During their long pilgrimage they lived for a time in England, Italy, Spain, France, Germany, and Austria, and Lawrence was contemplating a voyage to Africa when death put a stop to everything. The record evokes admiration as well as pity when one reflects that during the long quest he never stopped working. He enlarged his productivity too, when he got interested in painting; he argued that he would rather paint than write, but in fact he simply worked harder than ever at both arts. Barbara, who visited the Lawrences in the spring of 1927 at the Villa Mirenda in Scandicci, near Florence, thought his pictures definitely had something though they lacked technique. She called them "alive and mystical." They were also, she added, very shiny, because Lorenzo had a way of smearing on the color with his hands.

After a while Frieda, too, took up painting, with results that Barby admired: "Her wonderful colour sense gave her pictures life and gaiety," said Frieda's daughter. When she returned to England Barby stood one of Frieda's works, a picture of chickens at Kiowa Ranch which she particularly liked, on a mantelpiece in the house. Ernest noticed it immediately.

"I say, I like that!" he exclaimed. "Who did it?"

Barby said she could not remember.

A voice from the Lawrences' past was heard again at Scandicci, that of their one-time landlord Angelo Ravagli. Ravagli had been promoted and was now a captain, stationed at Gradisca. One day in the spring of 1927 he telegraphed Lawrence and Frieda to say that he was coming to Florence on duty, to serve as witness at a military tribunal; he suggested a meeting in the city. They all had a very merry lunch. But then, owing to a mix-up on the part of the army authorities, the trial was postponed and Captain Ravagli had to come back. This time he turned up unannounced at the Villa Mirenda, which, thought Lawrence, was too much of a good thing. Always aware to an uncanny degree of emotional undercurrents, he sensed that Angelo and Frieda were attracted to each other, and he didn't believe the postponement story. On some pretext he demanded a look at Angelo's travel documents. But when he looked at them he had to admit that the story was true, for there it was: "*Capitano Ravagli* deve *partire* [*must* leave] . . ."

To cover up his suspicions Lawrence shook his head and

said resentfully, "Why must? Why must? There shouldn't be any *must*." However, neither Frieda nor Ravagli doubted for a minute that he realized something was in the air. It was Aldous Huxley's theory on such matters that Lawrence always knew when Frieda was up to mischief and kept quiet about it as a matter of policy. One might say it was like his tuberculosis: he seemed to think that if he never mentioned it it did not exist.

Sometimes the tuberculosis, at any rate, could not be ignored. That June, for example, Lawrence suffered a bad hemorrhage. Though by the rules they had worked out the significance of this could not be mentioned, he and Frieda decided to move, as soon as he was strong enough, to some more salubrious climate. Once they went to Switzerland and at another time to Austria, from where they moved on to Irschenhausen for a holiday with Frieda's sisters. There in Bavaria one of Else Jaffe's friends persuaded Lawrence at last to consult a lung specialist, Dr. Hans Carossa of Munich, Lawrence being won over by the information that Carossa was a poet as well as a doctor.

The specialist managed his difficult patient well. He spoke soothingly and did not reveal his true opinion: later, however, he told the man who had introduced them that anyone else with such lungs would long since have died but that Lawrence would resist as long as possible. Carossa thought he might last two or three years longer.

Nevertheless, the disease had made inroads that could not be ignored. Back in Scandicci Lawrence complained a good deal about the weather. He spoke wistfully of Kiowa Ranch; he was sure he would get well there, and now and then he spoke of returning to New Mexico, though he knew in his heart that he wouldn't be able to pass through the immigration post on the way. By letter Brett urged him to try to sneak in, possibly through Canada, and he pretended to think about it, but it was only pretense. The other way was to get well first, and he seemed to think that he could. He wrote to Mabel of this daydream and pictured himself arriving in the coming summer with

the Brewsters, "Achsah in her long white robes and floating
veils" riding one of the horses.

Lorenzo had been working hard all spring on *Lady Chatterley's Lover* and was thinking of how to get it into print.
Clearly this would not be easy. He had already run into trouble
when it came to typing the manuscript. An Englishwoman in
Florence attempted to do it but was so scandalized by the text
that she refused to continue. In the end the typing was done by
two staunch friends, Catherine Carswell and Maria Huxley, but
what hope had he that any commercial publisher would touch
it? Very little. He resolved on a course of action often dreamed
of by troubled writers: he would publish it himself. Unlike many
such hopeful authors, Lawrence really had a chance to succeed
in this chancy venture, principally because of Giuseppe Orioli,
a friend of his in Florence. Orioli, whom everyone called Pino,
was a longtime intimate of Norman Douglas and a member of
what Frieda's biographer Robert Lucas has referred to as the
homosexual underground. As an antiquarian bookseller he was in
touch with printers; he had the technical knowledge necessary
and, through his shop, the means of distribution. When Lorenzo
approached him with his proposition, Pino readily agreed to a
partnership. They planned to print a first edition of a thousand
copies, to be sold at two guineas apiece. This was a lot of money
in 1926, but the partners were confident that the book would
sell. *Lady Chatterley's Lover* appeared in July, 1928.

All this was pleasantly exciting for Lawrence, and in spite
of his ill health he immersed himself happily in the business affairs of publication. Many of the volumes, sold privately to
friends abroad, were seized by customs inspectors when they
arrived in England or America. Other copies were haughtily
returned by booksellers. Soon the inevitable happened and the
book was pirated in the States, where some volumes sold for as
much as fifty dollars. Lawrence received a lot of hate mail,
some from erstwhile friends, but most of his circle were enthusiastic in their praise of the book. Bunny Garnett, though he

had long been estranged, wrote to tell Lorenzo how good it was, and Ottoline Morrell was one of the book's staunchest supporters.

All this was fun, and so was another project, a London exhibition of Lawrence's paintings. Barby suggested a new gallery run by Dorothy Warren, a niece of Lady Ottoline's, whom Lorenzo had met in Garsington days; Barbara herself had exhibited there with a number of contemporaries. When asked, Miss Warren professed herself more than ready to take on Lawrence's work, and there was a lot of correspondence on the subject. Dates in October, 1928, were first settled on, but the show was postponed until the summer of 1929.

We have a glimpse of Lawrence in 1928 through the eyes of a new admirer, a young girl named Margaret Gardiner whose brother Rolf was a good friend of the couple. It was during one of Frieda's absences in Germany that Miss Gardiner wrote to Lorenzo and arranged to come out to the villa and see him, and he met her at the car line and walked back with her. He seemed surprisingly shrunken and frail, she thought, and smaller than she had expected. As they climbed the steep hill to reach the Villa Mirenda he had to pause often to catch his breath.

They had a meal, during which she thoughtlessly left the potato pan on the table, making a black ring. Lawrence teased her about this, saying that she needed a lot of training about the house, and she was abashed. He laughed and said his wife was worse, or had been when they first married. Frieda, he gave her to understand, was incompetent, a true aristocrat. It was obvious that he was immensely proud of her. He told Miss Gardiner that he expected two elderly Englishwomen that afternoon, maiden ladies who were always referred to in his family circle as "the Virgins." They were coming expressly to see Lawrence's paintings, some of which hung on the walls of the villa. Lawrence showed them to his visitor; she didn't care for them but was afraid to say so. When the Virgins arrived and had their view of the art, it was apparent that they were of Miss Gardiner's mind, perhaps because they considered the subjects, and often the treatment of them, as sacrilegious. After hesitating painfully when the artist asked for their opinions, their relief was great when he brought out some water colors. Water colors were something they understood. But their relief did not last long.

"Here's one I particularly like," said Lawrence, grinning maliciously. "It's called *Le Pisseur.*"

"Really, Lawrence," said the younger sister indignantly. "You go too far."

They were shocked and hurt, and when they had taken their leave Lawrence was very angry with them. "The impudence," he stormed. "The incredible impudence. To speak like that to me. I'm a real artist."

"Oh, well," said Miss Gardiner as soothingly as she knew how. "Oh, well—the Virgins."

He seemed amused. "You're the real virgin, you know," he said.

However, some people did like the paintings. A man who worked in a firm that produced art books, the Mandrake Press, asked Lawrence to let them make a book of his pictures in reproduction, to be issued at the time of the Warren Gallery exhibition, and this was arranged. Lawrence wrote letters arranging these projects from Switzerland, where he and Frieda spent much of the early summer near the Aldous Huxleys, at Vaud. In time they left the resort hotel where they first stayed and moved into a chalet at Gstaad, then a little-known neighborhood. The Brewsters found lodgings nearby. The summer ended and it grew cold.

"The cows have now all come down from the high Alps—summer is over," wrote Lawrence on September 10, and a week later he and Frieda, Brewsters and all, descended like the cows and went direct to Baden-Baden to celebrate Earl Brewster's birthday at the hotel there. The old Baroness came over and

stayed, too; it turned into a house party. But all this failed to keep
Frieda contented. She was bored that summer and took a poor
view of her life. Nearly forty-nine, she was asking herself if this,
indeed, was all. Though it was an article of faith with her that
Lorenzo was a genius and that her duty was to take care of him
and save him for the world as long as possible, there were moments when she rebelled against fate. Not only was he extremely
difficult and getting worse, he was no longer her lover, since he
was impotent, and sex was the basis of her philosophy. If, as
Lawrence often said, she had "sex in the head," well, there it
was: Frieda needed sex, or at least was sure that she did.

Now in the early autumn she saw her chance to make a
temporary escape. The Lawrences' tenancy of the Villa Mirenda was coming to an end, and she had to attend to the practical details of getting out of the house. Lorenzo wrote to
Maria Huxley that Frieda would go to Florence and finish what
packing remained to be done, give up the house for good, and
rejoin him later.

"I, coward, am staying out of it," said Lawrence. He was
going direct to Le Lavandou near Hyères, Var, in the south of
France, and join Else Jaffe, who was there with her daughter
and Max Weber. Afterward they would be guests of Richard
Aldington on the island of Port-Cros near Le Lavandou.

Something went awry with the plans; Frieda did not turn
up when she was expected and was completely out of touch with
him for several days. Perhaps, thought Lorenzo, the formalities
of getting out of the villa took much longer than they had expected. The fact was that Frieda wasn't anywhere in Florence.
She had joined Captain Ravagli at some safe spot, probably
Gradisca, and it was October 12 before she surfaced.

"Frieda arrived with a raging Italian cold," reported Lawrence to the Brewsters, "—and of course passed it on to me, so
I've felt very cheap this week." But he asked no awkward questions. Once, according to Barby, he said something to his wife
that might indicate knowledge and understanding: "Every heart

has a right to its own secrets." If he suspected the truth, he preferred not to make a fuss about it.

Now, according to plan, they joined Aldington and his
party at La Vigie, Ile de Port-Cros. La Vigie was an old fort on
top of a precipitous hill, where they all lived in fairly primitive
conditions—too primitive for Lawrence, thought Aldington,
who was haunted by a sense of responsibility. Suppose their
genius suddenly took a turn for the worse, how were they to
get him down that hill, aboard a boat, and across the water to
the mainland? As it was they did not dare leave him alone, and
this put a crimp in their swimming parties and other expeditions.
Fortunately, nothing drastic happened, but the host thought he
saw a frightening worsening of Lorenzo's health, day after day,
which was not checked by the arrival of a great packet of
abusive reviews of *Lady Chatterley's Lover*. Lawrence took
them hard. Hoping to help him feel better, his friends read the
things aloud and shrieked with mocking laughter at the critics,
but Lawrence did not join in the merriment, and one of the
women heard him mutter, after reading one of the most violent
comments, "Nobody *likes* being called a cesspool."

Still, he was not always gloomy. In a more cheerful mood
he announced that he had made eight hundred pounds out of
*Lady Chatterley*, more money than he had ever owned all at one
time in his life. He and Frieda, he said, might take a villa at
Taormina and live like fighting cocks.

The house party dispersed when the weather got bad, in
November, and Lawrence and Frieda crossed the bay to
Bandol, where they moved into the place Katherine Mansfield
had liked so much, the Hôtel Beau Rivage. "I think we shall stay
here about two weeks," Lawrence wrote to a friend on November 18, but it was nearly four months before he could bring himself to move out, though Frieda would have preferred to find
a house in the vicinity. The hotel was perfectly satisfactory, he
retorted; always warm and bright. Besides, one could put up
guests without any trouble.

At the hotel they saw a good deal of Rhys Davies, the young Welsh writer. Davies was predisposed to like Lawrence, whose work he had always admired, but he found the writer's sudden storms of rage disconcerting. Once Davies and Frieda went to a nearby bar for apéritifs. Chatting, they forgot the time and were somewhat late getting back for lunch. They were met at the door by a Lorenzo insane with fury, dancing with rage, from whose mouth poured scalding words like lava from a volcano. Though he soon calmed down, Davies was seriously affronted. In the hotel dining room was a tray of fresh lobsters for which one had to pay extra, and Lawrence, now utterly charming, begged Frieda and Davies to have lobsters on him. The olive branch was rejected by Davies.

"*I* became cantankerous," wrote the younger man. "I refused to be wooed with lobsters. Frieda was not so silly. She enjoyed the fish with an unruffled air of 'however extraordinary my husband, one does not have lobsters every day.'" And in spite of such awkward moments, Rhys Davies concluded that it was a "prosperous" marriage:

> Frieda had a lioness quality that could meet his outbursts with a fine swing and dash: when really stung, she would shake her mane and grunt and growl; sometimes she charged. Their life together was an opulent one; her spirit was direct and generous, and his was laughing, malicious and subtle. Their notorious brawls were grand. She would lash out, and, gathering his forces with confident ease, he met her like a warrior. He would attack her for smoking too many cigarettes, having her hair cropped, taking a wrong line of thought, eating too many cakes in a café at Toulon, or for trying to be intellectual or aristocratic. He kept her simmering, subtly; for a natural inclination to a stout German placidity threatened to swamp her fine lioness quality.

Davies is the first if not the only observer to credit Lawrence with any charitable impulse in his attacks on Frieda. It is an interesting point of view. He described Lawrence's fury with

Frieda for reading a book on Rasputin with "fascinated avidity." Lawrence, it seems, did not care for Rasputin, so he found it disgusting that so many women did. He tore into Frieda for liking the book, until in the end she gave it up. Even then he couldn't let the matter rest.

"When she came down to dinner full of that Rasputin," he boasted to Davies, "I could have smacked her face across the soup."

Barbara arrived in Bandol the week after Christmas, but it was a calamitous time. Lawrence was obviously ill, Frieda was anxious for him, and Barby herself in a state of depression. It did not cheer her, of course, to learn that her mother had spent all Christmas Day weeping because nobody had sent her a present. Lawrence fulminated that he had no patience with such infantile behavior, and when Frieda put up a huge photograph of her son, Monty, to cheer herself up, her husband pulled it down again, saying that it was vulgar to have photographs around.

"Why don't your children send you presents?" he shouted at her jeeringly.

However, to do everyone justice, no amount of sweetness and light could have made Barbara feel better, and Lorenzo worried about her.

"I had a dreadful dream," he reported one January morning. "I was rescuing Barby from some disaster. She was in a fearful fix as usual."

The events of 1929, Lawrence's last full year, marched on at an increasing tempo. As spring came on in the south of France, he and Frieda discussed their next journey. Italy again? Corsica? Spain? In March he felt strong enough to venture without Frieda to Paris (though Davies went with him) to arrange a new edition of *Lady Chatterley*. Then they went to Majorca for two months.

A flurry was building up in England over *Lady Chatterley's Lover*, where the Home Secretary, William Joynson-Hicks, was waging a crusade against the book in the name of purity, collecting as many copies as he could find. He became so highly sensitized to the name of D. H. Lawrence that he seized a new manuscript by the same author, a volume of poems carrying the suspicious title of *Pansies,* as it came to the British Isles by post. He also grabbed an essay written by Lawrence, which happened to be harmless. Questions were asked about the actions in the House, but nothing definite was done, though it took Lawrence a long time to recover his papers. It was not the safest time, one would think, to open an exhibition of Lawrence's paintings, but events led inexorably to such an opening. Dorothy Warren, now Mrs. Philip Trotter, had been ill, but she had recovered; the paintings were there and so were the Mandrake books. The date was fixed for June 14.

Lawrence decided not to attend the opening but sent Frieda in his place. He himself moved to Lucca in Italy, there to stay near a house the Huxleys were occupying while he waited for reports on his work. Unfortunately for Frieda, she had sprained her ankle in Majorca. She was bathing when she suddenly notice a handsome officer in uniform riding a horse. He stared at her so fixedly, said Frieda, that she became confused and tried to get out of the sea too fast, stumbled on loose stones, fell, and sprained the ankle. It was still painful, but she managed to arrive in London in time for the private view at the Warren Gallery. Hobbling in, she was gratified to see a great number of friends. There was Ada too, who had come all the way from Ripley and greeted her with a proper semblance of affection. It was all very exciting.

That was on Friday. The show was opened to the public on the Saturday, and on Sunday there was one review, in *The Observer,* an unfavorable notice but quite a restrained one. Hysteria gained strength slowly. One by one the newspaper critics denounced the pictures, calling them abandoned, vicious, and *dirty*. Day after day the public came to see what was so awful about the show. So much prurient interest was aroused that people came in crowds; the Warren Gallery had never seen anything like it. Yet for days Frieda was simply unaware of the nature of the public's interest. Every day she dropped in, but the sight of all those people crowding in to gawk merely delighted her. She was not even surprised, feeling that Lawrence was at last coming into his own—and high time. The rest of the day she usually spent with the children, rejoicing especially in her new-found friendship with Monty. On the evening of July 4, she was guest of honor at a reception held by the Trotters, and she turned up, said Catherine Carswell, in a gay shawl, wearing red shoes and carrying a sheaf of lilies "to symbolize Lawrence's purity."

The show was scheduled to close on July 6. On the afternoon of the fifth, at about four o'clock, a band of police marched into the Gallery and removed from the walls thirteen of Lawrence's paintings, under the command of a leader who seemed to know exactly what he was doing and which paintings to take. It was alleged that the pictures would be burned, along with four copies of the Mandrake book. Frieda arrived after all the excitement was over to find herself facing thirteen glaring gaps on the walls. She was simply staggered.

"Let's all go to the Russian Ballet," proposed Dorothy, and that is what they did.

For days afterward the Trotter group discussed the raid. One of the things that mystified them was the nature of the criterion that was applied in the choice of paintings to be carried away. They thought it all over and came up with the solution: in those paintings, but not in the others, *Lawrence had delineated pubic hair.* Yes, that was it; that must be it. The next question was how to keep the seized paintings from being burned. The Trotters bent all their energies to preventing this bonfire, and after an immense amount of legal wrangling they succeeded on condition that the offending pictures be sent out of the country and put somewhere far away from English eyes. In the end this was done: the pictures were taken out of jail and shipped to Italy, where, long afterward, Frieda repossessed them.

Lorenzo had gone to Florence before the news arrived and was staying there with Pino Orioli. The tidings, possibly added to the fatigue of the journey and general debility, had a crucial effect on his health. As he lay in bed fighting for breath, his head and arms slipped over the edge of the mattress and hung help-lessly down. Pino was terrified and sent urgently for Frieda, who rushed to the scene, her ankle "still wabbly and aching," con-sumed with anxiety. The Trotters missed her "gusty visits" which, said Philip, were like champagne in the gloomy gallery, but Lorenzo, when he heard that she was on the way, brightened amazingly even before seeing her. He sat up in bed. Next to him stood a dish of peaches sent by some friend.

"What will Frieda say when she arrives?" asked Pino.

"She will say, 'What lovely peaches!' and she will devour them," Lawrence replied. Which is exactly what she did.

As soon as the patient could be moved they went to a *Kurhaus* at Baden-Baden, high on the mountainside. Again they invited the old Baroness to join them there, and she ac-cepted, but this was an unfortunate move because now, for the first time, she got on Lawrence's nerves. Of course he was ex-ceedingly unwell; as Frieda wrote to Dorothy Warren he was "as frail as one of those blue bird's eggs," but he was unusually irritable, even for him, writing in a letter to Orioli on August 2:

> It has rained and been bitter cold all the time we have been up here on this beastly mountain, and I have hated it, and only stayed because my mother-in-law got into a frenzy at the thought of going down. . . . She is 78, and is in a mad terror for fear she might die; and she would see me or anyone else die ten times over, to give her a bit more strength to drag on a few more meaningless years. It is so ugly and awful, I nearly faint. . . . Truly old and elderly women are ghastly, ghastly, eating up all life with hoggish greed, to keep themselves alive. They don't mind who else dies. I know my mother-in-law would secretly gloat, if I died at 43 and she lived on at 78.

Poor Frieda, caught in the middle between these egotists!

When at last they got off the mountain and down to the town hotel, and celebrated Frieda's fiftieth birthday with her mother's friends, it annoyed Lorenzo all over again to observe that, out of the nine people there, five were over seventy. Frieda too was irritable, wrote Lawrence to Maria Huxley, but then she always was when she was in her native Germany. The birthday party was quite nice, he admitted: "There are lovely roses on the table, and I dread the effect on Frieda of four huge boxes of chocolates."

Dr. Max Mohr, whom the Lawrences had met before in Irschenhausen, lived on the Tegernsee, where Frieda and Lorenzo went to stay after Baden. It was a fortunate thing for Frieda that they went, because Mohr called in a bone-setting farmer from the next village who fixed her ankle with one twist of the foot, but Lorenzo had a bad turn. Once again Frieda feared for his life, but he rallied. They went back to Bandol and this time took a house—"a nice little bungalow villa right on the sea . . . and a nice woman to cook and clean," wrote Lawrence to Else Jaffe on October 4. The only trouble was his health, he added, and said they would get a bigger house in the spring. Six weeks later he was writing to his friend Dr. Mohr, whom he had consulted in Germany:

"Frieda is happy. She is now singing Schubert at the piano: but the gramophone—'kiss your hand, Madame'—I only allow in the kitchen, with the doors shut. I do mortally hate it." Gramophones were a familiar source of contention; once Lawrence broke all the records he could find over Frieda's head. "Then we have pictures on the walls, covers on the 'divan' etc. etc.—and Frieda is proud of her little house, though I call it a little railway station, and Achsah despises it terribly, calls it a vulgar box." For the Brewsters had arrived and were living at the Beau Rivage, where their vegetarian habits caused puzzlement and consternation in the kitchen. "We had a very special octopus for supper on Saturday evening," continued Lawrence's letter, "and it was quite good, but still I had to shut my eyes."

Lorenzo held a little court in the bungalow villa. The Mohrs came to Bandol for a month that winter, as did Ida Rauh from Santa Fe and other friends. Frederick Carter, an artist from England with whom Lawrence had become friendly in 1924, came to see him, and Pino Orioli, with Norman Douglas, spent the Christmas season at Bandol, leaving on January 4. Everyone realized that the end was not far off; Lawrence tired very easily. A doctor, Andrew Morland, now came on the scene, charged by people in England to see Lorenzo and, if he possibly could, do something for him. Mark Gertler, who had been one of Morland's patients and was now cured, was most vociferous in urging the doctor to see Lawrence.

Morland managed to make some headway with the recalcitrant invalid. He was permitted to examine him and found, much as he had expected, that Lawrence suffered from pulmonary tuberculosis, which he must have had for a very long time, ten or fifteen years. Either he had never been properly treated, thought Morland, or—which was more likely—he had ignored such medical advice as he got, selecting only those details that he chose to follow. For example, he had been told by Mark Gertler that part of the cure was to drink plenty of milk and walk three or four miles a day. He had tried pathetically hard to do this, but had become too weak to walk.

Most of the time Lawrence lay in bed watching the sea from the window of the house, "Beau Soleil." The plants in his room flowered beautifully—"Why, oh why, can't you flourish like those?" Frieda asked him—and Earl Brewster came every day and gave him an oil massage.

"His worst time was before dawn when he coughed so much," said Frieda, "and I knew what he had been through. . . . But then at dawn I believe he felt grateful that another day had been given him. 'Come when the sun rises,' he said, and when I came he was glad, so very glad, as if he would say: 'See, another day is given me.' "

Even at this stage Morland did not think it an absolutely hopeless case. There was a chance if the patient could have the right treatment, but where was it to be found? Lawrence was utterly opposed to the idea of going to England or Switzerland, but in the doctor's opinion he was very badly off on the Mediterranean coast. He must go somewhere higher and drier, said the doctor. Lorenzo himself wanted to go to New Mexico, where he was sure he would get well. But quite apart from the immigration difficulties, of which Morland was aware, there was a strong doubt that the patient would survive the journey. The doctor recommended a small sanatorium he knew of in Vence, not far away, a place called "Ad Astra" which was not as institutional as most but more like a hotel, he said coaxingly.

Lawrence promised to think it over.

They would need an English nurse, said Dr. Morland, and Lawrence asked, "Can't I have Barby?" Frieda mentioned this to her younger daughter in a letter, and Barbara, touched, hastened to join them in Bandol. She was shocked at what she found —Lawrence staying all day in bed and exhibiting less and less patience with people, even Frieda.

"He felt Frieda could not help him any more, and this made him resentful," said Barbara. "Covered with rugs, and lying in the garden with a grey, drawn expression on his face, he said, 'Your mother is repelled by the death in me.'" They talked sometimes of going to New Mexico as if it were still a possibility; Frieda said Barby should go first and stay with Mabel until they arrived, but Lawrence was amazed and outraged by the suggestion. What on earth, he asked, would Mabel want with Frieda's daughter?

"You might just as well throw Barby into the sea!" he asserted.

About the first of February he made up his mind to go to Vence after all. He moved into the sanatorium on the sixth, with Frieda staying in a nearby hotel. Barbara remained at Beau Soleil for several days, then followed to join her mother. The Huxleys came up from Cannes to be near Lawrence, and Ida Rauh came to see him, as did H. G. Wells, who was staying on the coast not far away. The Aga Khan brought his wife, and Jo Davidson did a head of Lawrence, who complained that it was very tiring to pose.

Frieda used to stay as late as she could in the hospital before going back to her hotel room. She wrote:

> One night I saw how he did not want me to go away, so I came again after dinner and I said: "I'll sleep in your room tonight." His eyes were so grateful and bright, but he turned to my daughter and said: "It isn't often I want your mother, but I do want her tonight to stay." I slept on the long chair in his room, and I looked out at the dark night and I wanted one single star to shine and comfort me, but there wasn't one; it was a dark big sky, and no moon and no stars. I knew how Lawrence suffered and yet I could not help him.

Suddenly Lawrence announced that he wanted to leave Ad Astra. He said the place depressed him; he was sure that if he were in a house of his own he could get rested enough to go to New Mexico. Halfway convinced, Frieda and Barbara went out and found a house, the Villa Robermond on the hill behind Vence. Then Barby went down to Nice to see about passports. Lawrence was moved into the house and spent a night there—he hated the English nurse they had hired and made her very unhappy.

"Don't leave me," he said to Frieda, "don't go away," so she sat by his bed and read to him. She recorded what happened next:

> After lunch he began to suffer very much and about tea-time he said: "I must have a temperature, I am delirious. Give me the thermometer." This is the only time, seeing his tortured face, that I cried, and he said: "Don't cry," in a quick, compelling voice. So I ceased to cry any more.

The Huxleys were there. Aldous saw that Frieda bothered Lawrence by sitting on the edge of the bed and sometimes jiggling it, but toward the end she was quiet, holding his ankle, looking into his face.

It was ten o'clock at night, March 2, when Lawrence died.

# *16*

# *Frieda and Angelo: "What a good life"*

IT STARTLED HUXLEY to discover that Frieda, who had always seemed to him "such a powerful Valkyrie," was helpless on her own, without Lawrence. One comparatively unimportant matter seemed to occupy her mind to the exclusion of all other problems: would there be enough money in Lawrence's estate for her to take his body to Kiowa Ranch and rebury it there? In the meantime she arranged for a headstone to be placed on his grave in Vence, on which was portrayed a phoenix rising from the ashes, a design made by Lawrence himself years earlier. Frieda concentrated on these things with neurotic fervor until Angelo Ravagli, who had read of the death in a newspaper, got in touch and invited her to come and stay with his family in Savona. Frieda accepted and went away for a few days, and returned somewhat calmer from the visit.

Then she had to go to England to attend to various business matters, leaving Barbara alone at the Villa Robermond. Barby, upet by Lawrence's death, imagined that his spirit inhabited the house, and used to leave the door to his room open so that he could move in and out unimpeded, strong evidence of the impression the living man had made on that "little suburban nobody." Once it seemed to her that she distinctly saw his image bending over her, "made up of little shimmering particles. His

form, was filled out, glowing," and he looked at her "with a
very benign expression" before disappearing.

Soon after Frieda's return, John Middleton Murry appeared, saying that he had come to help out with advice. Then
at last he and Frieda became lovers, though only for the fortnight he stayed at Vence. They did not trouble to hide the facts
from Barby, and she was scandalized. After Murry had gone
Pino Orioli came to stay, and Frieda said she had a good idea.
Why didn't the three of them go for a holiday to Pieve di Tico,
just over the border in Italy? It was not a particularly attractive
spot, but Frieda had her reasons: Angelo Ravagli was stationed
not far away, and from the fact that he had taken a room for
the women at a local hotel it was clear that he expected them.
The place was horrible, Barby thought. It was here that a crisis
took place when Pino went off for a meal alone with Angelo
and came back to tell Frieda that Angelo wanted to break off
relations with her.

Frieda only laughed and refused to take it seriously. "You
don't understand Angelo," she said. "He is like a hummingbird."

Pino retorted that he didn't care if Angelo was like a hummingbird or a parrot: she'd better give him up.

Nonsense, said Frieda cheerfully, and went off to talk to
Angelo herself. Very quickly he allowed himself to be persuaded and all was well again between them, but the effect on
Barbara was acutely harmful. First Murry, then Angelo—what
sort of woman *was* her mother, anyway? Her mental health
deteriorated to such an extent that Frieda at last became alarmed
and took her to Baden-Baden, in the hope that a quiet stay with
her grandmother would settle her down. Barby remembered
how Lorenzo had laughed at the old Baroness's hearty appetite.
She too ate a lot while she was there; the apple cake and cream
were delicious. But then her grandmother said, "You ought to
speak German; your mother is German," the girl was angry and
retorted, "My mother left me."

It rained without stopping the whole time she was in Germany, and she caught bronchitis which hung on for weeks, even after she and Frieda returned to Vence. She ran fevers and had fits of delirium during which she ranted furiously against Frieda, abusing and threatening her. The doctor diagnosed a case of *grande hysterie,* and Frieda was in despair. One night when she was at the piano Barbara got out of her window and ran uphill to the cook's house, where the family of three peasants were eating supper. They took her in and comforted her; the cook gave her a glass of wine and put her to bed there, though she lay awake all night. One member of the family, a youth named Nicola, crouched under a tree in the moonlight and watched her window until Frieda came to fetch her daughter in the morning. Barbara threw a tin can at her, then allowed herself to be taken back to the villa, where she fainted.

One must remember Frieda's background in order to understand what she did next. She was terrified by Barby's illness, the continual series of deliriums and fainting spells. One night while the doctor was away Frieda called in Nicola and put him to bed with Barbara, and she repeated this "cure" every night until the doctor returned and made her stop. Barby's illness continued until late in the autumn, some weeks after the death of the old Baroness; then Frieda sent her back to England, and there, living quietly with an uncle, Barby recovered her senses.

"How *could* Frieda?" said a shocked Lady Ottoline Morrell when Barbara told her about Nicola. "She is obsessed with sex."

Well, of course. She had been trained by Otto Gross.

Angelo Ravagli had a wife, Ina Serafina, who taught school in Savona. He had three children of whom the youngest, Federico, was Frieda's godchild, and he had his commission in the army. All of these Frieda wanted him to give up, and he was not ready to do so. It is hard to understand why she was so determined to capture this dark little man, but these things are always mysterious to outsiders, and he seems to have been likable.

"His virile, open features betrayed his peasant origin, but

were otherwise in no way remarkable," said Frieda's biographer. "It was the face of a man who had worked himself up from below and who set great store on outward appearances."

After much discussion and some argument Angelo agreed to try out New Mexico with Frieda. He got six months' unpaid leave from the army and went with her to visit Kiowa Ranch at Taos, to see how he liked it. Most of the old-timers still talk of the day she arrived, when a group of friends from the old days, augmented by admirers of Lawrence, went to meet her train at Lamy. They had come well prepared to weep with her and to offer their shoulders, and then—then she stepped off the train beaming and not alone. Who on earth, they asked each other, was Captain Ravagli?

Frieda took him straight up to Kiowa Ranch. He looked disparagingly at the houses, which seemed to him ridiculously primitive; he knew about houses. It all seemed very lonely, too. But in a short time his imagination was fired by the possibilities of the place, the beauty of the scene, and the challenge of it all. Before his leave was up he had begun making plans and improvements. He was caught. They both returned to Europe then, Angelo to talk things over with Ina Serafina and Frieda to Vence, to prepare for a lawsuit over Lawrence's estate. His sisters Ada and Emily and his brother George were claiming a share in whatever Lawrence had left, but Frieda felt that she had a moral and legal right to the whole thing. Years earlier Lawrence had made a will leaving everything to her; now she couldn't find it, but she was determined to fight the case anyway. Aldous Huxley, for one, advised against it, saying that it would be far too expensive to go to law, but Frieda could not be persuaded to surrender without a struggle. Perhaps Huxley thought it stupid to fight for an estate worth at most £4,000, but that seemed to Frieda a very useful sum. No one could have foreseen that it would amount to much more than that in the end, but she insisted on fighting the Lawrences, and the case went to court.

Fortunately for Frieda, John Middleton Murry was able to remember the occasion on November 9, 1914, when Lawrence drew up his will and signed it, for the very good reason that Jack had done the same thing at the same time, and made a will leaving his all to Katherine Mansfield. He bore witness that the two documents were identical except for the names of the people involved. Better still, he still had his will and produced it in court at the hearing, which was held almost exactly eighteen years later, on November 2, 1932. Before the hearing Frieda had proposed settling £500 on each of the Lawrence claimants. But after the judge decided, as he did, in her favor, Ada angrily refuted her claim to anything; she did not wish to be beholden to the widow. The case marked the end of any pretense to friendship between Frieda and the Lawrences, which was probably a relief to all concerned.

For his part Angelo managed to get everything arranged satisfactorily. Ina Serafina agreed to let him go quietly on condition that she continued to get the same amount of money he had given her before. There was evidently no bad blood about the separation and no question of divorce at that time. Angelo resigned his commission and left the army, and the couple left again for Taos, there to build a "chapel" where Lawrence's remains could be laid. It was one of Angelo's first tasks, building that chapel. He crossed the Atlantic again to fetch Lawrence's ashes—they had decided it was easier that way—and brought them back to Taos in April, 1935, having stopped on the way for a visit with the family. He ran into a little difficulty with the American customs, where the officials could not seem to understand why anyone should want to carry mortal ashes into the country, but that was surmounted and Angelo moved on toward the West with his urn. At Lamy Frieda and a number of friends were waiting for him, and in the general joy and excitement the urn was forgotten; they left it on the platform. Halfway home they remembered it and turned back, to find it still there. In Santa Fe, on the way through, they stopped to see a friend, and once again the urn was forgotten, but next day they went back and fetched it. It is not hard to guess what any amateur psychologist would have to say about all this.

Frieda had planned a ceremony for the second interment. Barbara was there with her recently married husband, Stuart Barr, and friends were invited from miles around to come and pay their last respects. She was going to start the ceremony just at sunset, with Indians dancers from the Pueblo and a little reading over the grave. Just then rumor reached Frieda that Mabel disapproved. Lawrence, said Mabel, had said he wanted his ashes scattered over the Taos hills—a complete fabrication, said Frieda —and she, Mabel, would not stand for such a desecration of the remains of the great man as Frieda planned. Frieda and Angelo were going to capitalize on Lawrence, said Mabel; they would turn the chapel into a tourist trap. No! She would steal the ashes rather than let this happen. A trimming to the rumor was that Brett, who was working inside the chapel, had promised to help with the stealing. Forewarned, Frieda was able to frustrate this dastardly plot by keeping a guard over the urn night and day until the moment of the ceremony.

At the last minute the Pueblo Indians begged off. That same rumor had it that Tony, instigated by Mabel, had told them all that the great man's spirit would lay a curse on them if they danced for his funeral, so Frieda had to bring in Indians from another community, farther off. The judge who had promised to read the dedication sent his regrets, too; never mind, said Frieda, let Stuart Barr read it. Mabel did not come to the ceremony at all, but she sent flowers, with a letter telling Frieda that after Frieda's death she, Mabel, would have her way at last and scatter the ashes. Again she was foiled, for Angelo, always a handy man, mixed the ashes with concrete and produced from it a square block weighing at least a ton which stands firm and immovable in the chapel even today. Lawrence is safe.

As for Frieda and Brett, they made up their differences and became friends as soon as Frieda came back. After all, what had they to quarrel about now? Brett had become an old-timer herself, a familiar sight in her Levi's and boots and big hat.

The years passed peacefully. Angelo worked and worked on the house and brought it much nearer to his ideal, but there was no denying that the ranch was still too cold in winter, so Frieda bought a house a little lower on the mountain, near Questa, and they lived there in more bitter seasons. Lawrence's pictures, forwarded by Ina Serafina, were very useful for fixing up both places. Once they went to South America to visit Angelo's sister and brother in Buenos Aires, and in 1937 Angelo made another trip to Italy, to see the family and do some badly needed repairs on the Villa Bernarda. A letter Frieda wrote to him at this time has an interesting passage:

> You think I ought to give you more money. If I were rich, yes, but I am not and I don't think it is reasonable. I know there is only the 120 every month, but think of the money we spend. Going to South America and Boston and Hollywood. We spend quite a lot of money, but you don't think of that. Now I pay you for five months when you are away *and* the journey *and* some money for this time. . . . You never think of money, except when you think of Italy. But I hope that now that you are in Italy you realise what a good life you have in America.

However, she relented and added in a postscript that she would send another fifty dollars soon.

Trouble came, or at least was hinted at, in 1939, shortly before the beginning of the phony war, when an immigration officer from El Paso came to see Frieda and ask her personal questions about her relations with Angelo Ravagli. They were intimate, said Frieda cheerfully. But, persisted the officer, what were the financial arrangements between them? Was Frieda *keeping* Ravagli? Was he her gigolo? If so, he was liable to deportation on the grounds of moral turpitude. This sent Frieda into a panic. She remembered vividly the bad old days of the First World War, when she was suspected of being an enemy alien. Angelino was a foreigner, and if anybody wanted to make trouble for him . . . She was terrified, and she infected Angelo, too, with panic. Fortunately the matter did not go further.

We are given a glimpse of the household about then, in 1941, by Wolf von Eckardt of the *Washington Post*, who wrote an article about his experience in *Book World*, August 27, 1972. He was in Santa Fe in the summer of 1941 and decided to pay a call on Frieda, who was a distant relation of his. All his life he had heard the family legend, and he had built up a fantasy about this woman, widow of the man who wrote *Lady Chatterley's Lover*. She had snatched Angelo Ravagli from his wife and children just as D. H. Lawrence had snatched her from Ernest Weekley. Von Eckardt had always pictured Ravagli as a dashing *capitano* with a swagger stick, walking with his wife and children when suddenly he was transfixed by the vision of Frieda standing there in a white Gibson Girl dress and parasol, red hair shining in the sun, smiling at him. Next the youth visualized them together, naked on horseback, galloping across the New Mexico mesa into the sunset. Of *course* he went to see Frieda! He found the way to the ranch from the man who ran the bookstore in Taos, seventeen miles on a twisted road up the mountain, until he arrived at a meadow and a closed, very plain house. Von Eckardt knocked timidly on the door. Suddenly one of the upstairs shutters opened and someone called, "The chapel is up the hill!"

The woman who had called out was a witch, he said, with a big ruddy face and lots of white hair sticking out. She dropped a big key at his feet, and the visitor obediently walked up the hill and looked at the chapel, a "crude little hut, something like an outhouse," which he found touching. He examined a few pages of Lawrence's manuscript of *Lady Chatterley*, and looked at the big straw hat and the primitive chair that were on exhibit, and then came back to find that Frieda and Angelino had now recovered from their midday nap and were ready to receive him.

"She still looked somewhat like a witch, stout in a sort of

sackcloth and all that wild, white hair. Angelino was not my dashing *capitano* but—well, I thought I had seen him many times selling groceries on New York's Ninth Avenue."

The visitor told Frieda of their relationship; she did not seem much interested but offered him strawberries, which they all ate together. Angelo brought out some coffee cups he had just made and explained that he had taken up pottery. Von Eckardt liked them both. Later he brought his bride to meet the couple, and one way and another they all saw a good deal of each other. They went together to a fiesta, and the dashing *capitano*, still thinking himself utterly irresistible, tried to kiss Mrs. von Eckardt on the mouth.

"But they never did invite us to gallop naked across the desert," said Von Eckardt.

Having worried throughout the war about the immigration people and their equivocal position, Frieda and Angelo set about rearranging their marital status as soon as they could. The ever-obliging Ina Serafina agreed to divorce her husband in the Taos court, since in Italy divorce was still illegal, and as soon as the thing was done Angelo and Frieda were married, in August, 1950. The bride was seventy-one and the bridegroom fifty-eight.

Frieda was much richer at the end of the war than she had ever been before, for Lawrence's books had begun to sell very well and some were bought for the movies. In true Italian fashion the couple invested some of this money in real estate: Frieda acquired yet another house at Port Isabel, Texas, down in the most southern part of the United States territory, which they used as a winter resort. Angelino fished, Frieda sat, and everyone was happy. During the summer, of course, they went back to Taos, where Frieda saw a lot of Mabel as well as Brett. Old age heals all. Both Nusch and Else Jaffe managed to visit their sister in America, and in 1952 Frieda revisited England to check up on her children and grandchildren. Robert Lucas tells how Elsa's husband, Edward Seaman, took his mother-in-law past the family house in the family car, driving very slowly but not stopping, to give her as good a look as possible. She could not go in, it had been explained, because Ernest Weekley lived there. Now eighty-seven, he was bound to be at work in his study. He was never heard to mention Frieda.

"I am quite willing to talk to him," said Frieda in the car, but Seaman shook his head; it would not be advisable.

After this trip Frieda's health began to fail. She suffered from diabetes and asthma, but she continued to live in the way she and Angelino had worked out: Texas in the winter, Taos in the summer. Driving back from Port Isabel in April, 1956, they lost their way and had to go several hundred miles extra to reach Taos. That night Frieda had a small stroke, but she seemed to be on the mend when Barbara arrived a few weeks later, and she continued to improve. However, a month or so after her daughter had gone, on August 8, Frieda had a much more severe stroke. She died on her seventy-seventh birthday, August 11, 1956.

Her will was in order. Half the estate was divided evenly between the children and the other half went to Angelo Ravagli, who soon afterward went back to Italy to rejoin Ina Serafina.

# *Notes*

## Chapter 1: Lydia

| p. 14 | My father was a collier . . . | Ph 2:592 * |
| | . . . brutal and coarse . . . | AC:24 |
| p. 15 | My mother was, I suppose, superior. . . . | Ph 2:592–93 |
| p. 16 | . . . *clean* dirt . . . | EN 1:22 |
| | He was a highly skilled man . . . | ET:xv |
| p. 17 | Of this Mrs. Lawrence made much. . . . | ET:xv–xvi |
| | . . . poured her very soul into him. | EN 1:17 |
| | Dicky Dicky Denches . . . | EN 1:30 |
| p. 19 | . . . a short, robust woman . . . | EN 3:554 |
| p. 20 | They're gone! . . . | EN 3:559 |
| | Eh, child, tell your mother . . . | Ibid. |
| p. 21 | In her black dress . . . | EN 3:557 |
| | Skimp, skimp, I'm tired of skimping. | EN 3:558 |
| p. 22 | I marvel now at the housework . . . | AC:21 |
| | She struck me as a bright . . . woman . . . | ET:24 |
| | Her smallness was more than compensated for . . . | ET:36 |
| p. 23 | . . . clothed with a remnant . . . | EN 3:560 |
| p. 24 | . . . humping himself up . . . | EN 3:567 |
| | There was such a hateful feeling . . . | EN 3:568 |
| | He hates his father. | Ibid. |
| | Mother's wild . . . | EN 3:569 |
| p. 25 | A curious hollow voice . . . | RW:268 |

## Chapter 2: Jessie

| p. 27 | Miriam inherited her mother's . . . eyes. . . . | AC:44–45 |
| | I was the family drudge . . . | ET:28–29 |

* For an explanation of the abbreviations used here, see the list of works cited, which follows the notes.

| | | |
|---|---|---|
| p. 45 | Sallie, I gave Bert sex.... | HM:131 |
| p. 46 | I've tried ... | ET:155 |
| p. 47 | *You* are my luck.... | ET:159 |
| p. 48 | It isn't that I don't want to marry ... | ET:163 |
| p. 49 | Hurray, Fordie's discovered another genius! ... | EN 1:107 |
| | The artisan ... | EN 1:109 |
| | ... as one can well believe ... | EN 1:110 |
| p. 50 | He claimed moral support imperiously ... | EN 1:119 |
| p. 51 | Will she really like to see me? ... | ET:165 |
| p. 52 | You know, I could so easily peg out.... | ET:168–69 |
| p. 53 | You're a sort of Socialist ... | ET:170 |
| p. 54 | D. H. Lawrence brought his fiancée to | |
| | lunch.... | EN 1:127 |
| | It wouldn't be any good.... | ET:175 |
| | She'll like to hear ... | ET:176 |
| p. 55 | Well, it would be very interesting.... | Ibid. |
| | I was glad to be leaving ... | ET:177 |
| | I felt how sincere ... | ET:180 |
| p. 56 | I am ashamed ... | CP:94 |
| p. 57 | She was attractive ... | HM:122 |
| p. 58 | Lawrence implored me ... | ET:181–82 |
| p. 59 | The girl had launched me ... | Ph 2:593 |
| | ... a unique bond ... | HC:12 |
| p. 60 | ... rather as Mary of Bethany ... | Ibid. |
| | I must tell her ... | HC:13 |
| | Then I am afraid ... | ET:182 |
| p. 61 | When he cancelled out ... | EN 1:89 |
| p. 62 | ... stating to begin with ... | RA:109 |
| | I always feel ... | EN 1:136 |

## Chapter 4: Jessie and Louie

| | | |
|---|---|---|
| p. 64 | Oh, there's one thing ... | EN 1:138–39 |
| | She turned to me quickly ... | EN 1:139 |
| p. 65 | It is funny.... | LL:58 |
| p. 66 | You are like Canaan ... | LL:57 |
| p. 67 | I was in the train ... | CL:71 |
| | I have been to Leicester today ... | CL:70 |
| | You should not have drawn [Louie] into | |
| | things.... | ET:184 |
| p. 68 | My love looks like a girl to-night ... | CP:117 |
| | I suppose you will have seen [Lawrence] ... | HC:18 |
| p. 69 | I *did* think ... | HC:22 |
| | At times I am afflicted ... | CL:72 |
| p. 70 | You say you died a death of me ... | ET:186 |
| p. 71 | Somehow, I always feel sorry for her.... | LL:90 |
| | ... yet if I lay my hand ... | CP:158 |
| | ... push himself into correspondence. | LL:99 |

| p. 72 | I never want Lou to understand . . . | CL:77 |
| | I don't chuck money about . . . | LL:120 |
| p. 73 | Married! I don't *think* . . . | ET:188 |
| p. 74 | . . . he would thereby walk into freedom . . . | ET:192 |
| | He fell in absolutely with my suggestion . . . | ET:193 |
| p. 75 | . . . the long slow drag of hours . . . | LL:145–46 |
| | The most of the things . . . | LL:146 |
| | An' me as 'as kep' my-sen . . . | CP 2:919, 922 |
| p. 76 | . . . a big cottage . . . | EN 1:148–49 |
| p. 77 | . . . peculiarly disjointed . . . | EN 1:142 |
| | . . . often penniless themselves . . . | Ibid. |
| | . . . that insipid Sodom . . . | EN 1:143 |
| p. 78 | My girl is here. . . . | CL:90 |
| | I have been thinking . . . | LL:165 |
| p. 79 | By a cursed irony . . . | LL:166 |
| p. 80 | We were quite gay . . . | EN 1:144 |
| | I saw Louie yesterday . . . | CL:100 |
| | . . . and changed for the worse . . . | LL:xxvi |
| p. 81 | You really deserve someone better . . . | Ibid. |

Chapter 5: Jessie as Miriam

| p. 83 | There's nothing I admire like industry. . . . | ET:195–96 |
| p. 84 | Here was all that spontaneous flow . . . | ET:197–98 |
| p. 85 | [Ada] mustn't think she's mother. | ET:198 |
| | Are you going courting? | ET:200 |
| | Except in relation to beauty . . . | Ibid. |
| p. 86 | And after a week of love . . . | SL:355 |
| | Yours is the sullen sorrow . . . | CP:133–34 |
| p. 88 | His mother had to be supreme . . . | ET:201 |
| | I could not appeal to Lawrence . . . | Ibid. |
| | The events related . . . | ET:202 |
| | . . . gave the death-blow . . . | Ibid. |
| p. 89 | He had to present a distorted picture . . . | ET:203 |
| | Of course it isn't the truth. . . . | ET:204 |
| | It is as if he no longer wanted . . . | ED:119–20 |
| p. 90 | . . . concealed behind a more or less appropriate label . . . | ED:120 |
| p. 91 | . . . far too much a sick man . . . | ET:209–10 |
| p. 92 | She's wild with me . . . | ET:211 |
| p. 93 | Bill, I like a *gushing* woman. | ET:216 |
| | I'm sorry it turned out as it has. . . . | Ibid. |
| | *Pour vous seulement.* | Ibid. |
| p. 94 | This last year hasn't been all roses . . . | ET:219–20 |
| p. 95 | . . . direct and genuine. | HC:36 |
| p. 97 | Can you remember only the pain . . . | HC:43–44 |
| p. 98 | I am living here with a lady . . . | LL:171 |
| p. 99 | . . . a tall dark woman . . . | EN 3:448 |

p. 151   ... she simply had a horror of effusiveness ...          EN 1:233
         ... completely preoccupied ...                            EN 1:239
p. 152   Lawrence was apocalyptic ...                             Ibid.
         ... a horrid little cottage ...                          EN 1:258
         ... warm and complete ...                                EN 1:254
p. 153   I was still more shocked ...                             RL:5–6
         You must choose ...                                      EN 1:258
p. 155   ... as a sort of prophetess ...                          Ibid.
         You mustn't judge her lightly. ...                       CL:295
         You—I hoped never to see you again.                      EN 1:260
p. 156   ... the Jewish magpie.                                   CL:567
p. 157   I was glad you wrote ...                                 CL:305–6
p. 158   ... except that one night ...                            OM:272
         I want you to form the nucleus ...                       CL:311
p. 159   ... indefinite expressions of irritable dissent.         EN 1:286
p. 160   ... ignorant, jealous, irritable, hostile eyes.          HM:236
         ... very black and down ...                              CL:330
p. 161   Thank heaven we shall get out ...                        CL:333
p. 162   You didn't expect ...                                    NW:82
         And women shall not vote equally ...                     CL:349
         She had the feeling of being treated ...                 FL:129–30
p. 163   She was a great influence ...                            NW:82
         It's rather jolly ...                                    HM:247
p. 164   What is the good of being the Prime Minister's
         son?                                                     FL:146
p. 165   I want you to go and stay with Ottoline. ...             CL:381
         I want you to reserve to yourself ...                    CL:382
p. 166   I know America is bad ...                                CL:383
p. 167   He plagued and plagued me ...                            BR:16
         I, terribly shy ...                                      BR:16–17

### Chapter 9: H.D.

p. 168   He [Lawrence] was sex-mad, they said. ...                NW:83
p. 169   This is the first move to Florida.                       CL:405
         We have met one or two young people ...                  CL:401–2
p. 170   ... no more questioning and quibbling ...                CL:410–11
         But she is not really cross. ...                         CL:417
         ... the real blood connection ...                        CL:427
         ... for those who are whole and clear ...                CL:428
p. 171   For myself, thank God ...                                Ibid.
p. 172   I see Katherine Mansfield ...                            NW:84
         ... days of complete harmony ...                         NW:85
p. 173   He made the simplicities ...                             EN 1:293
         It is impossible to think of Lawrence ...                EN 1:306
         I shall *never* like this place.                         TW:403
p. 174   I am very much alone here. ...                           TW:404
         His relation to Frieda ...                               TW:409

| p. 174 | All the time, he recognized . . . | Ph 2:103–4 |
| | But I wanted a man friend . . . | WL:507–8 |
| p. 175 | If I love you . . . | RL:73 |
| | He'll kill me! . . . | TW:409 |
| p. 176 | Lawrence believed . . . | TW:413 |
| p. 178 | It would indeed be easy . . . | CC:63–64 |
| | You are not to *like* Mama . . . | FL:143 |
| p. 179 | He could talk by the hour . . . | NW:87–88 |
| p. 181 | I heard from Ottoline Morrell . . . | CL:488 |
| p. 182 | Stop it, stop it . . . | NW:86 |
| p. 183 | You are showing a light. | NW:89 |
| | When we were turned out of Cornwall . . . | NW:90 |
| p. 185 | What's this Orpheus . . . | HD:51 |
| | But she had . . . | Ibid. |
| | What does Frederick want . . . ? | HD:54–55 |
| | Listen, it's perfectly clear . . . | HD:56 |
| | We will go away together . . . | HD:57 |
| | It was not that she thought of Rico . . . | HD:58 |
| | Kick over your tiresome house of life. | HD:61 |
| p. 186 | He came several times . . . | HD:65–66 |
| | He is part of the cerebral burning . . . | HD:67 |
| | It's you, your fault . . . | HD:75 |
| | I'll leave Frederico with you. | Ibid. |
| | The mud was still stuck . . . | HD:77 |
| p. 187 | Elsa is there . . . | HD:77–78 |
| | . . . as if at a certain signal . . . | HD:81–82 |
| p. 188 | You are made for one another. | HD:140 |
| | You are really going to Cornwall? . . . | HD:136–37 |
| | Don't you realise . . . | HD:141 |
| | Friendship with Lawrence . . . | CG:137–38 |

Chapter 10: Cecily and Violet

| p. 190 | I am more than inclined to suspect . . . | CG:134 |
| p. 191 | Then, like a clock . . . | HR:106 |
| p. 192 | . . . cold, a little comfortless . . . | EN 1:453 |
| | . . . a tall, very slender creature . . . | EN 1:463 |
| p. 193 | A shock of mousey blonde hair . . . | Ibid. |
| | With this she wore . . . | Ibid. |
| p. 194 | . . . rich stew with mushrooms . . . | EN 1:464 |
| | Frieda was a good raconteur . . . | EN 1:465 |
| p. 195 | . . . a smallish bungalow . . . | EN 1:468 |
| p. 196 | With this strange attire . . . | CC:103 |
| | . . . the end of the war was in the air. | RL:92 |
| | These accursed people have put me . . . | CL 1:563 |
| p. 197 | Oh, there is something so lovable . . . | HM:310 |
| | So, you're here. . . . | EN 1:479 |
| | The hate and evil is greater . . . | Ibid. |

Chapter 11: Mary

Chapter 12: Mabel

| p. 243 | Mabel and Lawrence wanted to write a book ... | NW:136 |
| p. 244 | All women are alike ... | NW:137 |
|  | You *need* something new ... | ML:64 |
| p. 245 | There is something more important than love! | ML:69 |
|  | I wanted to seduce his spirit ... | ML:69–70 |
|  | ... solid and composed ... | ML:72 |
| p. 246 | A woman is a woman.... | ML:74 |
|  | ... yards and yards ... | Ibid. |
| p. 247 | Dear Mabel, I want you please ... | ML:105 |
| p. 248 | ... somewhere away from the city ... | EN 2:195 |
| p. 249 | He said a lot.... | ML:78 |
|  | ... the big voluptuous woman ... | ML:88 |
| p. 250 | I really can't bear to look at pictures! ... | KN:17 |
|  | ... tired of her, the bully ... | KN:28 |
| p. 251 | To think of it! | KN:30 |
| p. 252 | I think she needs more water.... | KN:53 |
|  | Why Mabel ought to go down on her knees ... | KN:65 |
| p. 253 | Mabel was too near a neighbour. | CL:731 |
|  | You have asked about Mabel Dodge ... | NW:158–59 |
| p. 254 | I saw, from our car ... | ML:111 |
|  | It's your own fault.... | ML:113 |
|  | He said you tried ... | Ibid. |
| p. 256 | Lawrence was completely out of his mind. | KN:173 |
|  | Best she stay with you. | KN:176 |
| p. 257 | Go away, Trip. ... | ET:65 |

Chapter 13: Frieda Again

| p. 258 | It's your fault, Frieda! ... | WB:2 |
| p. 259 | Her smile from the first ... | WB:4 |
|  | ... where Frieda, like an expanded Cleopatra ... | WB:23 |
|  | We are not staying here ... | WB:37 |
|  | Don't you feel it? ... | WB:37–38 |
| p. 260 | He looked extremely and childishly surprised ... | WB:38 |
|  | ... a smelly Italian hostelry ... | CB:186–87 |
|  | Her passivity merely incensed him ... | CB:187 |
|  | ... a very sick man ... | CB:187–88 |
| p. 261 | His bad manners shocked me ... | WB:184 |
|  | No, I shan't! ... | WB:185 |
| p. 262 | When he finds a place by himself ... | EN 2:233–34 |
|  | Mind you, I like Frieda ... | WB:137 |
| p. 263 | ... either on warm afternoons ... | EN 2:236 |
|  | All that time in Mexico ... | NW:139 |
|  | If you and Lawrence quarrel ... | Ibid. |
| p. 264 | Our craft moved ... | EN 2:240 |
| p. 265 | ... looking pale and pursued ... | EN 2:251 |
|  | I *like* Chapala! ... | EN 2:252 |

p. 265    I find my soul doesn't want to come . . .         NW:163
p. 267    Tell me, Frieda . . .                              MC:405–6
          . . . something ultimate and deeply
          satisfactory . . .                                 MC:407
          We might like to spend the winter . . .            KN:310
p. 268    He wanted desperately to help us paint. . . .      KN:312
p. 270    When I look at the ranches . . .                   KN:334
          He is longing for her. . . .                       KN:340
          He is always so concerned . . .                    Ibid.
          You know his ways . . .                            KN:343
p. 271    Gótzsche will have told you . . .                  KN:346
          He is afraid Frieda will avoid him . . .           KN:348
p. 272    I don't know how, but it gives me strength . . .   CL:763
          Oh, mother-in-law, you understand . . .            CL:763–64
p. 273    I am sure I will *die* . . .                       KN:350
p. 274    He slated it . . .                                 EN 2:271
          . . . a greenish pallor . . .                      CC:192
p. 275    I can't bear it. . . .                             Ibid.
p. 276    . . . terrible sadness . . .                       CC:200
          . . . a queer, unearthly creature . . .            EN 2:294–95
p. 277    . . . piquant and touching . . .                   CC:206
          Lawrence is a great man. . . .                     CC:209
p. 278    I love you, Lorenzo . . .                          RL:192
          You hate that house . . .                          BR:22
p. 279    They are dead. . . .                               BR:23
          The Lawrence party arrived very late . . .         SM:157
p. 280    Lawrence, you just can't leave Adam . . .          BR:30
          You expostulate wearily . . .                      BR:31
          . . . terrible to watch and hear . . .             Ibid.
p. 281    Frieda should not make me so angry.                BR:32
          Sometimes he went over the edge . . .              MC:341
p. 282    I saw on Saturday afternoon . . .                  DC:283
          . . . which is a state of U.S.A. . . .             DC:284

Chapter 14: Brett

p. 284    21 March 1924: Santa Fe. . . .                     WB:247
          I rather hope Murry won't come . . .               CL:778
p. 285    I don't know how to describe . . .                 ML:164–65
          . . . a tall, oldish girl . . .                    ML:166
p. 286    You know it will be good for us . . .              NW:152
          She doesn't count. . . .                           ML:167
p. 287    The cabin is built up slowly. . . .                BR:71
p. 288    You . . . say suddenly that I have no respect . . . BR:96
          Oh, it's wonderful . . .                           BR:104
p. 289    We will have to saw it. . . .                      BR:116–17
          I know, I know. . . .                              BR:129
          Brett, I'll give you half a crown . . .            NW:152

| | | |
|---|---|---|
| p. 290 | I don't want any shooting here.... | ML:204 |
| p. 291 | How *can* you treat me like that? | ML:206 |
| p. 292 | Why have you sent for the Doctor? ... | BR:139–40 |
| | It is all right.... | BR:141 |
| | ... everybody in this damned city ... | ML:279–80 |
| p. 293 | He is observant ... | BR:179 |
| | ... hot and sunny ... | CL:823 |
| | In spite of the beautiful climate ... | BR:185 |
| p. 294 | ... a huge Indian ... | Ibid. |
| | This is just the book for you.... | BR:186 |
| | Let us try.... | BR:192 |
| p. 295 | Here, let me have a try.... | BR:193 |
| | Frieda can't be coming ... | BR:194 |
| | ... a sort of apprehension ... | BR:203 |
| | Like the eye of the Lord, she was ... | NW:152 |
| p. 296 | Frieda broke out again ... | BR:204 |
| | In it she accuses us ... | BR:208 |
| p. 297 | ... an asparagus stick! | Ibid. |
| | She is astonished; so am I. | BR:209 |
| | I am wondering very much ... | EN 2:393 |
| | ... the remains of the old flu ... | Ibid. |
| | It's such an ugly cemetery ... | NW:149 |
| | But if I die ... | Ibid. |
| p. 298 | Mr. Lawrence has tuberculosis.... | NW:151 |
| p. 299 | She wanted to come up here but Frieda said no. | NW:175 |
| p. 300 | Oh, you get on my nerves! ... | BR:220 |
| | If Frieda starts her ... nonsense ... | BR:228 |
| p. 301 | ... plenty of money ... | BR:236 |
| p. 302 | Matthew, Mark, Luke and John ... | BR:239 |
| p. 303 | These mean, dirty little insults ... | EN 3:9 |
| | A real German *Hausfrau* ... | WG:254–55 |
| | These London girls.... | WG:256 |
| p. 304 | Horrid. | EN 3:16 |
| | ... a pink villa ... | NW:179 |
| p. 305 | ... that kind of man ... | EN 3:21 |
| | He has been horrid. | Ibid. |
| | Don't you imagine ... | NW:179–80 |
| | Look what I've done ... | EN 3:21–22 |
| p. 306 | Afterwards when someone told me ... | EN 3:22 |
| | I sensed that Lawrence did not share ... | EN 3:27 |
| | ... complaining to her about me ... | NW:180 |
| p. 307 | In the morning Ada and I had bitter words.... | Ibid. |
| | Somehow everything feels in a great muddle ... | EN 3:27 |
| | I only want to be quiet ... | BR:270 |
| p. 308 | I am so tired of it all ... | BR:271–72 |
| | ... a weary look of annoyance ... | BR:279 |
| | ... a vivid and very terrible picture. | Ibid. |

p. 309    I do not believe in a relationship . . .          BR: Epilogue,
                                                             pp. iii, iv *

p. 310    I don't know, Brett . . .                          BR:296–97
          Who is going to swallow whom?                      NW:181
          Now Mrs. L. . . .                                  Ibid.
p. 311    They are nice girls really . . .                   NW:184


Chapter 15: Frieda at the End

p. 313    . . . alive and mystical.                          EN 3:138
          Her wonderful colour sense . . .                   Ibid.
          *Capitano Ravagli* deve *partire* . . .            NW:195
p. 315    Achsah in her long white robes . . .               ML:334
p. 317    Here's one I particularly like. . . .              EN 3:280
          The cows have now all come down . . .              EN 3:243
p. 318    I, coward, am staying out of it.                   EN 3:247
          Frieda arrived . . .                               BB:182
          Every heart has a right . . .                      EN 3:189
p. 319    Nobody *likes* being called a cesspool.            EN 3:260
          I think we shall stay . . .                        EN 3:267
p. 320    *I* became cantankerous. . . .                     RD:201
          Frieda had a lioness quality . . .                 RD:202
p. 321    . . . fascinated avidity . . .                     Ibid.
          Why don't your children send you presents?         EN 3:283
          I had a dreadful dream. . . .                       EN 3:284
p. 323    . . . to symbolize Lawrence's purity.              EN 3:342
          Let's all go to the Russian Ballet.                EN 3:349
p. 324    . . . still wabbly and aching . . .                NW:199
          What will Frieda say? . . .                        Ibid.
          . . . as frail as one of those blue bird's eggs . . .   EN 3:378
          It has rained and been bitter cold . . .           HM:501–2
p. 325    There are lovely roses . . .                       EN 3:389
          . . . a nice little bungalow villa . . .           EN 3:401
          Frieda is happy. . . .                             EN 3:409
p. 326    Why, oh why, can't you flourish . . .              NW:287
          His worst time . . .                               NW:288
p. 327    Can't I have Barby? . . .                          EN 3:427–28
          You might just as well . . .                       EN 3:428
p. 328    One night I saw how he . . .                       NW:293
          Don't leave me . . .                               NW:295


* This revelation was made in the Epilogue of the second edition of
Brett's book, *Lawrence and Brett: A Friendship* (Sunstone Press, 1974).
On the advice of her friend and partner John Manchester of Taos, where
she still lives, Brett restored a passage that she excised from her journal
in the first edition, which was published in 1933.

Chapter 16: Frieda and Angelo

| | | |
|---|---|---|
| p. 329 | . . . such a powerful Valkyrie . . . | FL:254 |
| | . . . made up of little shimmering particles . . . | EN 3:466–67 |
| p. 330 | You don't understand Angelo. . . . | FL:256 |
| | You ought to speak German . . . | EN 3:466 |
| p. 331 | How *could* Frieda? . . . | FL:257 |
| | His virile, open features . . . | FL:242 |
| p. 335 | You think I ought to give you more money. . . . | MC:255 |
| p. 336 | The chapel is up the hill! . . . | WE:2, 8 |
| p. 338 | I am quite willing to talk to him. | FL:280 |

# Works Cited

AC    Ada Lawrence Clarke and G. Stuart Gelder. *Early Life of D. H. Lawrence*. London: Martin Secker, 1932.

BB    Achsah and Earl B. Brewster. *D. H. Lawrence: Reminiscences and Correspondence*. London: Martin Secker, 1934.

BL    D. H. Lawrence. "The Border Line." In *The Complete Short Stories*, vol. 3, pp. 587–604. London: William Heinemann, 1955.

BR    Dorothy Brett. *Lawrence and Brett: A Friendship*. Introduction, Prologue, and Epilogue by John Manchester. New ed. Santa Fe: The Sunstone Press, 1974.

CA    Cynthia Asquith. *Remember and Be Glad*. New York: Charles Scribner's Sons, 1952.

CB    Carleton Beals. *Glass Houses: Ten Years of Free-Lancing*. Philadelphia: J. B. Lippincott, 1938.

CC    Catherine Carswell. *The Savage Pilgrimage: A Narrative of D. H. Lawrence*. London: Chatto and Windus, 1932.

CG    Cecil Gray. *Musical Chairs or Between Two Stools: Being the Life and Memoirs of Cecil Gray*. London: Home and Van Thal, 1948.

CL    D. H. Lawrence. *The Collected Letters of D. H. Lawrence*. 2 vols. Edited and with an Introduction by Harry T. Moore. New York: The Viking Press, 1962.

CP    ———. *The Collected Poems of D. H. Lawrence*. 1-vol. ed. London: William Heinemann, 1933.

CP 2    ———. *The Complete Poems of D. H. Lawrence*. Vol. 2. Collected and edited with an Introduction and Notes by Vivian de Sola Pinto and Warren Roberts. New York: The Viking Press, 1964.

DC    Dora de Houghton Carrington. *Carrington: Letters and Extracts from Her Diaries*. Chosen and with an Introduction by David Garnett. New York: Holt, Rinehart and Winston, 1971.

DG     Douglas Goldring. *Life Interests*. London: MacDonald, 1948.

ED     Emile Delavenay. *D. H. Lawrence: The Man and His Work: The Formative Years: 1885–1919*. Translated by Katharine M. Delavenay. London: William Heinemann, 1972.

EN     Edward Nehls, ed. *D. H. Lawrence: A Composite Biography*. 3 vols. (Vol. 1: 1885–1919; vol. 2: 1919–1925; vol. 3: 1925–1930.) Madison: The University of Wisconsin Press, 1957–59.

ET     Jessie Chambers ("E.T."). *D. H. Lawrence: A Personal Record*. 2nd. ed. Edited by J. D. Chambers. New York: Barnes and Noble, 1965.

FL     Robert Lucas. *Frieda Lawrence: The Story of Frieda von Richthofen and D. H. Lawrence*. Translated by Geoffrey Skelton. New York: The Viking Press, 1973.

HC     Helen Corke. *D. H. Lawrence's "Princess": A Memory of Jessie Chambers*. Surrey: The Merle Press, 1951.

HD     Hilda Doolittle ("H.D."). *Bid Me to Live (A Madrigal)*. New York: Grove Press, 1960.

HM     Harry T. Moore. *The Intelligent Heart: The Story of D. H. Lawrence*. Revised and enlarged. New York: Grove Press, First Black Cat edition, 1962.

HR     Cynthia Asquith. *Haply I May Remember*. New York: Charles Scribner's Sons, 1950.

Kan     D. H. Lawrence. *Kangaroo*. New York: The Viking Press, 1960.

KM     Katherine Mansfield. *Letters to John Middleton Murry, 1913–1922*. New York: Alfred A. Knopf, 1951.

KN     Knud Merrild. *A Poet and Two Painters: A Memoir of D. H. Lawrence*. New York: The Viking Press, 1939.

LL     James T. Boulton, ed. *Lawrence in Love: Letters to Louie Burrows*. Nottingham: University of Nottingham, 1968.

MC     Frieda Lawrence. *The Memoirs and Correspondence*. Edited by E. W. Tedlock, Jr. New York: Alfred A. Knopf, 1964.

ML     Mabel Dodge Luhan. *Lorenzo in Taos*. New York: Alfred A. Knopf, 1932.

NW     Frieda Lawrence. *"Not I, But the Wind. . . ."* New York: The Viking Press, 1934.

OM     Lady Ottoline Morrell. *The Early Memoirs of Lady Ottoline Morrell*. Edited with an Introduction by Robert Gathorne-Hardy. London: Faber and Faber, 1963.

Ph 2     D. H. Lawrence. *Phoenix II: Uncollected, Unpublished, and Other Prose Works by D. H. Lawrence*. Collected and edited with an Introduction and Notes by Warren Roberts and Harry T. Moore. New York: The Viking Press, 1968.

RA     Richard Aldington. *D. H. Lawrence: Portrait of a Genius But. . . .* New York: Duell, Sloan and Pearce, 1950.

RD     Rhys Davies. "D. H. Lawrence in Bandol." In *Horizon: Review of Literature and Art* (edited by Cyril Connolly), vol. II, no. 10 (1940), pp. 191–208.

RL     John Middleton Murry. *Reminiscences of D. H. Lawrence*. Reprint. Freeport, N.Y.: Books for Libraries Press, 1971.

RW    Rebecca West. *Ending in Earnest: A Literary Log.* Reprint. Free-
      port, N.Y.: Books for Libraries Press, 1967.

SL    D. H. Lawrence. *Sons and Lovers.* Reprint. Harmondsworth,
      Middlesex: Penguin Books, 1948.

SM    Sarah Gertrude Millin. *The Night Is Long.* London: Faber and
      Faber, 1941.

TW    John Middleton Murry. *Between Two Worlds: An Autobiog-
      raphy.* London: Jonathan Cape, 1935.

VR    Martin Green. *The von Richthofen Sisters: The Triumphant and
      the Tragic Modes of Love: Else and Frieda von Richthofen,
      Otto Gross, Max Weber, and D. H. Lawrence, in the Years
      1870–1970.* New York: Basic Books, 1974.

WB    Witter Bynner. *Journey with Genius: Recollections and Reflec-
      tions Concerning the D. H. Lawrences.* New York: The
      John Day Co., 1951.

WE    Wolf von Eckardt. "Visiting Frieda: The Woman in D. H. Law-
      rence's Life." In the *Washington Post,* Book World, August
      27, 1972, pp. 218ff.

WG    William Gerhardi. *Memoirs of a Polyglot.* London: Duckworth,
      1931.

WL    D. H. Lawrence. *Women in Love.* London: Martin Secker, 1921.

# *Index*